AF477551

Popular Democracy in Japan

POPULAR DEMOCRACY IN JAPAN

How Gender and Community Are Changing Modern Electoral Politics

SHERRY L. MARTIN

CORNELL UNIVERSITY PRESS
ITHACA AND LONDON

This book has been published with the aid of a grant from the Hull Memorial Publication Fund of Cornell University.

First published 2011 by Cornell University Press
Printed in the United States of America

Library of Congress Cataloging-in-Publication Data

Martin, Sherry L., 1971–
    Popular democracy in Japan : how gender and community are changing modern electoral politics / Sherry L. Martin.
        p. cm.
    Includes bibliographical references and index.
    ISBN 978-0-8014-4917-8 (cloth : alk. paper)
    1. Democracy—Japan.   2. Japan—Politics and government—
21st century.   3. Political participation—Japan.   4. Political culture—
Japan.   5. Women—Political activity—Japan.   6. Community
power—Japan.   I. Title.
    JQ1681.M3   2011
    320.952—dc22   2010044421

Cornell University Press strives to use environmentally responsible suppliers and materials to the fullest extent possible in the publishing of its books. Such materials include vegetable-based, low-VOC inks and acid-free papers that are recycled, totally chlorine-free, or partly composed of nonwood fibers. For further information, visit our website at www. cornellpress.cornell.edu.

Cloth printing   10 9 8 7 6 5 4 3 2 1

For my extraordinary working mom...

Contents

Tables and Figures

Acknowledgments

This book is the product of a long and transformative journey. Along the path to its completion, I have been intellectually challenged, materially supported, and emotionally sustained by an expanding network of colleagues, friends, and family. I am most heavily indebted to the many Japanese women I interviewed for this project and the people who led me to them. I thank them for generously granting me access to their social and political worlds. I hope that they are able to recognize as their own the voices in this book that are defining Japanese democracy in new ways. If there is any misrepresentation, the fault is mine.

I began my journey in the political science department at the University of Michigan. In my earlier work I analyzed mass survey data and found that Japanese women were overrepresented among independent voters, a group of voters who were cynical about national political processes and constituted nearly half of the electorate. My conversations with women in the field were the backdrop to my survey data and merited only a short chapter. My adviser, John C. Campbell, commented several times that my focus group chapter was the most compelling. Ann Chih Lin, Ronald Inglehart, and Hiroko Akiyama suggested that someday I might think very differently about what my qualitative data were telling me.

Jointly appointed to the department of government and the program in feminist, gender, and sexuality studies at Cornell University, I began to hear my informants in a new register. Gender studies, an interdisciplinary enterprise fueled by an activist impulse, changed the questions I was asking, the answers I was finding, and the ways in which I was arriving at my conclusions. Mary F. Katzenstein has been a tireless mentor, thoughtful reviewer, and witness to my process of transformation from a political scientist concerned with how to include "absent" women in politics into one who listens to women's experiences with the political world to formulate a more complete picture of how politics works. Matthew Evangelista's feedback in the latter stages was invaluable in helping me to stay true to my disciplinary roots without compromising all of the important lessons that I have learned from gender studies.

Peter Katzenstein and Amy Villarejo encouraged me to get this project on track before I knew where it was headed. Both proffered practical advice for locating an editor and publisher for my book. Providence led me to Roger Haydon, whose tremendous skill as an editor surpasses his already stellar reputation. I thank all of these individuals for having confidence in my vision for this project.

This work would not have been possible without the institutional support that I have received. My original fieldwork was conducted between the fall of 1999 and the spring of 2001 with the support of a fellowship from the Japanese Ministry of Education. A residence with the program on U.S.-Japan relations at Harvard University in 2007–2008 provided me with time and material support to write my book while surrounded by a community of experts. A fellowship from Cornell University's Institute for the Social Sciences in the fall of 2008 helped me to bring this book to fruition. Members of my interdisciplinary writing group at Cornell were crucial throughout these latter stages. In 2009–2010, we were supported by the Brett de Bary Interdisciplinary Mellon Writing Group Grant at the Society for the Humanities. I thank current and former group members Durba Ghosh, Stacey Langwick, Rachel Prentice, Sara Pritchard, Marina Welker, Kathleen Vogel, Anindita Banerjee, Maria Fernandez, Sabine Haenni, and Sara Warner.

While in Japan from 1999 to 2001, I was affiliated with the University of Tokyo, where I was hosted by Ikuo Kabashima in the Faculty of Law. Kabashima-sensei, along with Ken'ichi Ikeda—also at the University of Tokyo—and Aiji Tanaka at Waseda, provided me with survey research resources in Japan and helped me to build a network of Japan-based colleagues whose support continues to be vital to my research. While Kabashima-sensei and members of his seminar helped me to think through my quantitative data, Hiroko Akiyama and her students helped me to brainstorm and frame the questions that I took into the field. Kaori Shoji and Karen Cox stand out as colleagues, peers, and friends who accompanied me into the field. They facilitated my initial forays into my new research settings, introducing me to critical contacts and supplying the proper words and turns of phrase when my Japanese language skills failed me.

Residence at the program on U.S.-Japan relations at Harvard University provided opportunities to continue and deepen the transformative conversations that I began during my first three years at Cornell among large and dynamic communities in gender studies and Asian studies. This book began to assume its current shape after Shinju Fuijihira, associate director of the U.S.-Japan program, with the assistance of William Nehring and Lianna Kushi, convened an author's conference that enabled me to invite scholars whose feedback I believed could strengthen my book. Susan Pharr, Virginia Sapiro, Robin M. LeBlanc, and David Leheny all encouraged me to revisit my qualitative work and offered strategies for listening to women's voices with new ears.

Each chapter in this book has benefited from constructive feedback from colleagues in political science, gender studies, and Asian studies. This group includes Eileen McDonogh, Shelley Feldman, Sidney Tarrow, Nicolas van de Walle, Valerie Bunce, Suzanne Mettler, and graduate students who read chapters. I am deeply indebted to the two anonymous Cornell University Press readers who made the review process an intellectually engaging and deeply satisfying experience. Their sharp eyes and generous suggestions helped me to produce the book that I envisioned.

I thank Hope Mandevelle in Feminist, Gender, and Sexuality Studies for lobbying to provide me with a quiet, sunny corner where I could work undisturbed. Aya Taniguchi, Weng Pong (Raymond) Woo, and Lily Deng provided hours of careful research assistance. I could not have worked so hard for so long without the support of numerous friends and colleagues: Kit Nichols, Josette Banks, Dyron Dabney, Gill Steel, Debbie Barrington, Kimberly Kono, and Jeannine Bell. Finally, I would like to thank my mother, Marcia Carr Martin, and members of my extended family who have had faith in my every step.

Abbreviations

CGP	Clean Government Party (Kōmeitō) (New Kōmeitō from 1998)
DPJ	Democratic Party of Japan (Minshutō)
EU	European Union
HC	House of Councilors (also called Upper House)
HR	House of Representatives (also called Lower House)
JCP	Japan Communist Party (Nihon Kiyōsantō)
JEDS	Japanese Election and Democracy Study 2000
JSP	Japan Socialist Party (Nihon Shakaitō)
LDP	Liberal Democratic Party (Jiyū Minshutō)
MEXT	Ministry of Education, Culture, Sports, Science and Technology
NET	Citizens' Network Parties (such as Kanagawa NET)
SCAP	Supreme Commander of the Allied Powers
SDP	Social Democratic Party (formerly the JSP) (Shakai Minshutō)
UNESCO	United Nations Educational, Scientific and Cultural Organization

Introduction

Why Don't They Stay Home?

On August 30, 2009, the Liberal Democratic Party of Japan suffered a dramatic defeat in the national House of Representatives election. This much-anticipated outcome was nearly three decades in the making. Wide-ranging political, administrative, and economic reforms and rapid demographic changes should have brought about the party's ouster long before this.[1] Voters were finally able to expel the LDP from power for the first time in fifty-four years.[2] But six decades of single-party dominance had taken a toll on Japanese voters.

---

1. An extensive literature examines how and why the LDP was able to continue winning elections despite changing institutional and structural conditions (Scheiner 2006; Tanaka 2003).

2. The LDP lost control of the government for ten months in 1993–1994 when an eight-party coalition government, consisting of every party other than the Japan Communist Party and the LDP, was formed and headed by Morihiro Hosokawa of the Japan New Party. The LDP's loss of power did not occur as a consequence of a definitive loss at the ballot box but rather through unanticipated behind-the-scenes bargaining among a highly fragmented opposition that was able to collaborate for a short period. Although the LDP remained the largest party in the National Diet, it failed to win a majority of seats and was unable to forge a coalition to govern. The party

In the two decades preceding the 2009 House election, public confidence that national elections were an effective means of influencing government had declined precipitously. Japanese voters at the turn of the twenty-first century were less likely than voters in other democracies to agree that voting makes a difference (Anderson et al. 2005, 39). Whereas a majority of American (63 percent) and British (56 percent) voters surveyed believed that their votes mattered, a majority of Japanese (54 percent) responded that their votes did not matter. Three-quarters of Japanese voters (as compared to one-third of British and American voters) complained that "many" politicians were dishonest (Yoshida 2002). Even though a majority of voters expressed strong feelings of dislike for the LDP, the party was entrenched and citizens were increasingly expressing frustration at their inability to alter the situation (Scheiner 2006).

The 2009 election brought about a rapid reversal in opinion. Japanese voters featured in Western news outlets reported a heightened sense of political efficacy: "I think people realized this time how powerful their one vote could be and that collectively, those votes could lead to something much bigger," said Nishibori, an unaffiliated voter originally from Japan's northern island of Hokkaido.[3] He continued, "Sunday gave us confidence that we, indeed, have a voice." A shopkeeper from Saitama Prefecture stated that "people had been fed up for a long time.... Their frustration reached a boiling point, and they finally rose up" (Hosaka 2009). This heightened sense of voter efficacy immediately after the election is itself worth exploring, but the primary concern of this book is the long period preceding the 2009 election, when people who had every reason to disengage from politics—and dominant theories predicted they would disengage—continued to turn out on Election Day. How do people who are angry, distrustful, discouraged, and estranged from politics remain people who think that participation in electoral politics is worthwhile? And what does this tell us about the groundswell in popular participation in 2009, the reversal in mass opinion about the influence of voting, and the change in governing party?

---

returned to power in 1994 in coalition with New Party Sakigake and its longtime rival, the Japan Socialist Party (renamed the Social Democratic Party in 1996).

3. Unaffiliated voters, also referred to as independent voters and floating voters, report that they do not support any existing political party.

In Japan, mass attitudes about democracy and its practice have changed, and voters have the resources to put their ideas into practice. Until the 2009 election, these attitudinal changes were more evident in particular places in Japan—local politics—and more prominent among specific groups—women and unaffiliated voters. Closer examination of unaffiliated women voters within local contexts helps us to think concretely about (a) new ways to engage underrepresented and marginalized groups, (b) citizen participation in different levels of politics, and (c) the long-term consequences for national electoral outcomes and the quality of democracy. A political system that alienates voters will not change if no action occurs, but the very conditions that foster and sustain political alienation often demobilize voters. Citizenship practices among Japanese women offer insights into this dilemma that are applicable to democratic politics everywhere.

In this book, I argue that institutional reforms, rapid demographic changes, and mass accumulation of socioeconomic resources such as increased income and education that facilitate political engagement have coalesced to produce a new style of Japanese politics. First, electoral reform and administrative decentralization have changed the relationship between local and national government, and that between residents and elected representatives, creating new incentives and opportunities for voters to change national politics through grassroots political action. Second, rapid economic growth during the postwar period equipped voters with the material resources (education and income) to participate in the democratic political process. At the same time, demographic changes such as rural depopulation and urbanization, a decline in extended family households and a commensurate increase in individuals living alone, a rapidly aging population, and a decline in fertility have altered the bases of party support. The quality of social networks has mutated in ways that strain political parties' traditional mobilization strategies. Third, higher levels of educational attainment, labor force participation, income, and other resources that promote political participation have changed how voters think about politics and about the quality of their participation. There has been an increase in elite-challenging attitudes about government accompanied by citizen demands for more direct participation in making the policies that govern them (Inglehart 1977, 1990).

This book uses a mixed-method approach to map out changes in mass political engagement in Japan that have unfolded over the course of the last decade. I use national survey data, focus groups, news reporting, statistical and archival data housed by the national and local governments, and a rich secondary literature. I discuss my methodological choices in detail later in this chapter, but first I would like to stress several features that make this research stand out.

I conduct a qualitative content analysis of open-ended responses provided by a national random sample of voters to the Japanese Election and Democracy Survey to explore the content of mass political attitudes about national politics. I explore a category of survey responses, "free answers," that are generally untapped in social science research. Detailed responses provide explicit reasons for the dissatisfaction of voters, whereas statistical analyses reflect only a change in public opinion, leaving causality to be inferred at best. However, in this rich data source, voters not only offer reasons for their dissatisfaction but also suggest solutions and provide information about what they—individually and in groups—are doing to change Japanese politics. Though I did not conduct the survey, I translated all of the Japanese-language responses to offer the first published analysis of these data.

I also relied on focus groups, which are seldom utilized in political science research. I conducted a total of seven focus groups in Tokyo and Nagano Prefecture, all with women of voting age. Since women constitute a majority of unaffiliated and distrustful voters, these group conversations provided an opportunity to probe attitudes about politics and to deepen our understanding of how and why this segment of the electorate remains, despite all odds, politically engaged. Yasuo Takao, in tracing the paths by which women become activists and develop higher political ambitions, finds that women's networks bring a different set of ethics to local political life: "Currently, there is an exceptionally high demand for an alternative politics, which is unparalleled in Japan's recent history. This has provided an opportunity for reformists and new political groups to work toward democracy-building. Already, forward-looking women's groups in Japan are proposing alternative forms of political renewal" (Takao 2008). Yet, what "women-centric networks" look like, how women become involved, what their practices are, and how such networks keep women politically engaged—these issues are less well understood (Lam 2005a). Talking to women points us in new directions: "communities of practice," supported by lifelong learning policy initiatives, offer risk-free opportunities for collective conversation, learning, and mutual support that may be important in helping people, especially women, to overcome obstacles to political participation and successfully enact change.

Finally, I use my combined data to talk about how mass attitudinal changes are being expressed in an increase in referenda, recall elections, and information disclosure movements; antiestablishment and citizens' parties; and the election of independent executives and outsider candidates. National survey data show that the attitudes and associated forms of political action are widespread but fail to capture underlying differences in how voters form their attitudes about politics and translate them into action. Case studies and media coverage of local political action frequently detail the contributions of women as the backbone of citizens' movements that spearheaded successful referenda and recall efforts and the electoral successes of outsider candidates. The average Japanese voter is a woman who is unaffiliated. She resurfaces frequently in accounts of local and national electoral upsets, but neither politicians nor political scientists in Japan have paid significant attention to what her participation tells us about enduring rather than ephemeral political change. Thus, I introduce focus group data and statistics mapping changes in women's socioeconomic resources and how they use those resources in order to identify the central role of women in bringing about political change in Japan. Existing accounts of the changing patterns of electoral engagement at the grassroots level treat women as marginal actors rather than a constitutive force in producing democratic political change. This book privileges the experiences of Japanese women voters within a general story about change in Japanese politics and democracy. Those experiences unlock answers to puzzles about political engagement that have been elusive because the role of women in politics has been underexplored.

This book contributes to research on the influence of institutions on citizen participation in society and politics with feedback effects that can drive elite political behavior in new directions. Placing grassroots citizenship practices and changing dynamics in subnational politics in the context of Japan's national political development (that is, the movement away from the LDP's money-power style of machine politics described in Joseph

Schlesinger's *Shadow Shoguns*) marks one of this book's distinctive contributions to the literature on Japan. There are studies of networks and associations (most notably, LeBlanc 1999), an emergent literature examining changes in civil society (Pekkanen 2006; Haddad 2007; Steinhoff 2008), and numerous accounts of electoral politics. My book provides an original analysis of electoral participation that links these studies. Patterns of political participation in Japan cannot be explained by dominant theories in comparative politics or in Japanese politics, and these puzzling outcomes set the course for this book.

Distrustful Democrats

The antiwar and social justice movements of the late 1960s and early 1970s marked the beginning of a downward slide in public confidence in political actors and institutions across established democracies—Western Europe, the United States and Japan (Putnam and Pharr 2000, Dalton 2006). This trend was attributed to multiple causes, among them an increase in elite-challenging attitudes accompanied by an increase in activist modes of political participation (Inglehart 1977, 1990); a widening disparity between voter preferences and policy outcomes (Miller 1974a, b, Weatherford 1991); increasingly scandal-oriented media sources (Norris 2000); negative campaigning; and a decline in civic engagement and a corresponding erosion of social capital (Putnam 1993). Deepening distrust has been correlated with a decline in voter turnout, a loosening of partisan identification and a corresponding increase in independent (or unaffiliated) voters, and increasing demands for more direct public participation in politics (Dalton 2006; Southwell 2008). Some political scientists forecast that these trends, should they continue, threaten to produce a "crisis of democracy" as regimes lose the legitimacy and public support that foster stable governance (Easton 1965; Crozier 1977).

Nearly half a century later political scientists are finding that widespread political cynicism can produce positive political outcomes. When political distrust is accompanied by a belief that participating in politics promotes change, citizens are more likely to mobilize in ways that reinforce and deepen democratic norms (Dalton 2006). Conditions in Japan are consistent with the alternative outcome—Japan should be caught in a downward spiral of deepening distrust and political disengagement.

Yoshida (2002) argues that Japanese voters are more cynical about politics *and* less likely than voters in the United States and European democracies to believe that their participation in national elections can make a difference. Cross-national election studies have shown that voters who do not identify with a political party are less likely to turn out and are more likely to express low levels of political efficacy (Verba et al. 1978; Dalton 2006). In recent decades, the percentage of unaffiliated voters has fluctuated from about a third to a little more than half of the Japanese electorate. And yet unaffiliated voters have turned out, and when they do, the long-dominant Liberal Democratic Party suffers historic losses: the 1998 House of Councilors election and the 2009 House of Representatives election are notable examples (Yoshida 2002). Yoshirō Mori, the most unpopular LDP prime minister in recent years (his public support ratings fell to single digits), aroused public outrage when he expressed his hope that unaffiliated voters would stay home. That unaffiliated voters turn out to exercise their voice at critical moments suggests a more complicated story—that they invest their political resources when the payoff is greatest.

In Japan and other established democracies, unaffiliated voters surmount higher thresholds to participate in the electoral process than partisans do. They have no preferred party that operates as an informational shortcut. They tend not to be integrated into candidate support organizations, professional associations, trade unions, and other associations that are linked to a national lobby that parties have traditionally used to distribute state resources and mobilize supporters. Unaffiliated voters in urban areas do not benefit from the friends-and-neighbors effect that obtains in rural communities. Further, unaffiliated voters tend to be members of politically underrepresented groups (women and minorities) and to have lower levels of resources, such as education and income, that facilitate participation. Consequently, the informational costs of voting are higher for these voters. What keeps voters who we would expect to abstain interested in electoral politics? What conditions help them to compensate for and overcome resource disparities that threaten to sideline them in the political process?

The Gender of Nonpartisanship

The average Japanese voter is a woman, and she does not support any party in the system. On Election Day, more Japanese women, whether measured in percentages or absolute numbers, turn out to vote than men; this has been true for every House election since 1969 (see table i.1). The gender gap in voter turnout extends to every election—local, prefectural, and national; executive and legislative—across Japan during this same period (see table i.2). Even as turnout declined, the gender gap remained an enduring feature of Japanese elections. The more local the election, the larger the gender gap in turnout. Even though the gender gap disappeared in recent national elections for both houses, higher turnout among women remains a distinguishing feature of Japanese politics.[4]

Yet the typical Japanese woman is also unaffiliated with any political party in the system. Figure i.1 shows that nonpartisanship is another enduring gender gap in Japanese politics. The bars represent the percentage of all respondents in national election studies who claimed to support no party in advance of the House of Representatives election in each represented year. The dark-shaded area represents the percentage of nonpartisans who were women; the light-shaded area represents the percentage of nonpartisans who are men. Women have made up nearly 60 percent of nonpartisan voters for over three decades; 40 percent of nonpartisans are men.[5] The length of time over which this trend has endured suggests that declining turnout in the Japanese electorate is not altogether attributable to an increase in nonpartisan voters; turnout has declined over the past thirty years, but nonpartisanship was no higher in 2005 than in 1976. In fact, nonpartisanship decreased.[6] What keeps unaffiliated women voters returning to the polls?

---

4. The slightly higher turnout among male voters in 2009 may be attributed to intensified party efforts to mobilize partisan voters, who tend to be men, in tight races between the LDP and the DPJ. The reasons for the fluctuations in the size of the gender gap in elections are beyond the focus of this book.

5. The survey data available to me is limited to the last three and a half decades. A secondary literature, however, suggests Japanese women have always been overrepresented among nonpartisans in the electorate.

6. Figure i.1 suggests that the proportion of nonpartisans in the electorate has declined significantly since the late 1970s. However, the proportion of nonpartisans tends to fluctuate depending on the proximity of polls to scheduled elections. When elections are impending and voters are primed by campaign messages, they are more likely to identify with the party they intend to vote for. However, between elections the weakest party supporters are more likely to say that they do not support any party in the electorate. Polls conducted by national newspapers such as the *Nikkei Shimbun* show large spikes in nonpartisanship throughout this same period. These poll results are not shown here, however, because available data do not control for gender.

TABLE i.1. Trends in gender and voter turnout in national elections, 1946–2009

House of Representatives elections				House of Councillors elections		
	Women	Men	Difference		Women	Men	Difference
1946	67.0	78.5	−11.5	1947	54.0	68.4	−14.4
1947	61.6	74.9	−13.3	1950	66.7	78.2	−11.5
1949	67.9	80.7	−12.8	1953	58.9	67.8	−8.9
1952	72.8	80.5	−7.7	1956	57.7	66.9	−9.2
1953	70.4	78.3	−7.9	1959	55.2	62.6	−7.4
1955	72.1	79.9	−7.8	1962	66.5	70.1	−3.6
1958	74.4	79.8	−5.4	1965	66.1	68.0	−1.9
1960	71.2	76.0	−4.8	1968	69.0	68.9	0.1
1963	70.0	72.4	−2.4	1971	59.3	59.1	0.2
1967	73.3	74.8	−1.5	1974	73.6	72.7	0.9
1969	69.1	67.9	1.2	1977	69.3	67.7	1.6
1971	72.5	71.0	1.5	1980	75.3	73.7	1.6
1976	74.0	72.8	1.2	1983	57.1	56.9	0.2
1979	68.6	67.4	1.2	1986	72.4	70.1	2.3
1980	75.4	73.7	1.7	1989	65.6	64.4	1.2
1983	68.3	67.6	0.7	1992	50.8	50.6	0.2
1986	72.5	70.2	2.3	1995	44.4	44.7	−0.3
1990	74.6	71.9	2.7	1998	59.3	58.4	0.9
1993	68.1	66.4	1.7	2001	56.9	56.0	0.9
1996	60.2	59.0	1.2	2004	56.5	56.6	−0.1
2000	62.9	62.0	0.9	2007	58.4	58.9	−0.5
2003	60.0	59.7	0.3				
2005	68.2	66.8	1.4				
2009	69.1	69.5	−0.4				

Source: Ministry of International Affairs and Communications (2009). Report of the Results of Elections. National Women's Education Center's Gender Statistics Database, available at http://winet.nwec.jp/cgi-bin/toukei/load/bin/tk_sql.cgi?hno=155&syocho=49&rfrom=101&rto=120&fopt=3, accessed January 20, 2010.

This abundance of evidence could lead observers to predict that women would disengage from politics, and this trend would be especially pronounced among unaffiliated women voters. Despite four decades of outvoting men and six decades of constitutionally guaranteed equality, the overriding perception is that progress toward gender equality in Japan

TABLE i.2. Trends in gender and voter turnout in subnational elections, 1975–2007

Gubernatorial elections (prefecture)				Prefectural assembly elections		
	Women	Men	Difference		Women	Men	Difference
1975	73.06	70.72	2.34	1975	75.17	73.00	2.17
1979	65.18	62.93	2.25	1979	70.63	68.05	2.58
1983	64.92	61.4	3.52	1983	69.92	66.90	3.02
1987	61.58	57.89	3.69	1987	68.35	64.85	3.50
1991	56.41	52.36	4.05	1991	62.40	58.45	3.95
1995	56.71	53.44	3.27	1995	57.85	54.49	3.36
1999	58.25	55.25	3.00	1999	58.08	55.21	2.87
2003	54.16	51.01	3.15	2003	53.81	51.05	2.76
2007	55.84	53.79	2.05	2007	53.09	51.34	1.75

Mayors (not designated cities)				Town or village assemblies		
	Women	Men	Difference		Women	Men	Difference
1975	78.54	75.13	3.41	1975	93.68	91.56	2.12
1979	77.28	73.25	4.03	1979	93.62	91.18	2.44
1983	74.44	70.21	4.23	1983	93.47	90.79	2.68
1987	72.44	68.02	4.42	1987	91.70	88.67	3.03
1991	69.24	63.72	5.52	1991	89.03	85.15	3.88
1995	62.28	57.63	4.65	1995	85.26	81.40	3.86
1999	63.01	58.58	4.43	1999	83.82	80.33	3.49
2003	58.95	54.87	4.08	2003	79.48	75.81	3.67
2007	55.02	52.00	3.02	2007	73.13	69.72	3.41

Source: Ministry of International Affairs and Communications (2009). Voting Percentages of Unified Local Election National Women's Education Center's Gender Statistics Database, available at http://winet.nwec.jp/cgi-bin/toukei/load/bin/tk_sql.cgi?hno=155&syocho=49&rfrom=101&rto=120&fopt=3, accessed January 20, 2010.

has been slow. The World Economic Forum's 2007 global gender gap report ranks Japan 91st out of 128 nations, reflecting women's limited access to resources and opportunities in politics, economics, education, and health. While Japan performs well above global averages in education and health, its overall score suffers due to the constraints women face in politics and economics. In politics, Japan has the lowest percentage of women parliamentarians among the G-8 nations. Economically, women are concentrated in temporary, part-time, and low-status jobs in the labor force.

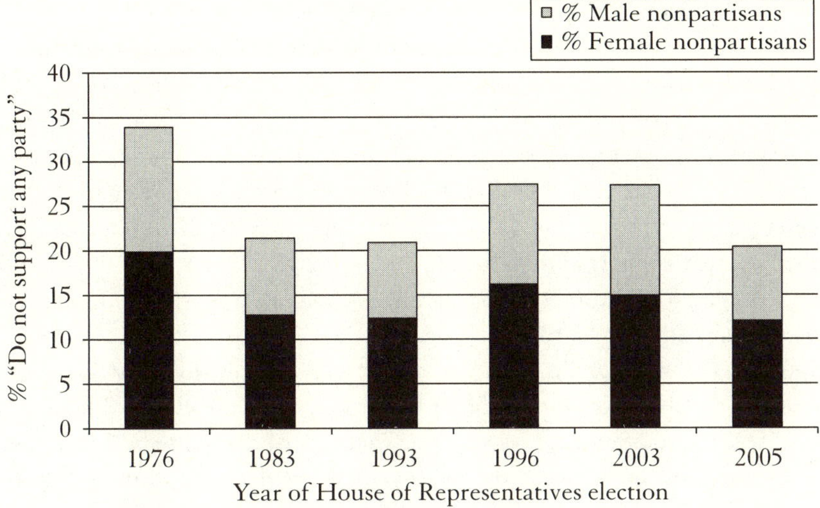

Figure i.1 Gender and nonpartisanship, 1976–2005
Sources: Flanagan et al. (1976); Watanuki et al., *Japan Election Study* (JES1) (1983); Kabashima et al., *Japan Election Study II* (JES2) (1993–96); Ikeda et al. (2007).

These disparities, which increase the cost of political participation for women as a group, presumably have a more intense effect on women who do not affiliate with any party. Further, the incrementalism of policies that promote gender equality might lead many women to conclude that voting is an ineffective tool for influencing politics (Gelb 2003). Why are women so politically engaged, especially in electoral politics, when they seemingly have little impact on a male-dominated political sphere?

The Dominant Explanation: Civic Duty and Social Networks

A strong sense of citizen duty is commonly offered as an explanation to the puzzle that I have just outlined. Survey research shows that women voters are more likely than men to agree that they know less about politics and are less interested, and these factors reduce the likelihood that a voter will turn out. This finding is offset by the fact that women are slightly more likely to agree that voting is a civic duty. However, some posit that male family members reduce the informational costs of voting by instructing women which parties and candidates to vote for (Flanagan 1991). In Japan, civic duty and family influences are reinforced by obligations to local opinion leaders who mobilize women to turn out and cast ballots for politicians and parties supported by members of their immediate social circles. The presumption that influence flows from men to women in Japan is sustained by the fact that there has traditionally been no gender gap in the choice of party. Even though women are more likely to be nonpartisans, they are just as likely as men to vote for the conservative LDP.

Cross-nationally, dense social networks play an important function in mobilizing voters to turn out (Rosenstone and Hansen 1993; Zuckerman 2005, 2007; Diani 2007). In Japan, the degree of embeddedness in social networks is the strongest predictor of turnout and vote choice (Flanagan et al. 1991). An abundance of research that describes the intensification of tight relationships between the bureaucracy, politicians, and the business elite over the postwar period demonstrates the centrality of social networks to the process of interest aggregation in Japan (Johnson 1982; Calder 1988). Political interests are expressed through traditional grassroots organizations that are integrated into peak associations at the national level that are, in turn, aligned with national party politicians and bureaucratic entities (Muramatsu and Krauss 1987). However, Japan is distinct in that networks are more likely to be organized vertically than horizontally. The conventional wisdom holds that Japan is a "vertical society," with organizations defined by hierarchical relationships that enable "higher-ups" to wield a disproportionate amount of influence in social networks (Nakane 1970; Ikeda and Richey 2005). "Traditional" organizations are geographically rooted (neighborhood associations/*chonaikai*), gender- and aged-based (women's associations/*fujinkai* and senior citizens' associations/*rojinkai*), occupationally differentiated (agricultural cooperatives, professional associations), or service-oriented (volunteer fire departments) (Haddad 2007).[7] Political bosses ask prominent community leaders to use their status and social capital to mobilize votes in their constituencies. Local opinion leaders use their ties to neighborhood associations, labor unions, professional organizations, PTAs and so forth in their district to mobilize votes for their

---

7. I am indebted to Mary Alice Haddad, who draws sharp distinctions between traditional and new-style associations in Japanese civil society in her new manuscript, *Making Democracy Real: Power to the People in Japan.*

candidate. Pork-barrel projects are channeled to constituents through organized networks in return for their support (Richardson 1974, 1997). One result is that ordinary citizens "may not develop citizenship skills due to the lack of deliberation and experiences negotiating outcomes with their fellow citizens" because they "almost exclusively follow the *meue's* [higher-ups'] judgments" (Ikeda and Richey 2005, 242).

Japanese women, when represented, tend to occupy lower-status positions in trade unions and professional associations and neighborhood associations. Even when women comprise the majority of the membership of groups such as PTAs and consumer cooperatives, the leadership tends to be male. Consequently, women are easily mobilized to vote by parties with strong "vote-gathering" machines such as the LDP. This leaves unresolved the question of why turnout for unaffiliated women voters is relatively high when conventional wisdom holds that these voters should be less likely to be integrated into organizations that mobilize voters (Ōtake 2000).

An Alternative Explanation: The Cognitive Mobilization of "Women-Centric Networks"

I began this research asking whether Japanese women have political resources that men lack or use differently. While existing literature recognizes that women and men belong to different types of social networks, social scientists have treated women's networks as though they are an extension of and subordinate to more professionalized and resource-rich networks that are male-dominated. In an account of the 2003 Saitama gubernatorial election, Lam identified "three modes of election campaigning: organizational mobilization based on interest groups (especially construction companies and farmers), *koenkai* (personal candidate support organizations), religious groups, trade unions, and party organizations; manifesto movements, which took off in Japanese politics in 2003; and women-centric, volunteer-based, horizontal network-style campaigning" (2005a, 80). The influence of women-centric networks has been overlooked, downplayed, and dismissed as highly localized.

These "women-centric networks" merit closer scrutiny because they are increasingly well-resourced. Women's average level of educational attainment is high, and more women are entering the workforce in higher-status jobs and staying in the workforce for longer periods of time. Outside of work and family, women seek new places for investing this reserve of human capital. New sites of learning and knowledge creation have been a primary outlet. In this book, I propose that women's citizenship practices in the thousands of study and hobby groups in local communities across Japan is fundamental to resolving the dilemma of how to keep disaffected voters politically active.

Political participation researchers dismiss study and hobby groups as politically inconsequential while simultaneously acknowledging their community-building functions. The proliferation of study and hobby groups outside of formal educational institutions provides opportunities for women to use educational resources acquired earlier in life to replace elite modes of knowledge production with their own, a process that affects how women reenter the political system. The internal dynamics and practices within study groups (a) deepen women's investment in a local, national, and global community; (b) enable participants to compare and contrast their own citizenship practices to "democracy" as practiced by political elites—and find the latter lacking; and (c) empower participants to use situated knowledge to challenge political elites to align elite decision-making practices more closely with those of the people. Understanding the practices inside these groups and their import for the type of political subject that is—or is not—produced through participation in a variety of learning experiences over the course of one's life makes evident how women contribute to community discourses that shift attitudes about politics in ways that affect patterns of political participation at the local, prefectural, and national levels. Study group participation increases women's confidence in using voting in combination with other forms of political participation to pressure political elites for a more inclusive democracy.

Changing Opportunity Structures

The Local Autonomy Law Amendment of 1999 expanded local tax bases and shifted fiscal and social welfare responsibilities to local governments, increasing incentives and opportunities for political entrepreneurship in local politics. New freedom of information laws enabled citizens to monitor local elected officials' management of public funds with greater ease.

Bringing more citizens into local politics has also been touted as necessary to root out local government inefficiencies generated by close ties among LDP politicians, bureaucrats, and politicians and creating greater efficiency through state-society partnerships in local governance.

Iwamoto suggests that the impact of administrative reforms on local budgets was felt as early as the 1980s, as "cutbacks galvanized women into action" (2001, 225). The high percentage of women participants in citizens' movements prior to administrative decentralization made women well-situated to escalate their efforts to change politics after decentralization (LeBlanc 1999; Takao 2008). By the 2007 Unified Local Elections, polls indicated that voters were following election campaigns with avid interest because highly publicized local government bankruptcies had raised consciousness about the importance of electing local officials who could be entrusted with revitalizing local economies. How voters, especially women, invest their political resources locally has consequences for national elections. Referenda, recall, and information disclosure movements; antiestablishment and citizens' parties; and the election of independent executives have increased since decentralization, and all present new challenges for national politicians and parties.

The Japanese state has also reduced the costs of women's mobilization by supplying material resources that legitimate existing citizenship practices by tying them to pragmatic goals. An increase in grassroots citizens' movements that rely on electoral politics coincides with an increase in women's educational attainment and an expansion of lifelong learning programs. The Japanese state has historically used adult education to shape citizenship practices. Education reforms adopted over the course of the last two decades actively seek to extend learning over the entire lifetime to mobilize citizens to develop grassroots responses to a range of social problems, from expanding social welfare services for children and the elderly to revitalizing depopulated rural villages. The state has also shaped the course of adult education by providing physical facilities and citizens' and women's centers across Japan, which lower the costs of group formation. In 1988, the Ministry of Education established the Lifelong Learning Bureau in recognition that citizens were already participating in lifelong learning activities because the formal education system was too rigid (MEXT, 1989–2002). In 1989, MEXT counted 159,721 social education courses offered in over seventeen thousand citizens' halls across the country. By 2004, the number of social education courses offered increased by a factor of two and a half, to 410,014 courses. The overwhelming majority of these courses were classified as "educational" (61.7 percent). Remaining courses involved recreation (12.6 percent), focused on home management (9.6 percent), transferred job-related skills (4.1 percent), promoted "civic-mindedness" (5.9 percent), and addressed an assortment of "miscellaneous" interests (6.0 percent) (MEXT 2008). This "official record" does not capture study and hobby groups that are formed by citizens and voluntary associations but does hint at an associational sphere that is far larger. A majority of participants in social education classes offered in citizens' centers in the mid-2000s (54.7 percent) were women (MEXT 2008). Under the right conditions, some study circles become launch pads for political action.

Methods

This book analyzes the content of "free answers" to a national survey and focus group discussions, bringing in current news reporting, polls, white papers, and a rich secondary literature to explore what voters think about politics and how they mobilize the resources around them to affect change. The Japanese Election and Democracy Survey (JEDS) provides an overview of the national distribution of attitudes about mass and elite political practices to establish the ubiquity of attitudes that have found expression in specific local political arenas. While Nagano, a locale that I focus on in this book, stands out as a hotbed of citizen activism, there is tremendous overlap of opinion between JEDS voters and Nagano residents. But Nagano voters have given voice to their opinion in patterns of local participation that have become increasingly common across Japan. This case helps me link national attitudes to specific types of political action to suggest that Nagano is not so far outside of the norm. The national survey also supports the generalizability of the narratives that emerge from all-women focus groups, which help us understand why women are so prominent among actors who are working for political change even though they constitute groups that we do not expect to be active. What previously overlooked or misunderstood factors keep them engaged? Is there a story about gender here and, if so, what is it? The focus group discussions deepen understanding of why voters remain engaged in politics even as they see the distance between themselves and elite politicians as widening. These groups and the spaces they occupy help me to generate a plausible explanation about how citizens mobilize knowledge for empowerment over the course of life.

The Japanese Election and Democracy Study

In April and May 2000, the principal investigators for the Japanese Election and Democracy Study (Nishizawa et al. 2001) conducted face-to-face interviews with a probability sample of eligible Japanese voters to understand the relationship between social capital and individual perceptions of democracy in Japan. "The main purpose of this survey is to understand the politically relevant aspects of social interaction among ordinary Japanese people by examining the diffusion of particular opinions between intimates such as spouses, close friends, and coworkers."[8] This initial wave of respondents was asked to supply the names of family, friends, and neighbors (up to three names) with whom they talked most frequently about politics to generate a "snowball sample" of respondents, who were then mailed questions, enabling researchers to compare opinions to test the strength of similarity in views between voters embedded in the same and overlapping networks. In October 2000, questionnaires were mailed to the initial probability sample after the general election in June. Of this group, 64.7 percent participated in the face-to-face interviews, and 39.2 percent followed up in the second wave.

I analyze three open-ended responses provided by the *initial* respondents (not the snowball sample); these questions were asked only in the face-to-face interview and the followup mail questionnaire that was not sent to the snowball sample of spouses and friends. Voters were asked to voice complaints about local, regional, or national problems and their proposed solutions; share what "Japanese politics" means to them; and state the reasons why they are willing to be involved in politics (when applicable). These two rounds not only ask questions that, fortuitously, are about precisely the issues I am interested in, they also allow voters to express, in their own terms, why they have remained politically engaged. The answers provide

---

8. Excerpted from the survey abstract, available from the Social Science Japan Data Archive. Available at http://ssjda.iss-u-tokyo.ac.jp/abstract/0247a.html, accessed February 21, 2003.

insight into how respondents pull together disparate pieces of information to develop a narrative about how politics works and about how that understanding shapes how they participate in the political world. Voters can tell us about the combined forces of civic duty, obligation to *meue* associates, self-interest, and democratic ideals that propel them to the polls.

These "free answers" allow me to explore the relationship between attitudes and action in several ways that traditional closed-response surveys do not. First, voters are not limited to predetermined categories that set the parameters for what constitutes the universe of appropriate answers. Consequently, voters can identify political problems that might not appear as an option on closed-response surveys, and they can offer solutions that fall outside of conventional response categories. Notably, respondents can make links between national politics and local action when the bulk of existing surveys privilege engagement in national politics. Second, voters have the freedom to describe connections between attitudes and behavior in ways that conform to or diverge from the predictions of dominant theories. Finally, these data allow me to get at the multiple factors that might get voters we would expect to stay at home to turn out.

Focus Groups

I use focus groups that I conducted with women voters and interviews with opinion leaders, combined with government reports, voter surveys, and communications from the prime minister's office to link changes in women's formal educational attainment to trends in education policy and women's participation in research and study groups. "Cognitive mobilization" among women correlates with the changing content of citizen demands and elite responses in Japanese politics over the past two decades.

My method for assembling groups resulted in a small sample of women with a wide variation in associational ties; this is important to the argument that I ultimately put forward—women's learning practices in groups that are encouraged by the state, but not institutionalized, provide opportunities to produce knowledge that empowers participants to challenge the state itself. This, however, was not my original intention. When I entered the field, mentors worried that I would be unable to recruit groups of unacquainted individuals and that they would be unwilling to express their views openly even if I could convene such groups. Consequently, I was advised to work through established women's groups and ask Japanese colleagues and friends to assist me in the recruitment effort. I tried multiple recruitment strategies. I posted flyers in women's centers, contacted women's advocacy groups with an online presence and/or a physical office space, and asked Japanese associates to plumb their own social networks. Table i.3 provides a descriptive summary of the seven focus groups I conducted that includes location, number of participants and their approximate ages, the common interest or group membership(s) that linked participants, and recruitment method. All three recruitment strategies were fruitful. Contrary to the earlier admonitions, I was able to convene a group of unrelated women. My only criterion for participation was that a participant be a woman of eligible voting age (over 20 years in Japan). My recruiting methods—the locations of my recruitment flyers, the kinds of groups I contacted, and the highly educated women whom I knew personally—enabled me to capture a slice of a dynamic and elusive associational sphere of women's activities and illuminate common practices across diverse groups.

The networks that were my point of entry to the field included relatively well-delineated *communities of practice,* that is, "groups of people who share a concern or a passion for something they do and learn how to do it better as they interact regularly" (Wenger n.d.). The women who became my focus group participants were involved in activities that yield networks and movements that Japanese civil society researchers would consider "new."[9] In contrast to "traditional" associations that are institutionalized and embedded in a neocorporatist framework that facilitates contact with the state directly or via intermediaries, new associations are more likely to work outside of the state and are more fluid in form, function, membership, and practice. My focus group participants belonged to "virtual" online communities, followed the development of nonprofit associations, participated in club activities in higher education, engaged in cultural and language exchange with the foreign community, and organized play dates with other mothers. These activities were not under the umbrella of a national organization, and the strength of their ties with other small groups varied enormously. Though the original aim of focus group conversations was not to replicate communities of practice in a controlled

---

9. See note 6.

TABLE i.3. Focus group sampling

Group name	Location	Number of participants	Type of group	Recruitment method
Women Now	Tokyo	6	Online community catering to women struggling to balance work and family responsibilities, aged late 20s to mid-50s.	Located group on the internet; informant circulated project description to recruitment site users to meet for the first time in a face-to-face meeting.
Neighborhood Friends	Tokyo	8	International friendship association affiliated with a student dorm, aged mid-40s to mid-60s.	Leaders mobilized membership to convene for the focus group.
Matsumoto City	Nagano	8	Women interested in the expanding nonprofit sector, aged mid-30s to mid-60s	A journalist helped to recruit women.
Dorm X	Tokyo	9	Graduate and undergraduate women representing an array of disciplines, aged 20–31	A graduate student attending one of the top universities circulated my informational flyer to recruiter members from her dorm.
WinWin	Tokyo	5	Fundraising organization for women candidates, aged late 20s to early 50s.	The head of the organization assembled staff members and volunteers.
World Café	Tokyo	6	Group of professional women who have traveled internationally and subscribe to an e-zine that targets women, aged 25–35	Active/dedicated reader recruited other readers in her network.
Small Town	Nagano	5	Women interested in the expanding non-profit sector, aged mid-40s to mid-60s	A journalist helped to recruit women.
Total		47		

setting, participants easily transferred habits developed in study groups to negotiate the interactions in this new site of knowledge production. The focus group itself briefly became another node in a large and loose network, providing insight to what happens in other settings.

My research method drew from feminist epistemologies that privilege "situated knowledge," that is, what the world looks like through the viewer's interpretation of her own experiences (Hartsock 1987; Lave and Wenger 1991; Kronsell 2005; Mahmood 2005). Women in my focus groups embraced their "standpoint" as a valuable source of information in a society that claims that women are not as politically sophisticated as men. Japanese women positioned themselves as equally knowledgeable as—if not or more knowledgeable than—predominantly male political elites who stand to learn a lot about how to improve government performance and increase public support if they take the everyday knowledge of women seriously. This is a radical move in a world that discounts women's knowledge. Empowerment for these women was in the value that they attribute to what they know and the process of understanding it in the context of their everyday lives. Women argued that their undervalued and marginalized perspective of the world is valuable because it is uniquely theirs and inaccessible to members of a privileged elite who refuse to engage with it. Government would be better if it embraced diverse perspectives. Not only would policy outcomes improve, political dynamics would also undergo significant changes because the incorporation of underrepresented perspectives demands greater transparency and accountability.

I conducted a total of seven focus groups in Tokyo and Nagano Prefecture, each with five to nine participants. These women are not representative of Japanese women and society as a whole. They are "self-selected"; that I invited women to talk about politics means by definition that women who already had strong feelings and opinions about gender and politics were more likely to participate. These women were slightly more educated, more civically engaged, and more politically progressive than women on average, but these traits also make them likely "opinion leaders." How these women negotiated and overcame the barriers to political action promised to tell me something about the how and why women who had fallen outside of traditional channels for political mobilization organized to influence national politics.

Aside from the depth that focus group discussions add to the range of perspectives that emerge in the survey data, focus groups are well suited to my book because they provide insight into the interactive, communal processes adopted by everyday voters that can potentially shift attitudes about politics in ways that influence behavior in the electoral arena.[10] Despite the

---

10. Madriz (2003) and Morgan (2004) provide in-depth discussions of the costs and benefits of focus group research.

secrecy of the ballot box and the tendency of survey researchers to identify and isolate factors that determine individual vote choice, voting is a collective activity. Focus groups not only provide ways to see how voters talk about politics among themselves, they also are an occasion to observe how participants manage power relations in communal settings. While my recruitment strategy produced groups made up of women who are more politically engaged than average, that I was outnumbered by participants means that the women I interviewed had more control over the space; the power relations that emerge are less likely to be those that privilege my goals as a researcher and are more likely to be those that participants bring with them from the outside world. Since status differences based on gender, age, education, occupation, and so on are considered central to the operation of Japan's "vertical society" and politics (Nakane 1970), focus groups provide an opportunity to observe the strategies Japanese women use to manage relations of power to create a space for productive engagement.

I have selected three of my seven focus groups for in-depth treatment—two in Tokyo and one in Matsumoto City, Nagano Prefecture. These three groups highlight themes and practices that were evident in the remaining groups. The other four groups are referenced throughout the book when they provide additional insights, but to avoid repetition they are not discussed at any length. While some might argue that seven focus groups is a small sample, the consistency of themes across disparate groups was a sign that I had reached a saturation point; in all likelihood, I would have heard mostly repetition if I had continued to convene additional groups using my same recruitment mechanism. Further, these groups were initially convened to provide context and content for aggregate statistics that showed that women were more dissatisfied with politics than men without providing reasons why. Thus, these groups were put together to generate possible explanations rather than to test a new theory. That said, my findings underscore a need for future research.

My focus groups represent a small slice of Japanese civil society but offer important insights into the forms that the politicization of women's groups can assume and the effects of this process on national-level politics. Though individual groups range from completely autonomous entities to loosely organized networks and can be purely social or explicitly political, what brings women into these groups provides an initial political spark that is ignited by an impulse to treat groups as a site of learning. Common paths for entering into gender-segregated groups that "educate" are as instructive as the experiences women have as group members. Both can lead to personal empowerment, with consequences for how members think about participation in national politics.

An Overview of the Book

The initial chapters of this book make Japanese politics accessible to newcomers to the field while linking disparate work on gender, state-society relations, institutional change, and political participation together in ways that should be of interest to Japanese politics specialists. This work bridges the local/national divide in analyses of voting behavior, links electoral and administrative reforms, and connects attitudes about politics to new forms of political action. My narrative about the substantive effects of demographic changes on citizen engagement in civil society and the operation of social networks is central to efforts to map and understand the changing nature of state-society relations in democracies. My focus on women's mobilization of resources to narrow disparities in political participation should be of interest to generalists interested in education and democracy; gender and politics; and the role of the state in supporting policies that build human capital.

In chapter 1, I analyze individual responses to open-ended questions posed to a national sample of voters in 2000, roughly the same time as my focus group meetings, to identify dominant trends in public opinion that remain as true now as then. Citizens across Japan use practices in their everyday lives to construct a definition of democracy that involves questioning the status quo and tradition, listening to diverse perspectives, encouraging participation and innovation, deliberating alternatives, and exposing the processes of decision-making. This definition conflicts with a widespread feeling that elite politics is exclusive, stagnant, and unresponsive and lacks vision, transparency, and accountability. Japanese voters complain that elite political practices are far removed from their understanding of what democracy is and how it should be practiced. Voters criticize closed decision-making processes and the inability of politicians to offer concrete, detailed policy alternatives to the problems that concern voters most. Changing attitudes about democracy and its practice provide a context for understanding observed patterns of participation in local politics and their implications for national political change.

In chapters 2 and 3 I argue that the types of political attitudes that emerge from surveys are consistent with trends in local political action—an increase in referenda and recall movements, demands for information disclosure and taxpayer suits, citizens' parties, and victorious independent and antiestablishment candidates. In chapter 2, I use the JEDS survey to highlight a central concern to voters—shortening the distance between everyday voters and national political elites. National elites' political practices do not conform to voters' expectations about democracy, and voters are struggling to bring elite practices into alignment with their own definitions of popular democracy. I provide examples of how grassroots political action consistent with the attitudes expressed in JEDS has slowly forced the national elite political establishment to respond to demands to deepen democracy. Political leaders across Japan are struggling to align their practices with public expectations about citizen-elite engagement.

In chapter 3, I develop a case study of politics in Nagano Prefecture that is informed by secondary literature, news reporting, election outcomes, and a focus group that I conducted in Matsumoto City. The Nagano data show how citizens are actively engaged in changing the politics of their everyday lives and communities in an effort to remake the state in their own image through the ballot box. Voter exclusion from national politics contrasts with the changes in the quality of local democracy that voters across Japan have been able to achieve through broadening and deepening their own citizenship practices. Voters' desires to extend these grassroots practices into the elite political sphere are reflected in patterns of local political action in Nagano and elsewhere that aim to change national politics from the grassroots level through referenda and recall, information disclosure movements, and local independent candidates and citizen's parties.

Chapter 4 introduces readers to two sets of focus group participants, all women of voting age living in the Tokyo metropolitan area. Women use emphatic narratives about education, self-improvement, community, and national development when talking about electoral participation. Women assume responsibility for teaching themselves and analyze their own interactions with the state in everyday life as their primary data source for evaluating national politics. Participants transform the focus group into a "community of practice" and through this process provide insight into how any study group, regardless of topic, upends traditional modes of knowledge production. Women's study groups yield alternative definitions of democracy and political practices that clash with "elite" national politics in Japan.

Chapter 5 examines the unexpected consequences of state efforts to harness women's educational attainment to its own developmental goals over the postwar period. Women's education was initially promoted to prepare mothers to socialize and educate a highly skilled and disciplined workforce for the future. A side effect is that women themselves constitute a highly skilled and underutilized pool of human capital that seeks alternative spaces for reinvestment and future growth. The Japanese state's promotion of lifelong learning, from the 1980s onward, to create a more flexible labor force generated opportunities for women to define new research and study agendas outside of a formal institutional setting.[11] Women engaged in study groups have the opportunity to shift popular understandings of what constitutes legitimate knowledge and expertise, how it is produced, and who is fit for teaching and being taught. In this chapter, I suggest that women's participation in spaces of learning in Japan is one key factor that explains how women voters mobilize to produce electoral upsets under conditions that should make them stay home. The book concludes with critical reflections on the potential and limits of lifelong learning in promoting political deliberation, a more inclusive democracy, and more representative outcomes.

---

11. Contemporary lifelong learning policy builds on, but is a clear break from, social education programs begun in Meiji era (1868–1912) and resumed after World War II.

1

THE POLITICAL DISTANCE BETWEEN CITIZENS AND ELITES

Nearly a decade after a short-lived eight-party coalition government unseated the LDP to reform the electoral rules of the House of Representatives in 1993–1994, Japanese voters remained deeply dissatisfied with national politics. The public mood shifted dramatically in the aftermath of the DPJ's August 2009 victory and the long-awaited alteration in government it brought, the first achieved through the ballot box in the postwar period. Voters reported that their votes had finally made a difference. What were the underlying dynamics of a landslide election and a rapid shift in public opinion about the influence of voters? In 2002, *Asahi Shimbun* opinions editor Shin'ichi Yoshida asserted that "distrust [in politics] has prompted change in the political process and the media as well. It has rocked the political establishment. It is changing ways of governing." A change in the "subsystems of government" provided angry voters opportunities to agitate for change in the "quality of governance." But Yoshida also hypothesized that "another decade or two will be needed before we can see how these developments have left their mark" on Japanese politics (Yoshida 2002, 14–15).

Yoshida's reference to changing "subsystems of government" calls attention to institutional reforms that shifted power relations among parties in a new era of coalition government; between politicians and the bureaucracy; and between local government and national government. Changes in these subsystems fundamentally alter the "electoral connection" between voters and elected officials, resulting in a "dismantling of conventional ways of governing" (ibid. 15). In this chapter, I examine the attitudes about politics that underpin mass expressions of distrust to begin the process of mapping out how citizens have left their mark on Japanese politics. I argue that distrust in politics is associated with a public discourse about how democracy should work that accompanies changes in how citizens practice democracy. These changes broke through the surface of national politics with the victory of the DPJ in the 2009 House of Representatives election.

I am interested in the content and structure of a public discourse about political discontent that emerges from a national sample of Japanese voters. Japanese voters express an ideology, a system of meaning that links "sets of beliefs that explain how [political] arrangements came to be and how they might be changed or strengthened" to a "cluster of values about what is right and wrong as well as norms about what to do," individually and collectively (Oliver and Johnston 2000, 44). In this chapter I establish that the concept of political discontent or distrust neatly encapsulates a detailed analysis of Japanese politics that is readily invoked by everyday Japanese voters. In this chapter and the next, I highlight how this ideology of discontent played a role in electoral upsets in local and national politics; it is commonly offered as a rationale for why citizens' groups rallied around unconventional and outsider candidates, and why successful politicians adopt populist strategies. In subsequent chapters, I argue that attending to women voters helps us to understand how this ideology is constructed and how the channels through which it circulates become so widespread. I argue that this system of meaning is discursively constructed in face-to-face encounters in communities of practice where ideas and opinions are exchanged and deliberated and is diffused through Japan's dense social networks and rich information and media environment. Looking at these practices, in turn, lets us see how patterns of civic engagement are changing in Japan and what these developments say about the changing quality of democracy.

This chapter organizes thematic content and structural elements present in political expressions voiced by a national random sample of voters in three categories borrowed from Benford and Snow (2000)—"diagnosis (how things got to be how they are), prognosis (what should be done and what the consequences will be), and rationale (who should do it and why)" (Oliver and Johnston 2000, 43). My point of reference is not the elite movement activist or political entrepreneur who makes strategic decisions about how to employ cultural values and folk wisdom as a means of framing grievances to mobilize public opinion and action behind a collective goal.[1] Rather, I am interested in the bottom-up process of "meaning-making" among everyday voters. My analysis of data sustains Oliver and Johnston's view of ordinary people "developing belief systems from a combination of reflecting on and interpreting their own experiences and learning ideas and idea systems from others. [Voters] are thinkers and interpreters" (51). I borrow the language of social movements as a tool to represent cognitive mobilization processes, which are associated with the wave of democratic citizens who use knowledge-based resources to construct a popular understanding of democracy that fosters a more critical engagement with the existing system and increasing demands for direct participation (Norris 1999; Dalton 2000; Dalton et al. 2000; Kabashima et al. 2000).

---

1. Oliver and Johnston (2000) argue that "frame" and "ideology" are often conflated by social movement researchers who consequently weaken the utility of framing as an analytical tool and leave the social construction of ideology unexamined. Ultimately, the connection between frames and ideology is undertheorized and tenuous. Frame, they argue, is not a synonym for ideology, though ideologies can function as frames. To draw a sharp distinction between the two, Oliver and Johnston cite Kristen Luker's 1984 work on the U.S. movements for and against legal abortion to demonstrate how the same master frame, "civil rights," was used by the pro-life and pro-choice activists, groups with "diametrically opposed ideologies." Oliver and Johnston deepen the distinction when they write, "framing points to process, while ideology points to content" (Oliver and Johnston 2000, 8). Here, I use *ideology* to highlight where conservatives and progressives find common ground in Japan while avoiding the need to juggle multiple ideologies. Framing enters my story in chapter 2, in which I argue that prime ministers, with varying degrees of success, try to "frame" their appeals to the public in ways that tap into the ideology of discontent to demonstrate that they are attentive to the public interest. The act of listening, evident in framing processes that "bring the public back in," becomes a sign of a commitment to bringing elite and popular democratic practices into closer alignment. I find Oliver and Johnston's distinctions between ideology and framing productive for the exercise presented here. Framing is about "renaming" or "repackaging" a system of beliefs, or some subset of a belief system, so that it sells better to a mass public. As frame is "an orientating principle that points in a direction of seeing things, and an ideology [is] a system of ideas arrived at through education, socialization, and debate" (Oliver and Johnston 2000, 12).

Discontent in the Electorate

In April and May of 2000, the interviewers from the Japanese Election and Democracy Study (henceforth JEDS) asked a national random sample of voters a series of open-ended questions in individual face-to-face interviews (Nishizawa et al. 2001). First, respondents were asked, "Have you had any dissatisfactions or doubts about matters of the nation, your prefecture, city/town/village, or neighborhood?" Those respondents who answered "yes" were then asked, "When you try to solve these problems, what kinds of means can you think of?" Respondents were invited to share an exhaustive list of problem-solving strategies. Respondents who expressed no dissatisfaction with the current state of affairs at any level were invited to imagine how they would respond if faced with a problem. Six months later, additional questions were posed to respondents in a mail-survey. First, respondents were asked, "What does the phrase 'politics in Japan' call to mind?" Second, they were asked why they participate in politics or not. Finally, the mail survey invited respondents to list the political and social activities they participate in. This chapter is concerned with the worldview that emerged from these questions. The following chapters link this view to actual patterns of civic and political engagement and proposed action strategies. The following analysis relies heavily on responses to the question about what the phrase "politics in Japan" calls to mind.

This survey and my own fieldwork were conducted as politics neared the end of a decade of flux, during which public distrust in and dissatisfaction with politics—in Japan and cross-nationally—mounted (Pharr 1997; Pharr and Putnam 2000). The opinion survey, it has been argued, is a "complement to, or even an alternative to voting, petitioning or protesting" (Tilly 1983, 262). This sentiment is evident in the response patterns that emerge. Respondents took advantage of the open-ended questions to voice frustrations that they said did not find expression in the political system. Several voiced the desire for more surveys exactly like the present one.[2] The open-ended format of the JEDS served as a mass outlet for

---

2. Given the size of the polling industry in Japan, the wish for more surveys is unusual. For instance, other respondents complained that politicians relied on polls too much. An overreliance on polls in decision-making poses a real threat to the public interest because polls can be designed to produce support for policies that serve politicians' self-interest. Further, polls rarely provide an

complaints about politics and offered a venue for respondents to suggest what they would do to solve communal problems; why they do or do not participate in the political process; and what types of actions they undertake to bring about change.

The entire population of survey respondents numbered 1,618 individuals for the first wave of face-to-face interviews and 635 individuals for the mail survey in the second wave. An analysis of the open-ended responses entails a dramatic reduction in the number of valid responses for any one item because proffering additional information and, in the case of the mail survey, writing in answers, imposes higher costs on the respondent. Figure 1.1 provides an overview of how many open-ended responses were analyzed for key open-ended questions in the face-to-face interviews of the first wave and mail survey of the second wave. Just over 40 percent (41.1 percent) of the 1,618 respondents in the face-to-face interviews (N=665) affirmed that they were dissatisfied with national or local matters, but only 261 individuals offered solutions. Though this leaves me with a dramatically reduced sample size, many individuals offered more than one solution, and many of the solutions were echoed by the 498 individuals who mailed in similar opinions about Japanese politics in the second wave and the 260 individuals who elaborated on why they want to become involved in politics (or not), also in the second wave. A benefit of the open-ended format is that many respondents offer answers that extend beyond the parameters of the question.

The free answers from each wave were stored in separate files that were also independent of the coded, quantitative data files.[3] While this ensured the confidentiality of respondents, this entry method made it difficult to link different open-ended responses to the same individual. There is significant overlap for the 261 respondents who shared their solutions for national and local problems, the 498 respondents who described their image

---

outlet for people to express the rationale that underlies their positions, thereby potentially masking illiberal tendencies. I can only suppose that the desire for "more surveys like this one" means more surveys that provide opportunities for respondents to elaborate on their positions in a quasi-structured format.

3. I assume that the quantitative and qualitative data were stored separately in formats that made matching difficult in order to ensure the confidentiality of the identities of individual respondents. Some of the qualitative data may have contained information that could have made certain respondents identifiable once combined with coded demographic information.

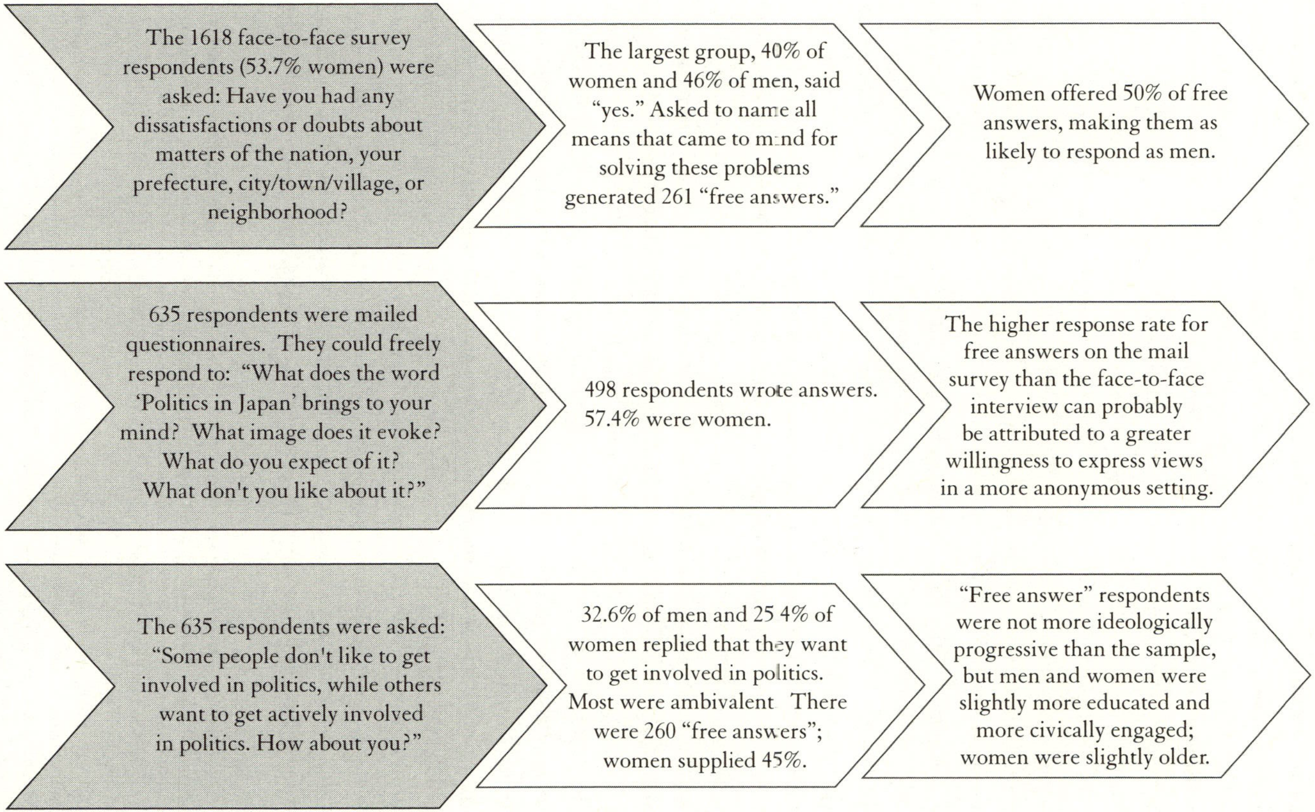

Figure 1.1 Sampling discontent

of Japanese politics, and the 260 respondents who offered their rationale for wanting to get involved in or stay out of Japanese politics. Some participants responded only in the face-to-face interview, some answered only the mail survey, and some responded to both. In each wave, some respondents answered every open-ended question while others answered one or none at all.

Finally, different data entry and storage methods for the open-ended (qualitative) and closed-ended (quantitative) data makes linking the open-ended respondents to the demographic data needed to provide a comprehensive statistical reporting of their descriptives unfeasible. Nonetheless, I compared some key demographic and attitudinal data of respondents who responded only in the face-to-face interviews (N=983, that is, N=1618–635) with those of respondents who also followed up by completing the mail-in survey (N=635) to draw some inferences about whether the answers provided by the mail-in respondents differ significantly and, if so, in what ways. Figure 1.1 reports some statistics to situate the small number of respondents who offered "free answers" within the sample as a whole to highlight any systematic biases that set these individuals apart.[4] Voters who followed up in the second wave, the mail-in survey, were not more ideologically progressive; on a scale of one to ten where one represents the "most progressive," the mean for both groups (approximately 5.5) indicated that most voters were moderates or centrists. There were almost as many LDP identifiers and nonpartisans in the first group (35.2 percent and 40.8 percent, respectively) as in the second group of respondents (40.8 percent and 40.6 percent). However, with the exception of labor unions, the second group of respondents had slightly higher rates of membership in every group listed as an option: residential associations, PTAs, trade associations, consumer cooperatives, volunteer groups, residential movements, religious groups, alumni associations, and candidate support

---

4. Again, my ability to provide a comprehensive report of descriptive statistics for those respondents who answered open-ended questions was limited, because these data were not entered and stored in a manner that allowed me to manipulate them with ease. If the open-ended question was preceded by a closed-ended question, as in the case where respondents were asked whether they wanted to be involved in politics, I was able to generate descriptive statistics that provided insight into the kinds of respondents who then continued to offer open-ended responses. On a very limited basis, I used case ID information to pull out relevant socioeconomic data for questions that were not preceded by a closed-ended question, as was the case when respondents were asked about their image of Japanese politics.

groups (*koenkai*). Not only were mail-in respondents more likely to belong to groups, they also reported slightly higher levels of involvement. A higher percentage of respondents to the mail survey reported that they were interested in politics (60.6 percent expressed an interest in politics, compared to 48.5 percent of face-to-face respondents). Consistent with their higher rates of participation, respondents in the second wave were slightly older and more educated, which translates to more experience and access to knowledge-based resources that, combined with higher rates of group participation, bolster engagement. Although there is variability across responses, for the most part men and women were as likely to respond to the open-ended questions as men.

Though respondents to the mail-in survey and the open-ended questions are among the more engaged and better-resourced respondents, they are not outliers. In fact, they are likely opinion leaders whose attitudes should be of great interest because they may tell us something about whether and how these voters differ from our conventional understanding of local opinion leaders as invested in maintaining the LDP's money-power style of politics. Taken individually, the interpretation of any one response is necessarily limited to what is written on the page; I can attribute no further meaning to what is offered. In the aggregate, these responses form a rich, coherent, and consistent narrative about the limitations of the democratic process in Japan and citizen strategies—individually and collectively—for attending to democratic deficiencies.

The Frog in the Well

Japanese voters use the idiomatic expression, "it's like a frog in a well" (*I no naka no kawazu*) to express their image of politics in Japan. A frog in a well does not know the sea (*taikai o shirazu*). Like a frog in a well, a person with few experiences is incapable of having a broad perspective on the world.[5]

---

5. Teachers in Japan often use this proverb to encourage students to broaden their horizons and to get ahead in life through hard work and achievement. Maynard and Maynard (1995) explain the meaning of this proverb in a text designed to acquaint Japanese-language learners with culture through idiomatic expressions. The expression resonates on several levels at once: it is used to talk about individuals as well as Japan as a nation. The frog in a well is someone who is too comfortable within the limited confines of his or her daily existence, so is ignorant of how wide the

The "frog in the well" is a culturally resonant symbol available as a "frame" to political entrepreneurs for mobilizing ordinary Japanese to turn out to vote, petition, or protest politicians, parties, and political practices that are not in the public interest. The expression plays an important role in defining "we the people" against "self-interested elites" and "shaping grievances into broader more resonant claims" (Tarrow 1998, 21). This frame is a point of entry into an underlying ideology of discontent. The frame is discursively shaped in a particular context (a national survey) and political moment (the Mori administration in 2000 and 2001), but the worldview that it expresses helps to account for patterns of mass political participation unfolding in Japan over the course of the last two decades.

In this section, I use the "frog in the well" to enter into, examine, and describe the content and structure of this political worldview. To elaborate its meaning as fully as possible, I looked at the statements that preceded and followed this declaration. I asked how often statements that were synonymous with "frog in the well" were echoed throughout the sample by voters who did not invoke the idiom. I divide the underlying ideology into its constitutive parts—the common problem, its source, its potential solutions, and strategies for its resolution. A "distance frame" connects these constitutive parts of the particular ideology of discontent expressed by ordinary Japanese. The problem with politics is that it is far removed from the everyday experiences of the average voter. The solution is to bring elite political practices into alignment with popular understandings of what democracy is and how it should be practiced. The rationale is that when citizens cultivate democracy in everyday interactions, they prepare themselves for deeper engagement in local politics, and better democracy in local politics opens new channels for changing national politics from the ground up.

The Limited Vision of Japanese Politicians

The question "Do you have any dissatisfactions or doubts about politics?" elicits complaints. In face-to-face encounters, the respondents were happy to

---

world is and what it has to offer. The frog is parochial, not cosmopolitan. The Japanese are self-conscious about their identity as an island nation. As an island nation, the Japanese must travel widely and think about their place in the world to avoid succumbing to isolationism. After noticing the frequency with which this expression was used, I asked a colleague and native speaker how to interpret it within the context of politics.

comply. But the question "What images come to mind when you hear the phrase politics in Japan?" allows respondents to offer positive or negative assessments. The latter question was asked in a mail survey conducted in late 2000, six months after the initial face-to-face interview. The intervening period of time offset the chance that the first set of questions would affect the content and tone of the second set of answers. But the tone of the responses was overwhelmingly critical and consistent with what voters said when interviewed face to face. When respondents replied to both sets of questions, the consistency in their answers—spaced six months apart—is high. Individual images of Japanese politics and political dissatisfaction are interchangeable, synonymous. Voters went off topic in the open-ended questions, seizing any opportunity to talk about and critique the political process and elites.

That voters characterize politics and politicians as dirty and corrupt is not news. National politicians are seen as self-interested, short-sighted, inexperienced policy-makers with no sense of innovation who waste the taxpayers' money on useless public works projects that are not in the interest of the common good, because they (politicians) have no sense of what the public interest looks like. Politicians in the LDP, the ruling party at the time, are out of touch because long-term single-party dominance has insulated them from mass political pressures while firmly tying them to a narrow constituency base that includes the construction industry, farmers, and big business.[6] No, this characterization of Japanese politics is not new. What is new, however, is the sentiment that ordinary voters occupy a qualitatively different political practice space that they are struggling to extend into the elite political sphere.

Voters fervently "wish [politicians] could understand and carry out politics from the common people's point of view." Or, as one voter put it, "Because politicians are elected by the people as representatives, the people are not below the politicians, the politicians are below the people. I think it's wrong that we should call them *'sensei,'*" a common term of respect. Voters watch the deliberations of the National Diet (the most important legislative house in Japan) on television, "notice that many seats are empty," and "wish politicians attended and participated in Diet discussions since they are elected by the people in order to listen to people's voice and work for

---

6. In reality, "special interests" to voters are district-specific and include whichever group(s) any individual voter does not self-identify with.

them." The contrast between national politics and local citizenship practices make up the body of facts that citizens marshal in pitting "us" (ordinary voters) against "them" (unrepresentative elites) and leads ordinary voters to rally around a vision of politics for the people and by the people. There is a consensus that national politicians are unable to represent voters' interests, because politics is "happening too far from the places we live in," and the places ordinary Japanese live in have changed considerably over the course of the postwar period. National "politics remains the same," but everyday people have changed. One voter states simply that there can be no "Japanese politics" without the people.

Turnout has been falling and distrust in politics has been increasing for approximately three decades (Kabashima et al. 2000). These trends suggest that public opinion about democracy and elite democratic practices have been divergent for a long while and that the gap between mass and elite visions of democracy is large. Voters argue that bringing ordinary people back in would make politics and elites more representative, responsive, and accountable—all dimensions that political researchers use to make assessments about how well democracy works (Diamond 1997; O'Donnell 2007). Japanese voters complain that the national political process falls short on every dimension.

Voters use several measures to mark the distance between "ordinary Japanese" and political elites, between "real" democracy at the grassroots level and the mockery that elites make of democracy on the national level— the depths of political stagnation amid mounting expectations for change; the amount of collective effort it takes to kick the miscreants out; the demographic differences between the National Diet and the population; the number of check-points voters must navigate to contact elected officials; the difference between a top-down and bottom-up political process; the difference between national policy outcomes and personal policy preferences; the difference between public opinion and elite practices; and the difference between the lived experiences of elites and "ordinary Japanese." LeBlanc, too, uses a distance metaphor to capture the differences in the routes that taxi citizens (men) and bicycle citizens (women) must travel to express their voices in the political world. Men have a direct path to political influence while women must follow a more circuitous and indirect path (LeBlanc 1999). In recent work, LeBlanc puts forward an "autonomy principle," wherein local citizens exercise their right to greater self-determination in this unitary state. Local citizens are increasingly saying "no" to unpopular national public work projects because Tokyo's distance from local conditions demands closer consultation with locals when making decisions that affect local communities (LeBlanc 2008). This national sample of voters indicates the multiple dimensions by which political distance can be measured as well as the ways that distance impinges upon how democracy works.

For voters as well as political observers inside and outside the Japanese system, LDP dominance was the most obvious sign that there is more continuity than change in Japanese politics after electoral reform. At the time of the JEDS survey, the LDP had been in continuous power throughout the postwar period, except for a brief fall from power from 1993 to 1994. Many voters were still awaiting a system whereby electoral power would alternate between two moderate, programmatic parties, an important goal of electoral reformers (Reed and Thies 2001). In the post-reform period, the LDP returned to power, first in a coalition of "strange bedfellows" with the LDP's longtime rival, the Social Democratic Party (formerly the Japan Socialist Party), before developing a more lengthy collaboration with the New Kōmeitō, a small party that draws its membership from the Buddhist organization Sōka Gakkai. At the time of the JEDS survey, a majority of voters had voted in the June 2000 House of Representatives election for a different party than the LDP; the winner-take-all single-member district seats allowed the LDP to translate a narrow plurality of votes into the largest bloc of seats in the lower house of the Diet. A coalition with a "religious" party that was unpopular with the LDP base enabled the LDP to hold on to power (Tanaka 2003). In sum, the LDP government was, in 2000 and the years to follow, showing signs that Japanese politics was falling short on multiple dimensions of democratic performance. Voters' ability to hold an unrepresentative, unresponsive, and exclusive government accountable was limited.

In 2000, voters used socioeconomic and "descriptive" markers of difference to inform the argument that elites who do not listen to everyday voters do not have the experience or knowledge to legislate in the public interest. National politicians are a tangible embodiment of major substantive problems with Japanese politics. Japan lags far behind other advanced stable industrial democracies in the representation of women in elected decision-making assemblies. Even as the social management of women's identities long has been an important state apparatus for conveying messages about Japan's progress and cosmopolitanism to the Western world (Garon 1998), these messages are undercut by the chronic underrepresentation of women in public life. With women holding 11.3 percent of lower house seats, Japan ranks just below Azerbaijan and Romania in its percentage of women elected to office, far behind the top ten nations, all of whom exceed a critical mass (30 percent) and are approaching parity.[7] In the absence of common experiences that link elites and ordinary voters, the importance of listening to the public to assess and weigh competing interests increases.

Though some voters voice a wish for more women in politics, few voters in the survey frame their argument for more women in terms of gender equality or argue that women would legislate on behalf of a female constituency. When it comes to women in politics, voters are as likely to mention the sexual exploits of male politicians as they are to talk about female officeholders or how social welfare policies affect women. When the private behavior of male politicians erupts into public sex scandals, the status of women in society and the futility of pursuing gender equality, given the climate in political parties and the National Diet, becomes clear. A young, nonpartisan woman stated, "I don't think leaders can be born in this kind of environment," where "politicians are implicated in bribery and problems with women." For this voter, criminality among politicians contributes to a vicious cycle. Gender aside, it is difficult to breed a new generation of citizens and politicians when current politicians are such poor role models. An environment that is hostile to women, in which male and female politicians across the partisan divide break the rules, cannot socialize its members to new values and norms. Undemocratic legislative

---

7. See the Inter-Parliamentary Union's 2010 report, "Women in National Parliaments." The United States is ranked 73rd, with 16.8 percent of House of Representatives seats held by women; women hold 15.3 percent of Senate seats. After the July 2007 House of Councillors election, Japan soared ahead of the United States in electing women, to 18.2 percent of seats. Even though political observers see stark differences in the status of women in both of these societies, they are more alike than not in the representation of women in national political office. The United States, too, is arguably far behind other long-term, advanced industrialized democracies. Women hold 47 percent of seats in Sweden's lower house, 41.5 percent in Finland, and 32.8 percent in Germany. The United States falls behind Iraq, where it instituted regime change; Iraqi women hold 25.5 percent of seats and the nation is ranked 41st. Neither the United States nor Japan has elected a woman as head of state.

norms are driving elites and voters farther apart. Changing legislative norms entails bringing in more people, including women, with "outsider" perspectives on politics.

Even though there is widespread recognition that politics is "male-dominated," it is the age and socioeconomic backgrounds of politicians, more than their gender, that pose the largest concerns to voters. Political insularity is a matter that cuts across the gender divide. The Diet is almost as unrepresentative of the male electorate as it is of women. One disgruntled voter complained that Diet members are "just a bunch of old men, and I think that the whole crew, even old women, above seventy years should not be allowed to run in elections." Age is a problem because older politicians perpetuate autocratic practices that are inconsistent with democratic ideals—they enforce seniority norms that do not allow young, talented politicians to influence the course of decision-making; in the words of one respondent, "They suppress the younger generation so they cannot voice their opinions." Older politicians, who came to prominence in an earlier era of political development, are out of sync with the contemporary challenges that the nation faces.

Voters assert that there is something qualitatively different about "junior" politicians, in their fifties and sixties, who represent the postwar generation, and this difference would make a difference in their style of governance and, relatedly, the policies that would emerge. The human capital that has accumulated in the generations raised during the early postwar and high-growth periods should produce politicians with "broader perspectives" that challenge the "conservative and exclusive" character of national politics. The political generation born and socialized after World War II participated in the social movements of the 1960s and 1970s. Like the young people who fueled social movements in the advanced industrialized democracies in the 1960s and 1970s, this generation of Japanese is seen as more elite-challenging and progressive and in solidarity with less powerful groups in society (Inglehart 1990, 1997). Generational change holds the promise of a new period of leadership. One JEDS respondent, a fifty-year-old women who voted for the LDP gives voice to voters who "hope for more people like Yasuo Tanaka, governor of Nagano Prefecture, who wants to change the traditional, bureaucratic system into a new, more open form of government." But political change is not a waiting game. Ordinary voters are changing their citizenship practices to influence patterns of citizen-elite engagement, the focus of chapters 2 through 4.

The lived experiences of representatives are so far outside of the mainstream that they are unable to relate to common problems faced by everyday voters. One nonpartisan woman in her early forties complained, "Diet members are elites without any sense of how everyday people think." And a male nonpartisan nearly two decades older agreed, "Since there are so many rich politicians, they don't understand what it means to be poor." Hereditary politicians, second- and third-generation Diet members who succeeded a male relative to office, are evidence of a system that is literally reproducing itself because the institutional mechanisms that evolved under the 1955 system have persisted into the post-reform period. For example, fiscal centralization is a feature of the Japanese system that encouraged voters to elect hereditary politicians because they have preexisting connections to business and political elites that make it easier for them to redirect funds to their home district (Scheiner 2005, 2006; Taniguchi 2008). With administrative decentralization, there are tensions in small rural districts between citizens reluctant to let go of these practices for fear of the burden that administrative functions will impose and others who see this as an opportunity to change local relationships with the national government.

The socioeconomic distance between citizens and political elites was arguably a mounting problem by 2000, for the same reasons, ironically, that these differences were largely ameliorated during the high-growth period; elites are no longer able to redistribute income as effectively as they once did. In 2000, voters were already feeling the effects of "the gap" (*kakusa*); after enjoying high growth and one of the most equal distributions of wealth in the world from the 1970s through the early 1990s, the income disparities between rich and poor had begun to widen once again, after the speculative economic bubble burst. The combination of administrative decentralization to rationalize social care costs and the erosion of the social welfare system brought on by demographic changes has worried many voters, who concluded that the relative security of elites meant that the future did not pose similar threats to their well-being.

In the midst of a protracted recession, respondents claimed that affluent politicians could not grasp the depth of widespread anxieties about the future of the pension system and social care services for the young and aged. One woman voter, a nonpartisan in her mid-thirties, complained that "pension-related issues are never discussed seriously in the Diet because most politicians don't need to be worried about their lives after retirement.…I sometimes think I could do better for the people if I were a politician. If politicians increased the qualifying age for child care allowances because they really think it will improve the declining birthrate, then they really are idiots. Double-income families can't benefit from taxes they've already paid." When self-interested politicians take action to address livelihood issues, they are unable to pass legislation that successfully tackles quality-of-life issues because they cannot understand the experiences of average Japanese voters.

The distinction between "descriptive" and "substantive" representation is an argument frequently heard in debates globally about whether members of majority groups are able to represent adequately the interests of underrepresented groups, for instance, women and ethnic or racial minorities. Japanese voters echo these concerns but take the matter a step further by including socioeconomic markers beyond gender and ethnicity as well. Additionally, voters invoke descriptive representation as an explicit symptom of how informal, often unobserved, practices limit the range of voices heard in politics, thereby impeding the functioning of democracy. The people understood as belonging to underrepresented groups move from the margins of the political stage to its center. Voters discursively expand the group boundaries of underrepresentation to include ordinary Japanese and exclude the elite political establishment, a tactical move with the potential to facilitate mass political mobilization.

Voters also measured the disconnect with elites in terms of the narrowing spectrum of ideological perspectives represented in the Diet. By 2000, the scope of representation in the Diet had indeed narrowed. The largest traditional opposition parties—the JSP and the JCP—had virtually disappeared from the national political scene, and the DPJ had not yet filled the void. Moreover, as a conglomeration of ideologies from across the political spectrum, the DPJ was both more centrist and less defined than any of the traditional opposition parties. This left many opposition party supporters without any clear party to support at the national level. Consequently, voters complained that they had no electoral choices.

A weak opposition means that there are fewer veto points in the system for voters to express their views. Linkage structures have broken down, increasing the number of hurdles voters must surmount to voice their interests and distancing them even further from national political elites. The

LDP has so much power that government ends up running more like a dictatorship (*dokusaiteki na seiji ni natte shimau*) than a democracy. When the opposition is excluded from decision-making, "isn't this," questions one voter, "an abuse of democracy?" He continued, "I wish there was more discussion when problems are addressed." During earlier points in the postwar period, a stronger opposition—though still out of power—was able to use delaying tactics effectively to protest publicly, thereby raising consciousness about their exclusion from decision-making; this gained them concessions from the LDP. But over the course of the decade leading up to 2000, the opposition has become increasingly fragmented, parties have disappeared, and their collective share of Diet seats has diminished. While majority norms prevail in legislative politics, they are not legitimate if minority views are not represented at all. Or rather, elites are cast as a minority suppressing the rights of a majority of voters, who gain no representation. Some voters do not see parties at all but a collection of individuals who are all pursing their own personal interests. The opposition's voice has weakened dramatically, but people's expectations that there should be an opposition remain, because their own experiences are proof that there is an alternative point of view. There is a collective sense that better democracy entails a reworking of the relationship between elites and the public at large.

Old Politics under the New DPJ

In 2001, Junichiro Koizumi, who the media dubbed a "maverick" politician, moved from the periphery to the center of the LDP when he appealed directly to local party chapters and the mass public to win the post of party president. As prime minister, Koizumi vowed to revitalize Japanese politics by destroying traditional bases of power within the party and creating greater transparency, responsiveness, and accountability in government. He retained and honed the populist strategies he used to win the party presidency to advance his policy agenda over the course of his premiership (to be discussed in chapters 2 and 3). Koizumi shortened the distance between the prime minister and the electorate. JEDs voters finally had their "transformational leader" (Samuels 2003).[8] However, Koizumi

---

8. Richard Samuels finds that "transformational" leaders "stretch their constraints," mobilizing available resources to reshape social and institutional norms, thereby altering the range of future political possibilities.

did not set Japanese politics on a new course. After five years in office, Koizumi stepped down and old patterns of governance returned. Political observers such as Yoshida (2002, 18–19) noted that even as the LDP reaped the electoral benefits of Koizumi's popularity, voters maintained a separation between their evaluation of the prime minister and the LDP. Even though the prime minister had moved closer to voters, the LDP was still considered distant. Consequently, voter dissatisfaction with national politics returned full force in 2005.

In 2009, voters finally built enough momentum to exercise the power of the ballot box to decisively oust the LDP. However, voters' excitement following the DPJ's victory, read as a public mandate in favor of "change," was short-lived. Between 2005 and 2010, Japan observers have maintained that the success of administrations post-Koizumi is contingent upon the ability of prime ministers to use the media to build public support (Krauss and Pekkanen 2008). Kan, too, is advised to do "what Koizumi did: [appeal] to the public directly in order to break the resistance of opposition parties and opponents within his own party" (Harris 2010).

However, the DPJ has been hampered by leadership problems. Instability at the top hints at problems internal to the party's organization that have real consequences for governing. The party had two prime ministers in its first year in power. Yukio Hatoyama resigned in June 2010 and was replaced by Naoto Kan. Internal struggles for power were a constant during the DPJ's first year, placing considerable constraints upon the party's leadership. Further, Hatoyama's failure to deliver on his campaign promise to relocate the Futenma Marine Corps Air Base led to mass protests on Okinawa that threatened to destabilize the long-standing U.S.-Japan security alliance, a relationship that has popular support on the mainland. Efforts to resolve the Futenma issue detracted from the new government's ability to tackle economic and political issues that were more important to the majority of voters. In its first year, the DPJ failed to shorten the distance between political elites and everyday voters, resulting in Hatoyama's early resignation and loss of the party's majority in the House of Councillors in the July 2010 election.

Kan spent his first months in office defending his position from DPJ cofounder and former secretary general Ichiro Ozawa, who challenged him for the positions of party president and prime minister in the DPJ's presidential election in September 2010. The specter of Ozawa, whose political roots are in the LDP, signaled to voters that old political practices survived under the new administration. Media reporting fueled public suspicion that Ozawa operated as the power behind the throne during the Hatoyama administration. Kan's decisive victory over Ozawa provides him and the DPJ another opportunity to lead Japan. Thus far, he has excluded members of Ozawa's political group from the cabinet in a renewed effort to change how Japan is governed while laying the groundwork to tackle economic challenges that speak directly to the quality-of-life issues that most concern voters.

Ordinary People in Elite Politics: A Prognosis and Rationale

The distance between national elites and ordinary Japanese distorts democratic processes and outcomes. The narrative that ordinary citizens know more about collective problems and problem-solving and are thus better suited to govern than elites is present in voters' perceptions of the "distance" separating "us" from "them" and their solutions for closing the gap. Extending inclusive citizenship practices from the grassroots level into elite political spaces offers a means for aligning democracy in theory—politics for and by the people—with practice. Converting "them" into "us" is the best means of shortening the distance, and it can be achieved through making political discussion public. Public discussion raises consciousness and changes attitudes with implications for everyone's political practice.

The "only way to solve problems is to talk, talk, talk." Unfortunately, this JEDS respondent's image of politics is that politicians, especially members of the opposition party, avoid conflict by not attending Diet sessions when contentious topics are scheduled for debate. Absent from their elected duties, opposition politicians violate their responsibility to their constituents when they do not voice and defend their views, and a sizable proportion of the voting public is excluded from the ground floor of decision-making. Politicians are not extending the parameters of a necessarily *public* debate in the most fundamental of ways. In their failure to engage in a public discussion, opposition politicians are not reshaping the terms of the debate by giving citizen observers new ways of thinking and talking about common problems and, in doing so, creating opportunities for alternative outcomes. In not talking, problems remain unresolved.

The deliberative practices that political elites do, or do not, adopt affect the quality and content of public information, which JEDS respondents overwhelmingly deemed poor. The poverty of public information, in turn, constrains ordinary voters' ability to hold elected officials accountable. Political exchanges during elections and from the floor of the Diet are not meaningful to voters, who complain that politicians hide behind jargon-filled language, omit and obscure relevant facts, assign blame to others, and pay more attention to private scandals than to public business. The impenetrable nothingness of elite political discourse deepened voters' beliefs that the real discussions and decision-making were happening somewhere "inside the organization, and never presented to the people." Closed decision-making bred self-interest and corruption among elites. The cumulative impact, voters complained, of a shortage of substantive public discussions that feature clearly articulated positions, concrete facts, and identifiable actors is that it produces a national politics that lacks beliefs and a well-articulated philosophy. Many voters, consequently, expressed vague, yet deep, anxieties about the "future of Japan" and its identity as a people and a state.

The political information that voters are left to work with are questions about why elite deliberative practices fail to produce the substance that voters require to make informed choices and assume their rightful place in the democratic process—above politicians. The distance between democracy as practiced in national politics and democracy as defined and practiced by voters in the context of their everyday lives is vast. When asked how they would solve local, prefectural, or national problems, JEDS participants offered solutions that placed talking with others and broadening the scope of *public* discussion at the center. JEDS participants proposed talking to friends, family, and neighbors; writing letters to the editor; making internet contacts; starting study groups; and contacting local officials and opinion leaders. Democratic politics seeks a common good that is negotiated within a large community of diverse interests.[9] Voters are taking responsibility for retrieving and exchanging the information that they need

---

9. A long tradition of work by scholars such as Pateman (1970), Bickford (1996), Bowler and Donovan (2002), and Walsh (2004), stresses the importance of deliberation to making democracy work, and how political discussion as a form of direct citizen participation in democracy can lead participants to deepen their engagement with the political world.

to create political knowledge, to contribute to an enriched public debate, and to exert control over elected officials in their local communities. JEDS respondents look to themselves to "study politics and be smart," "boost people's interest in politics," and "express opinions through elections," because "at the end of the day, politics reflects our opinions."

National Engagement through Local Practices: A Way Out

Japanese voters are less likely than voters elsewhere to agree that politicians listen and that their views are reflected in politics. According to data from *The Comparative Study of Electoral Systems* (2007 version), in 2004, 23.9 percent of Japanese voters felt that elections ensured that their views were represented in the political process, compared to 72 percent of American voters, 61 percent of French voters, 46 percent of Italian voters, and 49 percent of British voters. Not coincidentally, Japanese voters were also less likely to say that there was some party that represented their views and less likely to say that their government was performing well.

The large percentages of voters expressing the opinion that their voices are not represented in national politics is a problem because research also shows that when citizens are not included in making political decisions that affect them, they are more likely to question the legitimacy of political decision-making processes and policy outcomes (Hiskey and Bowler 2005). In extreme cases, citizens can become less compliant and more likely to break the rules over the long term. Conversely, inclusiveness—the feeling that you have a say in the decisions that affect you directly—promotes a sense of legitimacy with regard to political outcomes, even those that are contrary to one's own position (Hiskey and Bowler 2005; see also Bickford 1996; Young 2002). Legitimacy, in turn, fosters compliance and promotes positive feelings toward government. Even though Japanese voters are far more cynical about politics and far more likely than voters in other electorates to feel excluded, the good news is that Japanese voters, at 70 percent, are just as satisfied as voters in other electorates with their democracy. These two opposing views—satisfaction with democracy and distrust in national politics—can coexist because grassroots citizenship practices sustain the belief that voters can exercise greater control over political elites, starting from the ground up.

This chapter has been concerned with what types of evidence everyday people assemble to conclude that their voices are not represented, and how this sense of exclusion shapes their attitudes about national politics—what's wrong with it, how to fix it, and who will fix it. The open-ended responses to the JEDS survey reveal that the distance between voters and national politicians, and between normative democratic ideals and actual practices, are serious problems. Voters are pleased with democracy but dissatisfied with the practices. When asked how to solve community, regional, or national problems, these same voters propose that deepening democratic norms in their everyday patterns of civic engagement is the basis of extending these same norms into the political sphere so that Japan's democratic machinery produces more democratic outcomes. The problems do not lie with the institutions of democracy but with the practices that elected officials have evolved over time to reproduce the status quo.

Chapters 2 and 3 link the attitudes about politics expressed here to patterns of local political action increasingly observed over the course of the last two decades—referenda, recall, and information disclosure movements; electoral victories by independent and antiestablishment candidates; and the proliferation of citizen's parties in local politics. Hiskey and Bowler (2005) argue that the depth of local democratic practices is important because local politics is a training ground for national politics, and positive experiences with democracy close to home build individual-level confidence in mass ability to collectively influence the course of national politics over the long term, sustaining engagement even through periods when conditions encourage disengagement. Local political context matters because it provides civic experiences that help citizens to develop a popular understanding of what democracy is and the conviction that democracy can be built from the ground up.

Voters' ability to change their immediate environment through civic engagement builds confidence that these local practices can be extended to national politics. Democratic practices on the ground incite efforts to change the center from the periphery. People still have faith that democracy works because they opt to use existing tools to work within the system to change it from within; what is different is their starting point. Instead of working to replace national elites, everyday people are working from the ground up to move popular practices into elite politics. By developing their own democratic practices on the ground, they build a stronger foundation for national democracy, since democracy becomes ineffective if the people are not doing their job to produce a politics of the people, by the people, and for the people. Once people are holding up their end of the contract, they have necessarily created the momentum to demand that national politicians follow suit (Yokoyama 1999).

2

New Styles of Political Leadership and Community Mobilization

My image is that politics is a world where people's voices cannot be heard.
I can't support any parties because I don't understand what each party
wants to accomplish because they keep dividing and regrouping.
Elections are meaningless because I can't find any candidates I can
trust to exhibit strong leadership to make Japan a better place. I envy
nations like the U.S., with a system that allows people to directly
elect their nation's top leader. Prime Minister Mori's selection was
the complete opposite. I feel a deep sense of unease.

Nonpartisan female JEDS respondent, 37 years old

The Japanese Election and Democracy Study survey coincided with the tenure of Yoshirō Mori, who became president of the LDP and prime minister of Japan in April 2000, following the death of Keizō Obuchi, who had been in office just shy of two years. Japan went through six prime ministers in the seven years after electoral reform. The 1990s witnessed a proliferation of small reform parties formed by defectors from the LDP and the traditional opposition parties on the left. Parties splintered, merged, and dissolved at a dizzying rate, as voters waited for the system to reach a new equilibrium. The instability of the party system meant that party labels did not convey meaningful information to voters, and rapid turnover at the top level of government made it difficult for any administration to push forward a policy agenda. Japan entered a period of coalition government, beginning in 1993 with an eight-party coalition that included all parties except the JCP.[1]

---

1. The LDP was also excluded from this grand coalition that was formed precisely to unseat the dominant party. The LDP took control of government once again in 1994 when it entered into a coalition with the JSP, its longtime rival.

Coalition government further muddied accountability and made strong leadership essential, since so many players had to be satisfied in order to maintain the stability of the coalition. In coalition, first with longtime rivals the Japan Socialist Party and then with the New Kōmeitō, the LDP was able to regain and retain power in 1994 despite its unpopularity. The fragmented opposition was unable to consolidate into a viable party (or coalition) that could offer coherent policy alternatives. By 2000, the 1990s were being dubbed Japan's "lost decade" to reflect mass sentiment that, amid this disarray, national political and economic elites had missed an opportunity to implement a strong reform agenda and had instead relegated the country to a protracted period of "economic stagnation and political convolution" (Kikkawa 2000). Against this backdrop, the quality of political leadership, specifically prime ministerial leadership, became increasingly salient for voters who craved strong, decisive political decision-makers to guide them through these turbulent political and economic times: "Koizumi was swept into power because of the desire among voters for change in politics" (Yoshida 2002, 15).

Prior to the Koizumi administration, public confidence in government was low, turnout was falling, and the rate of nonpartisanship was approaching 50 percent of the electorate. Citizens were disengaging from national politics. National leaders tried to anticipate, respond to, and borrow from changes in local politics to keep their jobs. Many of the JEDS participants who responded to the question, "What image do you have of Japanese politics?" used the prime minister—the office or person as the public face of the LDP and the nation—to structure a largely negative assessment of Japanese politics. When not talking explicitly about the prime minister, participants invoked the names of iconic leaders past (Shigeru Yoshida) and present (Shintarō Ishihara and Makiko Tanaka) or referred to an all-inclusive national "political establishment" to compare and contrast contemporary political styles in an exercise to articulate a vision for better leadership. Narrowly focusing on the prime minister—for voters and political observers alike—is a form of shorthand, a convenient way to alert listeners to a host of problems that plague Japanese politics without having a broader conversation. Targeting specific leaders helps ordinary voters to focus their claims about a national political establishment run by an undifferentiated mass of politicians catering to powerful, and often corporate, interests who are far removed from the everyday lives of voters.[2] Talking about leaders temporarily narrows the distance between ordinary voters and a corrupt political establishment by locating identifiable and familiar targets. By tying specific acts to identifiable actors, ordinary voters are able to focus and strengthen the claims they bring against "them."

This chapter examines political leaders' efforts to align their practices with public expectations about citizen-elite engagement. Changes at the grassroots level—the success of citizen party candidates in local assemblies, the election of independent mayors and governors, the increase in referenda and recall in opposition to national government policies, and the increase in nonpartisans in the electorate—have created pressures for the national leadership to change how it connects to everyday voters. I use JEDS respondents' demands for better politics that are achievable through building stronger connections between voters and elected representatives to contextualize the popularity of independent, maverick, antipartisan, and antiestablishment challengers for political office throughout the Japanese system, the most prominent being prefectural governors, former LDP prime minister Junichiro Koizumi and, more recently, former DPJ prime minister Yukio Hatoyama. In this chapter I focus on the prime minister because the presidentialization of this post provides insight into the success everyday voters are achieving in bringing the local and national political practices into closer alignment. Administrative decentralization can empower local executives to use their positions as bully pulpits to assume a more prominent role in setting policy agendas, building legislative coalitions, and assembling independent support bases.

Political outsiders who are elected are indebted to voters in ways that traditional politicians are not; without a party or an organized base of support, reaching out to a broad segment of the voting population is the only way that these candidates can overcome the barriers to office. In cases where candidates for local offices have not served in the national bureaucracy or the Diet, they are able to distance themselves from the scandal-laden, interest-driven environment that the young, nonpartisan, female JEDS voter, quoted in chapter 1, said could not produce quality leaders.

---

2. When not talking about Mori or charismatic figures such as Makiko Tanaka and Shintarō Ishihara, politics for Japanese voters, much like their American counterparts, becomes "an undifferentiated block of interlocking selfish interests" (Gamson 1992, 62).

Because independent and citizens' party candidates' paths to office differ from those of traditional candidates, voters have good reason to expect that, once elected, these candidates will practice democracy differently from traditional politicians.

In the first section of this chapter, I attend to the seeming contradiction between calls for strong leadership and a more participatory democracy. Next, I describe the main themes and linkages that structure comments about leadership from the JEDS respondents and form a diagnosis of Japan's democratic deficit, offer a prognosis for change, and propose a rationale for how and why better leadership can serve as a impetus for changing national democratic practices and deepening democracy. I then shift focus to examine briefly the constraints—formal and informal—that Japanese prime ministers face in approximating the type of engagement that increasing numbers of citizens demand.

Local politicians, in contrast, do not face these same constraints. Even though Japanese voters are unable to elect their heads of state and government—their votes are for apportionment in legislative bodies—they do directly elect local and prefectural executives. As argued in chapter 1, shifting patterns of engagement with local elites shape voters' expectations about new arrangements for citizen-elite engagement in national politics. Leadership styles at the subnational level vary and provide alternative models for citizen-elite engagement that voters can use as a point of reference when evaluating national elites. I use an interview with a local politician, Ms. Takagi, as an example of a style of citizen-elite engagement that resonates with JEDS voters' demands for better leadership and direct participation. Assembly members such as Ms. Takagi use a style of leadership that voters want to extend into the upper reaches of the political establishment. Transforming patterns of local leadership is part of voters' strategy of changing national politics from the bottom up.

From local politics I redirect attention to national leaders' efforts to shorten the distance between themselves and voters over the course of the last decade. Increasingly, national politicians are coopting successful styles of citizen-elite engagement seen in local politics. Former prime minister Koizumi was able to use the official resources of the office to circumvent traditional, unofficial constraints that the LDP placed on prime ministers and launch direct appeals to an approving public. National politicians, including Koizumi, responded to calls for a more open politics by launching websites, introducing party manifestos, and appearing on political "wide shows" to signal their commitment to a more open political process. The extent to which politicians engage in these practices is not purely symbolic; rather, it reflects an underlying change in the relationship of prime ministers to their party in which the former act with greater independence from the latter in setting and pursuing their policy agendas. Public support becomes a mandate that empowers prime ministers to pursue policies that citizens want in defiance of party elites.

Leadership and Participatory Democracy: A Contradiction?

Calls for strong leadership in Japan have traditionally been cause for alarm. Strong leadership is associated with nostalgia for a militarist, ultra-nationalist prewar past that is incompatible with democratic institutions and norms. In the aftermath of World War II, the Supreme Commander of the Allied Powers (SCAP) took explicit steps to inculcate democratic norms and attitudes in the population to speed the consolidation of democracy in Japan so that the nation could serve as a bulwark against communism in Asia. SCAP purged wartime officials while mobilizing previously silenced civil society actors—labor unions and women, for instance—to counterbalance authoritarian norms and attempted to level hierarchical social relationships through the education system and land reform.

At regular intervals throughout the postwar period, political scientists working within the "civic culture" tradition (Almond and Verba 1963) have polled the Japanese public to assess the extent to which a participant political culture has supplanted a subject political culture (Richardson 1974); traditional cultural outlooks have been replaced by modern views (Verba et al. 1978; Flanagan et al. 1991); and more citizens were accepting the postwar constitution over prewar political arrangements (the emperor system) (Richardson 1997). Researchers have sought evidence that the balance of political attitudes and norms had shifted from a passive acceptance of political decisions handed down from elites to an elite-challenging, participant culture that demands a more active role in decision-making for everyday people.

Voters at the turn of the twenty-first century clearly cast themselves as the principals and elected executives as the agents who lead in close and ongoing deliberation with a mass public. JEDS respondents' definition of strong leadership sustains this vision. In fact, there are several themes that emerge from the open-ended JEDS data that suggest that, for voters, strong political leaders can facilitate a collective journey toward a more participatory politics. First, voters complain that in the absence of parties that offer clear policy alternatives, candidates remain the best available source of information in helping them to clarify their electoral choices. A strong leader with a vision can negotiate with the different factions in his or her party and establish a consensus around a clear mission supported by a policy slate. Second, as indicated in the statement of the voter at the outset of this chapter, focusing on parties and policies during campaign season is ineffective when candidates keep switching parties; candidates remain the same, while parties shift continuously. Third, strong national leadership plays an important role in keeping voters rooted through rapid demographic changes that have weakened the role that local elites and "traditionally intimate forms of social organizations" such as neighborhood associations and trade unions play in mobilizing voters (Richardson 1997, 30). One consequence of this is that candidates must rely more heavily on personal support organizations and direct requests and endorsements as substitutes for the role that local elites and traditional organizations used to play in mobilizing voter support. A strong leader with a vision can impose an organizational frame on politics that can make it easier for everyday people to engage with the political system.

Rather than reaching back to into their own authoritarian past, Japanese voters present the U.S. president as a model for strong national leadership. One voter argues, "I think we can choose better politicians if we can choose our prime minister directly, like the [president] in the U.S." Many voters take umbrage at the indirect selection of the national leadership by the LDP, a party they see as moribund and corrupt. A directly elected leader would have a popular mandate, which would allow the public, through the prime minister, to bypass an unpopular party and parliament. The global influence and visibility of the U.S. presidency arguably evokes a widepsread desire for Japan to attain world prestige commensurate with its economic status. On the domestic front, voters' expectations about the ability of directly elected heads of government and state to deepen democracy are more optimistic than what we might expect given evidence from the United States.

Voters contend that a popularly elected national leader would enable everyday people to bring about change at the top level of politics and help usher in a new era in politics. A JEDS respondent vocalized a plan for "the local values to penetrate Japan as a whole. I hope there are more politicians with strong leadership to lead Japan. I think the most important characteristic for a politician is clearness, and politicians should keep in mind that their reputation is heavily dependent on a clean image. I hope more politicians bring a fresh perspective to current politics." This one statement is laden with parallels between "local values" and normative democratic values. Politicians are called upon to "speak clearly and directly" in terms that everyday people understand to enable them to engage authentically with processes that appear to be remote but nonetheless have consequences for their quality of life. The demand for "fresh perspectives" is consistent with calls for a more inclusive politics that is, by extension, more representative. And the demand that politicians maintain a clean image is a backlash against widespread scandal and corruption, which, complains the Japanese public, diverts attention from salient issues and the public welfare.

A strong national leader, with the U.S. president as a prominent and readily available example, is a foil that underscores the weakness of contemporary leadership in Japan. Strong leadership means establishing order, but not in the authoritarian sense. Order is attained through providing voters with clear alternatives that facilitate public deliberation and build the public support needed to empower leaders in taking decisive policy stances. Weak leadership, discussed below, is a symptom of institutional constraints that promote undemocratic elite political practices that shut out everyday people and impede economic and political change.

Strong Institutional Norms and Weak Leaders

Prime Minister Yoshirō Mori shattered all records for low public support. He began his administration with an approval rating of only 36 percent. Over the remainder of his administration, Mori's public approval ratings never again exceeded 30 percent, and he departed office with single-digit ratings.[3] JEDS respondents expressed their displeasure with contemporary leadership and politics through the figure of Mori, who was in office at

---

3. Nikkei Net Interactive maintains an archive of cabinet approval ratings based on a monthly Nikkei poll. Available at http://e.nikkei.com, accessed August 18, 2010.

the time. A woman in her early thirties who is a high school graduate and urban nonpartisan voiced a common sentiment when she declared, "I hate Prime Minister Mori. A prime minister should think about the nation, be willing to make it a better place, and have a strong political philosophy and beliefs." However, Mori was the norm rather than the exception in a polity that is known for lackluster leadership.

The prime minister is typically the leader of the largest party in the Diet, and that party has, with few exceptions—notably current prime minister and DPJ leader Naoto Kan—been the LDP. The president of the LDP traditionally is a position that rotates with frequency to reflect seniority norms and factional balance within the party. This means that the prime minister is often not the person who is best suited for the position (Hayao 1993). The difficult task of maintaining a delicate equilibrium among factions means that prime ministers tend toward risk aversion. Consequently, it has long been noted that the Japanese selection process fails to produce dynamic leaders, and the low visibility of the prime minister in Japanese politics impedes the development of a positive affective attachment to politics within the public. The Japanese prime minister is a "missing leader" who fails to evoke the same degree of positive sentiment as the U.S. president or the British prime minister (Massey 1975).

Real institutional constraints, in addition to constraints imposed by party structures and legislative norms that grew up under one-party rule, are at the root of voters' gut reactions to the prime minister. The Japanese prime minister operates under institutional constraints and party norms that traditionally made it difficult for the office to operate as a site for revolutionary vision and political change. Japan scholars Hayao (1993) and Mulgan (2000) have discussed in detail how limited resources within the prime minister's office (for instance, small staff size) limited his ability to assume leadership on important policy matters when confronted with a professionalized bureaucracy and legislative policy tribes. Japanese voters' disdain for Prime Minister Mori and their later enthusiasm for Prime Minister Koizumi correlates with institutional changes and corresponding changes in legislative and party norms that empowered Koizumi relative to other prime ministers. Koizumi was the first prime minister to take advantage of resources placed at his disposal by administrative reforms that streamlined the bureaucracy and expanded the size of the prime minister's office. Similarly, the post-1993 legislative environment created incentives for a more visible and proactive style of leadership; coalition government, for one, required more coordination than pure one-party dominance.

Though the discourse about leadership that emerges from a national sample of individual voters is imprecise, voters' intuition about the nature of political change at this moment in Japanese politics and the opportunities that it presents for redefining political leadership styles is highly accurate. Japanese politics had become less transparent, less inclusive, less responsive, and less accountable to everyday voters, culminating in the figure of Yoshirō Mori. According to *Asahi Shimbun* reporters, the public could observe the intense battles and campaigning within the LDP that preceded the election of Takeo Miki, Kakuei Tanaka, Masayoshi Ōhira, Takeo Fukuda, and Yasuhiro Nakasone (*Asahi Shimbun* 2001). Politics became increasingly closed from the late 1980s onward, as the opposition weakened and its traditional supporters found themselves without a party to represent their interests, while conservative voters fell outside of the LDP's distributive channels (Otake 2000, 129–30).

In 2000, the LDP leadership faced intense criticism for choosing Mori in a Tokyo hotel room, behind closed doors. "Covert action is increasingly dominating the political world," giving voters the impression that prime ministers are chosen before the election (*Asahi Shimbun* 2001). A rural JEDS respondent, a nonpartisan man in his late forties who complained that "ordinary people don't know and can't see what politicians do," agrees with his urban counterpart, a forty-year-old nonpartisan woman who similarly complained that political "discussions are all inside the establishment and never open to the people." Mori's selection as prime minister suggested that a fundamental flaw in the decision-making processes—the exclusion of everyday voters—had reached the very top of the democratic political establishment: "What the party leaders are currently doing is far from the wishes of many party members, to say nothing of the general public" (*Asahi Shimbun* 2001).

A politics without the people is more than a politics incapable of reflecting the public interest; it is a politics that has lost its way. Voters are unable to envision a future for the nation and hence anticipate a total loss of control. One man, a New Kōmeitō supporter in his twenties, described politics as "fuzzy, with no leader," a situation that causes him to "get panicky when something serious happens." Another JEDS respondent, a man in his seventies, was equally anxious: "I guess that Japan is going to play out a worst-case scenario because of economic collapse, environmental destruction, poor foreign diplomacy, and so on. I don't know how long it will be before a strong political party emerges. I hope for the arrival of great politicians with strong leadership for Japan and the Japanese people." A distant and closed political process deepens the sense of a nation entering a state of crisis.

Powerlessness is intensified because closed-door politics deprives voters of an opportunity to define collectively "who we are" and "who we want to be." The absence of public discussion about a common future involving concrete plans implemented by identifiable actors robs citizens of autonomy and self-determination and contributes to a sense of insecurity. Politicians who focus on narrow partisan interests in pursuit of their own reelection in the short term "don't seriously consider the future of Japan one hundred or two hundred years later," as one JEDS respondent, a sixty-five-year old female nonpartisan, put it. Moreover, according to another nonpartisan woman in her mid-forties, an inward-looking political establishment is "weak-kneed" and unable to advance its own interests among stronger global players because it has not assessed its own best interests and the resources available to pursue them.

Direct elections would require the prime minister to forge a national consensus to keep his or her job, loosening the ties between the prime minister and an unpopular party while strengthening the ties between the prime minister and the public. Japanese voters would have a representative accountable to the nation as a whole. Many voters propose a directly elected president to replace the prime minister because it would ensure that the top person in power is directly accountable to the people, a national constituency, instead of the party. Independence from the party, "presidentialization," would amount to a mandate to reorder politics to achieve policy outcomes with broad-based appeal.[4]

Reforming the premiership is an opportunity to bring substantive change. As JEDS respondents complained about the weakness of national leadership, reforms adopted under earlier administrations coalesced to

---

4. The "presidentialization" of the prime minister refers to a slow-moving, cross-national trend whereby prime ministers are mobilizing resources to strengthen their individual bases of support. This trend is supported in part by the demands of globalization and "increased demands for government action…in welfare, inflation, unemployment, [and] national security" that require a more active leadership role for heads of state (Hayao 1993, 43).

provide the tools to strengthen the premiership. Administrative reforms reorganized and streamlined the bureaucracy, channeling more money and staff into the prime minister's office. Koizumi made significant efforts to use available resources to consolidate power in his office. For example, the 1994 political campaign reform set up public funding that is dispersed through the governing party's secretary general. This change enabled Koizumi to demand that backbenchers shift their loyalty from faction bosses to the party leader if they want the party's endorsement and campaign funding. With the aid of the new Council on Economic and Fiscal Policy, Koizumi was able to assert more control over the policy-making process. Finally, Koizumi changed politics by showing that "the way to gain and hold power is by appealing to the public, by making gestures of leadership and by favoring change" (*Economist* 2005).

In 2000, however, national politics seemed mostly unchanged in the post-reform period. In the years before the Koizumi administration, voters began working from the bottom up—replacing local leaders with those willing to stand up to Tokyo. These grassroots efforts to revitalize local politics and leadership have continued, even as popular fears were realized when the bad, old patterns reasserted themselves after Koizumi stepped down.

Leadership Models in Local Politics

On the afternoon of January 18, 2001, I met with Ms. Mako Takagi (a pseudonym), a representative in the Kanagawa Prefectural Assembly and a member of Kanagawa NET, a local citizens' party that runs women candidates to increase the representation of women on local decision-making bodies. I met with Ms. Takagi in the NET office in Kannai, Yokohama, after reading about her in the news. There was a policy study group in her home district, and I was interested to learn how she made sense of the various demands emanating from constituents and translated them into policy proposals in the prefectural assembly. Ms. Takagi stressed that asking constituents for input was important to involving citizens in decision-making, but listening to what they have to say was even more vital. Listening often entailed putting aside a preconceived agenda, an action that deepened citizens' engagement with politics. As an example, Ms. Takagi related her experience conducting a survey to explore popular opinion on waste disposal and recycling, bread-and-butter issues for the female candidates who run under the NET banner. Residents' answers revealed that transportation was a far more salient issue than waste disposal and recycling, while equally consistent with other goals that the party emphasizes in its literature—the environment and building a human network.

Ms. Tagaki's district, City A, is located along a crowded commuter train line that feeds into Shinjuku Station to connect suburbanites with their jobs in central Tokyo. City A is set up to facilitate easy transport between individual neighborhoods and the train station. Neighborhoods in City A are self-sufficient, with their own schools and shops, and the transportation network reflected this atomistic arrangement. Buses tended to run from individual neighborhoods to the train station, but they did not link the neighborhoods to one another in a direct and convenient way. Consequently, local residents had to rely on their own cars to travel between neighborhoods; those who did not have cars had to take the bus to the station and transfer to another bus going in the direction of the neighborhood they wished to visit. Visiting friends and associates in the same town was nearly as timely and costly as making a trip into Shinjuku itself. Students living and attending schools in different neighborhoods had a hard time interacting with one another outside of school. Furthermore, the transportation network was particularly hard on the elderly residents who comprised a growing proportion of the population. Ms. Takagi could easily relate to residents' concerns, as she did not have a driver's license. She put the issue before the Kanagawa prefectural assembly and set up carpools to facilitate transportation and communication between the separate neighborhoods.

Ms. Takagi is a local leader who epitomizes "strong" leadership to contemporary voters. Ms. Takagi reached out to her constituents, listened to their grievances, included them in crafting an interim solution, and took leadership in bringing her constituents' concerns before the prefectural assembly. There is nothing exceptional in what Ms. Takagi did as an elected official except that, according to voters, most elected officials do not involve the general public in all—or any—parts of the decision-making process, from setting the agenda to debating alternative solutions to implementing policies and assessing their impact. For the Kanagawa NET and its members, advocating direct communication between political elites and voters and blurring the boundaries between elite and citizen participation in politics is what it means to be a citizen party that works to make politics by the people and for the people.

Ms. Takagi deviated from standard practice among Japanese politicians in creating a new infrastructure that would enable local citizens to build new social capital. JEDS respondents, along with the focus group participants that I cover later, complained that politicians were self-interested and catered only to the most powerful interests in their own constituencies. Mobilizing citizens to solve the local transportation problem required Ms. Takagi to reach out to a broader constituency to link citizens who lived in different neighborhoods in different parts of the city that were not easily accessible, strengthening and expanding the boundaries of existing communities.

The language of citizens' parties, with its emphasis on open and direct communication between citizens and elites, has been adopted by political executives at the prefectural and national levels, with Koizumi its most effective practitioner. While some voters have no expectation that everyday people should be more directly involved in decision-making processes, most voters complain that they are stuck on the outside looking in. A new grassroots consensus about citizen-elite relations in democracy emerged before Koizumi assumed office, and Ms. Takagi is one of many local politicians who met those evolving public expectations. Koizumi's appeals to the public won him widespread support because he shortened the distance between national decision-making and everyday life.

Koizumi's "Populist" Politics

Koizumi fulfilled many of the hopes that focus group respondents and a national sample of voters voiced for the future of democratic leadership in Japan. Koizumi was elected LDP president and Japanese prime minister shortly before my departure from Tokyo. He entered office with unprecedentedly high approval ratings; Koizumi's approval rating was 80 percent immediately following the April 2001 House of Representatives election.[5]

---

5. The *Nikkei Weekly*'s online subscription service provides access to a database of cabinet support ratings based on regular public opinion polls at e.nikkei.com/e/fr/freetop.aspx.

Even when public approval fell, at its lowest nearly half of the Japanese public approved of his cabinet. Koizumi's lows were other prime minister's highs. No other postwar prime minister has enjoyed so much support for such an extended period of time. Koizumi coopted the rhetoric of "us versus them," reframing public political discourse in terms of the "new" LDP against the "old" LDP, successfully running against his own party to secure its future in politics by placing himself firmly in the reform camp and on the side of everyday voters. The "new" LDP would include everyday voters in its deliberations over the future of Japan.

Openness, public discussion, simple language, direct contact, the importance of public opinion, and clear and justifiable policy positions constitute voters' definition of a more open politics. One JEDS respondent, a twenty-one-year-old woman, demanded "to know where and when politicians listen to and elicit the opinions of the people." "Publicity" is one of the three defining characteristics that are common to most theorists' vision of democratic deliberation, and it is arguably fundamental to achieving two other characteristics of deliberative democracy—deliberation that is not coerced or swayed by powerful groups, and the elimination of procedural and substantive barriers to equal participation (Conover et al. 2002, 24). Deliberation is public when decision-making is accessible to everyday citizens who are able to weigh options rationally and offer a "public" reason for their preferences in public spaces. Public deliberation tempers the expression of extreme views and particular interests by inviting the expression of diverse perspectives. Publicity ensures that discussion revolves around commonly shared interests that are communicated in a fashion that is easily understood by all parties while allowing participants to respond in their own terms.

"Openness" became a trademark of the Koizumi administration. Though previous prime ministers also used media outlets to promote their agendas,[6]

---

6. Yasuhiro Nakasone (1983–1987) appealed directly to the public in an effort to increase his leverage relative to the faction leaders within the LDP: "He used it to portray an image of an effective leader in domestic, and especially foreign affairs," (Krauss and Pekkanen 2008, 23). Similarly, Morihiro Hosokawa (1993–1994) used the media to garner public support to push forward electoral reforms. Though Nakasone's popularity did not approach that of Koizumi, he enjoyed high public support relative to the prime ministers that succeeded him; he also enjoyed the longest tenure in office in the postwar period.

Koizumi used the media to create an air of openness and transparency. The Koizumi administration, through the media, provided the public unprecedented access to elite political circles. The first administration was dubbed the "Wide Show Cabinet," because "watching politics" became mainstream under Koizumi. "Wide shows," TV programs that focus on public interest topics, are televised at peak viewing hours, and women and older viewers are their primary audience (*Asahi Shimbun* 2001). Politics has typically not been a subject for the wide show audience. However, from the moment that he declared his candidacy for the post of LDP president and prime minister of Japan, public interest in Koizumi soared and the press responded. Prior to Koizumi, the press provided routine coverage of the prime minister in the Diet and significant diplomatic and public appearances. However, with the arrival of Koizumi the press began to cover all of Koizumi's activities, providing a view into the prime minister's private life. When the press was not covering Koizumi, it was covering his foreign minister Makiko Tanaka, whom the public found equally riveting. When Koizumi and Tanaka became embroiled in a political dispute, the public tuned in even more. Naturally when allegations surfaced that Tanaka had been embezzling funds earmarked for her political secretary, the public kept watching that as well.

This administration earned its "wide show" designation for openness along several dimensions. First, the media was able to attract the attention of an audience that is ordinarily uninterested in national politics (women aged thirty-five and up). Second, the media gained unprecedented access to the prime minister and provided viewers with in-depth discussion of policy content and disagreements among political personnel. Third, traditional and nontraditional media outlets were used to engage the public and mobilize public opinion. Furthermore, the message of openness was embodied in the composition of the cabinet that was the center of the media blitz: across three cabinets and four reshuffles, Koizumi appointed more women, more younger politicians, and more factional outsiders, all of whom represented a fresh perspective in Nagatachō, the Tokyo district synonymous with national politics.

Housewives appreciated the plainspoken manner adopted by Foreign Minister Tanaka. At a time when voters were complaining that politics was hard to understand, that some politicians adopted intentionally vague language to avoid taking responsibility for unpopular decisions while other politicians avoided details to cover up their lack of expertise, Tanaka packaged complex political information in an easily digestible format for voters. The appearance of politicians on wide shows in particular made their viewers—primarily housewives—feel that their views mattered enough for politicians to talk about politics in this forum. When asked, slices of the electorate that had been disengaged from politics for a long time—women and youth, both overrepresented among unaffiliated voters—were now responding, "Of course we're interested in politics." What is more, they were interested in national politics (*Asahi Shimbun* 2001).

Koizumi also launched an e-magazine. Readers could sign up for a free subscription service to receive a weekly update on "what's going on around the prime minister." The magazine had over 870,000 subscribers when its first issue was transmitted, and traditional newspapers reported that it was one of the largest email magazines in the world. His first message to the public: "My first impression is that I no longer have freedom of my own. It is like a bird trapped in a cage 24 hours a day" (*Japan Times* 2001). Yet Koizumi had already demonstrated, with his grassroots campaign for the party presidency and his disregard for factional balance in appointing his cabinet, his independence from the party and his commitment to a struggle to strengthen his own autonomy as a leader. In the inaugural issue of his weekly e-magazine, Koizumi invoked the constraints that the prime minister traditionally faces to empathize with voters who feel similarly constrained by limited political choices that inhibit their ability to influence the course of national politics. Koizumi appealed to the public to "free" him from the constraints of his office, symbolically elevating the public over elite politicians.[7]

Voters saw Koizumi's "outsider" characteristics as a way to select a national representative who was from the establishment, yet committed to the substantive changes that would engage everyday voters. Scholars such as Nyblade and Krauss (2005) have demonstrated that Koizumi used the media to mobilize public opinion to create pressure to push forward his

---

7. Koizumi used the email magazine to communicate his views directly to the public and as a means of marketing himself as a political product for mass consumption. The one-way nature of the communication, that is, the failure to utilize the interactive potential of web-based technologies, speaks to the effort to bolster perceptions that government was more open even if reality fell short of normative expectations (see Mackie 2003).

legislative agenda. How prime ministers engage with the media communicates information about elite political practices that shape voters' opinions about whether or not democracy works in the ways that they think it should. Prime ministers' use of media resources sends a strong public message about the real nature of unobserved constraints within the ruling party and coalition that are inextricably related to how open the party and government is to voter pressure. Koizumi's usage of the media to frame issues for the public in a way that provides substantive information sent a message about real procedural change under his administration.

The strong reformist strains that characterized Koizumi's campaign for the party presidency and the premiership remained constant over the following five-year period and were backed up by political and economic reforms that altered norms, widely cited as antithetical to democracy, within the elite political establishment. The Koizumi administration responded to grassroots efforts to halt wasteful government spending on unnecessary public works projects. Koizumi cut public works spending and capped government bonds and, after a battle within his own party, passed a reform package to privatize the government-run postal system and reorganize government-affiliated financial institutions. These measures also had the desired effect, from the public's point of view, of weakening factions, loosening the bureaucracy's control over the budget and policy, and cutting off a source of corruption in politics (Krauss and Pekkanen 2008). Furthermore, Koizumi's dogged pursuit of his policy agenda reinforced the sense that he, unlike other politicians, would keep his promises to the public. When his efforts were obstructed, Koizumi pointed to constraints within his own party, reinforcing his identification with ordinary voters engaged in a struggle to move the political establishment.

Throughout the market reform process, Koizumi asked the public to do the very thing that JEDS respondents demanded from the political elites—that they "endure today's pain for a better tomorrow" (Sugeno 2008). In 2005, as the economy was showing signs of recovery, Koizumi successfully framed the snap election, called after members of his own party voted against his postal privatization package, as a public referendum on a reform process hamstrung by LDP politicians' reluctance to abandon pork-barrel politics to advance the public interest; voters were asked to decide whether they wanted to continue or halt reform.

In calling a snap election to push forward his postal privatization reform package, Koizumi took a risk that was bold, quick, decisive, and justified in clearly articulated terms to the public. Significantly, he used "referendum," a buzzword associated with direct participation in local politics. In doing so, Koizumi referenced grassroots activism and underscored the House of Representatives election as an opportunity for direct engagement in national politics. But this was not the first time that Koizumi had responded to public calls for strong leadership. In response to the 2003 nonperforming loans crisis, the government strengthened the criteria for evaluating bank assets, took control of Resona Bank, and triggered a realignment of the banking industry while holding interest rates down and buying dollars to halt the sharp appreciation of the yen (Sugeno 2008). In a retrospective of the Koizumi administration, a *New York Times* reporter wrote, "Overseas, Koizumi has led the most serious postwar movement yet to transform Japan from a vassal state of the U.S. into a leading player in global politics, one that might one day have a fully functioning military, a revised constitution that renounces pacifism, and a permanent seat on the U.N. Security Council" (Frederick 2005). In contrast to Japan's widely criticized response to U.S. aid requests during the first Gulf War, Koizumi passed legislation to allow the Maritime Self-Defense Force to refuel U.S. vessels in the Indian Ocean to support antiterrorism missions and dispatched the Ground Self-Defense Force to Iraq on a humanitarian mission.

Koizumi "excelled in speaking to the public in short, plain language" (Sugeno 2008). Though prime ministers after Koizumi enjoy heightened media visibility, they have not successfully used the media to engage the public. LDP prime ministers who equivocated in public heightened the sense that politicians are reverting to old, undemocratic practices. Yukio Hatoyama, the DPJ's first prime minister, rapidly succumbed to the media's double-edged sword. Campaign finance scandals, broken campaign pledges, and the rocky transition period discussed below and in chapters 1 and 6 subverted a larger message about shortening the distance between voters and the elite establishment to restore popular sovereignty. Naoto Kan's political career has been shaped by early experiences as a grassroots organizer and a campaign staffer for the late women's rights activist and Diet Member Fusae Ichikawa. These populist roots might serve him well over the course of the next two years as the DPJ tries to retain public support while pushing through difficult economic policies.

Politics after Koizumi

Each prime minister after Koizumi has used the e-magazine established under the Koizumi administration as a "hotline" that links voters directly to the prime minister. Each has gone through the motions of appealing to the public, but none has been able to lead in a way that sustains a belief that government is moving closer to the interests of ordinary voters. This publicly accessible channel of communication is presented to voters as a tool to increase transparency in decision-making processes, responsiveness to voters' demands, and public accessibility. In his inaugural issue, Koizumi's successor Shinzō Abe publicly shared plans to use the e-magazine to "provide people a clear vision of what the Government is thinking and what it is trying to accomplish in my own words" (October 5, 2006).[8] This web forum would enable the administration to think more pragmatically about the problems that ordinary Japanese face and tailor policies accordingly: "Rather than mere theoretical discussions I believe opening our ears to what various people have to say is important to understand the people's needs, what troubles them, what gives them a hard time, or what stands against them. Understanding these points will lead to the measures that the people truly want."

In one of the initial pronouncements of his administration, Prime Minister Yasuo Fukuda, who succeeded Abe, used the e-magazine to tie widespread cynicism about politics to the failure of politicians to include citizens' voices in the decision-making process. In this regard, voters' voices are "loud and clear," and Fukuda understood "what they are saying without reservation" (October 4, 2007). Fukuda asserted his belief that "it is important that I put myself in the shoes of the Japanese people to see things from their viewpoint" as a way of restoring trust in politics. To communicate his strength of commitment to engaging with voters, he assured readers, "I look forward to receiving many different opinions and hearing about anything that you would like to share. I very much hope to make this e-mail magazine a platform for interactive dialogue with all readers."

A year later, Prime Minister Taro Aso ended his first issue of the e-magazine with statements designed to shorten the distance between himself and

---

8. Email magazine issues for all administrations are available at www.mmz.kantei.go.jp/foreign/m-magazine/index.html, accessed August 18, 2010.

ordinary voters: "Over the past year, I have toured 161 locations around the country in order to listen directly to what the people in the regions have to say" (October 2, 2008). Aso, too, established the e-magazine as a venue that linked everyday voters directly to the prime minister. By virtue of this close connection, voters would be able to participate directly in deciding the course of national politics under this administration: "This e-mail magazine is not just to express my ideas; it also provides an opportunity to listen to your views, so that I can reflect them in the conduct of the affairs of state. I hope each and every one of you will think of yourselves as members of the Aso Cabinet, and share with me your frank opinions."

During his tenure, Yukio Hatoyama sent a weekly "Yu-Ai" message, using the Japanese word for *fraternity* because it can also be read phonetically in English as "you and I." In his first issue of the magazine (October 1, 2009), Hatoyama capitalized on the DPJ's landslide victory to link this historic alteration in national politics to voters "who seek to change conventional politics." Change is defined as what conventional politics is not. Conventional politics were ineffective and did not address voters concerns because politicians were disconnected from "the minds of the people" and, consequently, could not "directly affect people's voices." The new administration promised change, but Hatayama pledged that it would pursue national "ideals" that previous administrations had lost sight of. In hindsight, the Hatoyama administration made a rapid and dramatic departure from its stated commitments. Naoto Kan has not used the e-zine as a venue for garnering public support.

The conduct of prime ministers in the post-Koizumi period contradicts the public promises made within the texts of the e-magazine. Abe's "right-wing political agenda over-looked the bread-and-butter issues of most voters" (Fackler 2008), leading even business elites to complain that he was unable to read the public mood, a sin akin to not knowing "that your guest wants another cup of tea or that you should be serving cold tea because it is a hot day" (Ito 2007). While Abe focused his energies on passing education reform bills to inculcate a stronger sense of patriotism in children, voters were worried about their missing pension records and the future of the social welfare safety net. The incoherence of foreign policy revealed the Abe administration's inability to enforce internal party discipline.

Abe started his administration with a desire to continue Koizumi's reforms, but this commitment was undercut when he readmitted the postal rebels, the "old guard," back into the party, a move that "made him appear beholden to the LDP's old backroom chieftains and seem deaf to voters' calls for a more modern approach to politics." Readmitting the rebels to the party created the impression that he would retreat from the reform agenda (Wallace 2006). Factions, though weakened, made a comeback under the Abe administration. Policies substantiated this impression. In the 2006 supplemental budget, the administration spent $38.6 billion of tax revenues on public works projects, a reversal of Koizumi's reduction of public works spending (Krauss and Pekkanen 2008). The Abe administration was marred by successive corruption scandals that implicated several cabinet-level ministers in the weeks preceding the July 2007 House of Councillors elections, a referendum on his leadership.[9]

Fukuda's low approval ratings were linked to his efforts "to bring back the politics of closed doors and faction-led decision-making" (Fackler 2008). After Abe, Fukuda was chosen for his capability in steering the government through legislative roadblocks. But Fukuda was unable to negotiate with the DPJ to pass major legislation. Upon gaining control of the House of Councillors in 2007, the DPJ adopted obstructionist tactics—especially on security and defense issues related to U.S. military forces stationed in Japan and government support of the U.S. missions in Iraq and Afghanistan—in an effort to force a general election and increase its number of seats in the House of Representatives.

Taro Aso was the third prime minister in as many years. Aso, who had lost his earlier bid for the premiership to Abe, spent the months preceding his run to follow Fukuda distancing himself from his image as a foreign policy nationalist and moving closer to voters. Aso traveled around Japan to talk directly to voters and build a strong base of public support. He acknowledged that Abe's nationalism had blinded the government to bigger economic issues and promised to adopt economic measures that would address long-term problems such as the pension system: "Aso's bold embrace of higher taxes and radical reforms conjures memories of Koizumi's

---

9. Since the House of Councillors has traditionally been considered the weaker of the two houses of the Diet—any legislation that it does not pass can be enacted with a super majority in the House of Representatives—voters have supported opposition parties to send a message to the ruling party when its decisions and practices are out of sync with public opinion. Opposition control—or a narrow ruling party majority—in the Upper House can force the ruling party to compromise more with the opposition parties in order to avoid legislative delays.

political style: breaking with the inherent caution and stagnation of the ruling party power brokers by going over their heads to appeal to voters" (Ueno and Wallace 2008).

Though Yukio Hatoyama represented change, the new DPJ-led administration fell far short of voters' expectations. Within ten months of winning control of the government, approval ratings for the DPJ plunged to 25 percent from a high of over 70 percent (Curtis 2010). Gerald Curtis reported that neither the prime minister nor his cabinet members was able to sustain the types of leadership styles promised during the campaign and evident during the administration's first weeks. Political observers were allegedly "stunned by cabinet ministers speaking in their own words rather than reading from scripts prepared by bureaucrats" and believed that "Japan was going to have a new kind of politics—more open and responsive to average citizens than to the special interests that had captured the Liberal Democratic Party" (Curtis 2010). Hatoyama had difficulty commanding the unity of his cabinet members and voters suspected that he was being supplanted by Ichirō Ozawa.

Naoto Kan represents the DPJ's second chance to establish a firm foothold in the Japanese party system as the party of change and a viable alternative to the LDP. A cofounder of the DPJ with Hatoyama, Kan has nonetheless established a reputation as a politician who is qualitatively different from his predecessor. Even though his political career has not been without scandal, with vast media coverage given to his extramarital affair and failure to pay into the pension system, they have been offset by concrete measures he has taken to assert political power over the unelected bureaucracy. His popularity soared when, as health minister in 1996, he exposed how collusion between health bureaucrats and the pharmaceutical industry exposed the public to HIV-tainted blood. More recently, Kan's forthright admission about the unavoidability of higher taxes cost the DPJ its majority in the July 2010 House of Councillors election.

Despite the early unpopularity of Kan's economic policies, voters interested in changing Japanese political culture and stable national leadership supported Kan over Ozawa, whose candidacy was seen as antithetical to both goals. Immediately after his re-election as party president, Kan reshuffled his cabinet to assert control over and restore order to internal party dynamics by eliminating Ozawa's supporters from the line-up. This move was broadly interpreted as an indication of a renewed commitment to voters to change how elites practice politics. Public support for Prime Minister Kan reached a public approval rating of nearly two-thirds, an increase of approximately 15 percentage points over his pre-election rating (*Mainichi Japan* 2010).

Prime ministers who followed Koizumi have not enjoyed a similar public rapport and have paid the consequences in low public approval ratings and a high rate of turnover. The inability of Koizumi's successors, five prime ministers in five years, to attain and sustain the level of public support that Koizumi enjoyed over the course of his five-year tenure indicates that while they have understood the political importance of direct communication, they have not followed through with substantive political changes (Sakamoto 2008). Naoto Kan has two years before his party *must* face voters in the next scheduled House of Representatives election to demonstrate that, unlike his direct predecessors, his commitment to changing the political culture is not a hollow promise.

Changing Patterns of Citizen-Elite Engagement

In the 1970s, Massey (1975) concluded that a strong public commitment to democratic political processes in Japan was important because a weak prime minister meant that the nation did not have a highly visible unifying figure that could deepen the cognitive and affective engagement of a mass public with democracy. In lieu of a strong leader, public confidence in vehicles of interest articulation such as parties and elections became more important. If the public was unable to maintain its confidence that these linkage structures—parties and elections—helped citizens' voices to be heard in the political process, then a crisis of legitimacy could ensue. By 2000, voters had neither strong leaders nor any confidence that they could influence national politicians and, through parties and elections, the course of their collective future.

During a period when national politics has grown more distant from everyday voters, the local political arena becomes an important field of practice that keeps citizens engaged in politics; local changes, a product of citizen participation, build confidence that citizen's voices can matter. Grassroots citizenship practices that yield local political change produce a vision for national political change and concrete strategies for achieving it. Electing leaders who break the political mold is one strategy that has worked well in local politics. As with the election of progressive mayors in the late 1960s and early 1970s, the 1990s witnessed an increase in independent and antiestablishment governors and citizens' party assembly members, which signaled a renaissance in local politics. Progressive local governments in the 1960s and 1970s introduced popular and innovative quality-of-life reforms (social welfare and environment) that were coopted by national political elites. Contemporary local executives and citizens' parties advocate for a more open and inclusive politics, and national leaders struggle to coopt their styles.

National elites pay close attention to the results of unified local elections results because they serve as a barometer of grassroots changes that may affect their own electoral futures. In this chapter, I have argued that evolving grassroots citizenship practices are important to national political elites, as is evident in recent prime ministers' struggles to establish open channels of communication between themselves and the national political establishment. Voters advocate for strong leaders, whose strength derives from a mass public rather than from party elites. The ability of independent, antiestablishment, "maverick" leaders to bring about change in the top levels of the political establishment with the help of grassroots support not only reaffirms voters that their voices matter but also serves as a indicator of the nature and extent of substantive underlying changes in party and legislative norms, norms that make Japanese democracy work better.

3

National Attitudes and Local Action

Changing the Center from the Periphery

One-party dominance in national politics has propelled voters to seek new opportunities to influence politics at the local level. Local political entrepreneurs—independent politicians, citizen activists, and emerging nonprofit organizations, among others—have worked to widen existing channels of interest articulation, while administrative reforms have created new opportunities for citizen participation by shifting the balance of power between the national government and local government. The Information Disclosure Law (1999), the Nonprofit Organization Law (1998), the Law to Promote Decentralization (1995), and the Revised Local Autonomy Law (1999) are vital tools. Administrative decentralization has revived debate about the meaning of local autonomy and how it is best achieved. At the same time, it has underscored the gap between local administration under the 1955 System and constitutionally defined local government power. Local political entrepreneurs critically reassess conventional interpretations of the constitutionally proscribed relationship among different levels of government administration in Japan, locating new bases of power while recovering existing ones that have been underutilized to date. Local governments have not realized the full potential of their power relative to the national government, and decentralization provides a framework and incentives for local administrators and citizens to craft a new relationship between themselves and the central government that tips the balance of power more firmly in the direction of ordinary voters. The decentralization process has opened new opportunities for political participation while unleashing multiple pressures to take advantage of them (Machidori and Soga 2007).

Administrative decentralization has shifted the burden of responsibility for social welfare and associated costs from the central government to the local government. It is especially difficult for depopulated, rural districts with small tax bases to shoulder this shifting burden. Consequently, small rural communities are merging with or are being absorbed by the closest cities to expand their tax bases and enjoy economies of scale. But the new wave of municipal mergers that has accompanied administrative decentralization has incited anxieties at the very foundations of Japanese civil society. Voters in the smallest towns and villages worry that their absorption into larger units will erode their identities and silence their voices on municipal and regional representative assemblies. Further, the amalgamation process is robbing formerly independent municipal units of property rights, resulting in the erosion of autonomous control over lands and other resources.[1]

Decentralization can thus be said to be occurring on multiple fronts. Yoshisuke Tajima (2003) observed that the Great Heisei Merger (1999–2006)[2] prescribed the devolution of power from the central government to regional and municipal governments but has incited additional demands for further devolution to the previously existing villages, towns, and cities in newly amalgamated areas. Citizens, arguing that democratic self-government works better in smaller units, advocate maintaining executive authority over the original jurisdiction of town and villages absorbed to create larger municipalities (Tajima 2003). As in the aftermath

---

1. I extend many thanks to the incredibly thorough reader from Johns Hopkins who reminded me that I was understating what is at stake with municipal mergers.

2. Under the Law for Exceptional Measures on Municipal Mergers, the central government has encouraged small towns and villages to combine into larger municipalities to expand the local tax base in order to ease the financial burdens that local governments will assume with the transfer of administrative power. The number of municipalities was reduced from 3,232 in 1999 to 1,820 in 2006 (Kohara 2007).

of the Showa mergers (Kohara 2007), the Great Heisei Merger has been a catalyst for community building (Tajima 2003). Whereas the handful of referenda carried out between 1996 and 2000, discussed below, were almost exclusively concerned with wasteful or potentially hazardous public works projects, 418 referenda were held on merger plans between 2001 and March 2005 (Kohara 2007, 10). The Great Heisei Merger encouraged residents to demand information disclosure and greater participation in municipal decision-making, "side effects that the central government had never intended" (Kohara 2007, 10). Increasingly, ordinary Japanese are talking about politics as a multilevel game—what happens in the local political arena influences national politics, and vice versa. This reciprocal relationship is a departure from the conventional characterization of Japanese politics as a top-down system.

Japanese voters make different calculations about where best to invest scarce political resources—locally or nationally—based on the predictions about how much their efforts will matter. Though voters are disappointed by the stagnancy and insularity of national-level politics, they remain committed to deepening democracy from the ground up. Voters undertake participation in local politics because it is here that they can see immediate change in their daily lives. Engagement in local politics makes sense for a host of well-established reasons. Grassroots politics is closer to home, so decision-making at this level is more immediately relevant to everyday life, and the issues are easier to understand. Smaller electorates increase the sense that individuals can affect outcomes.

Yet local political participation is nationally oriented. Everyday people engage with local government as the most immediate means of influencing decisions that shape everyday life while simultaneously asserting indirect and escalating pressures on the national government. Headlines broadcast local "rebellions" against unpopular national policies and citizen action plans to change the character of national politics from the ground up (Tajima 1996, 2003; Sugita 2003).[3] The costs and benefits of participation

---

3. A search of Japanese periodical indexes such as MagazinePlus and Oya-Bunko show that, starting in the early 1990s, national public opinion magazines such as *Aera, Sekai,* and *Shukan Kinyobi* began printing articles about a range of citizen action at the local level. One might compare these magazines, in terms of their readership and quality of reporting, to the *New York Times Magazine.* While reporting on local politics is not unusual, a critical mass of articles on local politics that directly challenged the authority of central government actors is unusual in this unitary

in national and subnational politics differ, but the two processes are intertwined. There is mounting public expectation that local practices can produce a groundswell of pressures that will infiltrate national politics over the long term.

A rich secondary literature examines the vibrancy of local politics in Japan as measured by several interrelated trends: referendum and recall movements (Jain 2000; Lam 2005b; Numata 2006; LeBlanc 2008); antiparty movements and the wave of elections in the 1990s that seated independent governors in prefectures across Japan (Lam 2005b); the rise of citizens' parties in local government (LeBlanc 1999, 2008, 2010); an increase in nonprofit organizations (Pekkanen 2006; Kawato and Pekkanen 2008); and information disclosure movements that produced an increase in taxpayer suits to combat governmental waste (Marshall 2002). All of these local efforts to increase the responsiveness, transparency, accountability, and inclusiveness of local government also had as a goal to shake up national political practices through the ballot box. Existing research has investigated the disparate patterns of local political engagement and national disengagement to establish a connection between the two political spheres and the different calculations that voters make about engaging in either one. The case study approach that characterizes this work, the specificity of the cases, and the limited frequency of these events confounds generalizability. Scarce events like the anti-dam referendum movement in Tokushima (Jain 2000; Lam 2005b; Numata 2006) and the election of independent governor Yasuo Tanaka in Nagano Prefecture (see Lam 2005b) do not tell us how widespread the underlying attitudes that produced these movements are.[4] Work on isolated cases does not establish a link between events in one locale and those in another. However, citizens who have participated in these grassroots movements, who are informants for these case studies and are represented in the national media reporting of these movements,

---

system. The late 1960s and early 1970s mark the last period in Japanese politics when local opposition governments posed a challenge to national politicians. Political scientists such as Steiner (1965) and Scheiner (2004) detail the conditions that traditionally encouraged local politicians to follow the LDP party-line, and factors—relatively rare in postwar politics prior to the last decade—that explain when local politicians exercise greater local autonomy.

4. Similarly, the low frequency of these events does not inform us about how the intense media attention given to these movements shapes public opinion, nor how the threat posed by these movements is sufficient to bring about changes in elite behavior that effectively deter the need for more movements elsewhere.

frame their motivations and goals in terms that are echoed nationally by the JEDS respondents, introduced in chapters 1 and 2.

Mikiko Eto (2007) notes that "collective action" in the broad, noisy, confrontational, discontinuous, and public sense of the term is not practiced on a national scale in Japanese politics, and continuity at the top masks underlying changes in how people think about politics, changes that are expressed in patterns of grassroots engagement and a spreading national discourse about the relationship between local and national politics.[5] In chapters 1 and 2 I used voters' "free answers" in the Japanese Election and Democracy Study to examine the rationale that underlies public dissatisfaction with national politics. In chapter 2, I examined changes in executive leadership styles that reflect the interaction between voters seeking to elect leaders unencumbered by partisan constraints that make them more responsive to entrenched interests than to ordinary citizens and leaders who are building independent power bases by circumventing parties with populist appeals. Voters' diagnoses for what is wrong with Japanese politics and their visions for how to achieve a new politics are consistent with what I found when I conducted a focus group in Nagano Prefecture, a hotbed of grassroots political activity. In this chapter, I use the focus groups to ground the aggregated views from the national JEDS survey in a specific locale. Having used the survey to establish the generalizability of attitudes, Nagano is a place where many of the behavioral outcomes that we might expect to emanate from the types of opinions expressed coalesce. The last part of this chapter enlarges the scope to talk about how an expanding repertoire of local action stands to influence national political practices.

All Politics Is Local

When queried about how best to solve communal problems—whether local, prefectural, or national in scope—few JEDS respondents suggested

---

5. Eto (2007) argues that "contentiousness" has become a fundamental characteristic of social movements as defined by Western researchers, to the exclusion of social movements in Japan and elsewhere that do not use disruptive tactics such as occupying public spaces. Grasping the full range of social movement activity requires looking at nondisruptive and civil tactics such as lobbying, lawsuits, and the creation of new values at the grassroots level to bring about a decision-making environment that is conducive to social justice.

direct engagement with national political elites. Few voters threatened to change their support for a national party or candidate or proposed to run for office at any level of politics. Nor did voters propose contacting their Diet representative. Voters' reluctance to engage with national political elites to solve common problems at any administrative level is consistent with the high level of distrust expressed throughout the survey; it is particularly evident in the responses to the query about the images that politics in Japan brings to mind—corruption, self-interest, and a disregard for the common good. Voters expect national politicians to confront problems with indifference. Diet members, when spurred to action, veer between self-interest and ineptitude, fueling voters' sentiments that problems are best resolved when citizens collectively organize to address them. When asked to explain what factors inspire or inhibit political participation, one JEDS voter, a forty-year old, nonpartisan women responded, "I can't entrust my life to the politicians."

When faced with a common problem, Japanese voters strive to mobilize public opinion to influence the local political discourse and local elites. JEDS respondents proposed broad, complementary, and mutually supportive solutions for problem-solving. They sought to mobilize public opinion through editorials, petitions, study groups, and conversations with family, friends, and neighbors. Others offered to take personal responsibility for gathering more information to help them to establish their own position on issues and contribute to the public debate. Respondents indentified a well-delineated set of information resources, from internet-based research and the views of well-informed neighbors to direct consultations with local public officials to pressure them into offering answers and disclosing information. Expanding public debate by engaging ordinary citizens and local politicians, each of whom is expected to provide more information and to reflect a diversity of perspectives, yields better deliberative outcomes while also transforming mass and elite attitudes.

Voters, offering hypothetical responses to what they would do if confronted with a common problem, prioritize local mobilization over individual participation in national politics. But they do not regard their efforts to engage a broader public to respond collectively to a common problem as a form of political participation. As one JEDS respondent put it, "Although I don't participate in political activity, I participate in local activities. We think about how to improve our own futures and how to live together better." If political participation is synonymous with participation in national politics and elite political practices that do not improve the quality of life for ordinary Japanese, then citizens' participation in their local communities does not fall into the same category as the "dirty" and "corrupt" practices that they observe among political elites. Voters describe several distinguishing characteristics that separate "local activity" from "political participation."

First, political participation is action that is directly aimed at influencing national politicians and bureaucrats. Second, local activity is beneficial to residents and improves their quality of life, whereas participation in national politics involves complicity with corrupt politicians who ignore the public interest. Third, whereas citizens' voices are heard locally, they fail to reach national politicians because there are fewer opportunities to influence national politicians, and the enduring stagnation in national politics signals to voters that their efforts to exert influence at this level are insufficient to bring about change. JEDS respondents "don't see any meaning in being involved in political activities since no politicians work for the public interest." Locally, citizens craft their own small-scale solutions and mobilize public opinion to pressure local elites. Local activities, while political, are not termed as such because doing so would blur the distinction between "us" and "them," grassroots politics and elite practices.

JEDS participants are responding in the hypothetical, proposing what they would do if confronted with a problem that affected their community locally, regionally, or nationally. It is telling that they confine their proposed action to the lowest political unit—local politics. This does not mean that voters do not see themselves as citizens of the region, nation, or even the world. Citizens consider themselves members of these larger publics as well, but they frame local politics as the nucleus from which action has the potential to radiate outwards to influence political processes in these larger arenas. The focus is on community building rather than political participation; if the former succeeds, it enriches the latter and paves the way toward better political outcomes.

JEDS respondents' readiness to work collectively to solve problems is consistent with a rich local civic tradition. Survey respondents are involved in a broad range of activities that can nonetheless be organized under three broad, overlapping categories—volunteer activities aimed at helping the weakest members of society, participation in study and hobby groups, and membership in "traditional" associations. They are hobbyists, residents, and activists (Rausch 2004). The boundary separating the work of volunteers and members of traditional associations is blurry. Members in both types of activities visited elderly residents, sponsored health awareness programs, supported disabled citizens, facilitated youth activities, and worked in child care facilities. Both volunteers and traditional associations assumed social welfare functions that emphasized bridging the generational divide to link older and younger citizens, focused on the maintenance and development of public space, and encouraged regional growth and development. While some respondents limit their participation to one type of activity, more often their community involvement spans all three categories. Although I am most interested in study groups and volunteer efforts that are independent of the state, studies of all three venues have shown that some subset of participants prioritize changing how everyday people think about their relationships to other citizens—locally, nationally, and globally; to the state; and to their material environments. Haddad argues that over time, members in "traditional" associations increasingly struggle to reorganize the internal structures of their organizations to make them less hierarchical and more tolerant of a diversity of views and practices, with greater autonomy from the state and elite political actors. In short, even members of traditional organizations are struggling to "make democracy real" (Haddad forthcoming).

The local orientation of citizen engagement and voters' efforts to differentiate their practices from those of national elites should not lead to the conclusion that voters have abandoned national politics altogether. Empowerment at the local level has given rise to a two-pronged strategy whereby voters are able to reach immediate goals locally while using participation in a local political arena to influence the course of national politics from the ground up. Attitudes about the distance between local and national politics coexist with the belief that this distance can be bridged through community building and participation in local politics. As discussed below, private attitudes that find public expression through the survey are consistent with the attitudes of opinion leaders and everyday citizens that find their way into the local and national press. Whenever information disclosure movements uncover an unexpectedly large scandal or stimulate legal activism that extends beyond the locality, whenever a referendum or recall movement succeeds, or whenever citizens' parties enjoy a rapid expansion of seats during local elections, opinion leaders invoke narratives about changing national politics from the local level. These examples of local activism draw the attention of similarly situated localities across Japan as well as that of a national and international public. The specificity of these events masks the ubiquity of privately held attitudes that do not necessarily erupt into noisy contention but nonetheless reshape the political sphere by producing a quieter change in mass and elite attitudes that influences the types of candidates that run for and are elected to office, voters' decision-making calculus, the tenor of local politics, and, by extension, the relationship that local governments have with the national government. JEDS respondents' attitudes about politics provide insight into the kind of climate that gives rise to the patterns of political action that have been increasing over the course of the last decade in local politics in Japan. Understanding the attitudes that produce local political actions is an important analytical tool for reevaluating the small-scale changes in national-level politics during this same period. They help us predict the future course of national Japanese politics and the potential for changes of larger magnitude. Further, they force us to reassess the utility of voting to ordinary Japanese.

The Nagano Model of Popular Democracy

Nagano was an important research site for several reasons. I was initially motivated by Nagano's more rural and traditionally conservative population, a demographic profile that enabled me to test the generalizability of the data provided by the more progressive urban groups in Tokyo. I expected salient attitudinal differences, if they existed, to appear along the rural-urban divide, as this is an enduring cleavage in modern Japanese politics. But, prefectural politics in Nagano had entered a transformative period with the election of former novelist and independent, antiestablishment candidate Yasuo Tanaka as governor in October 2000. Tanaka's election came on the heels of electoral successes by other reform-minded, independent, and victorious gubernatorial challengers that spanned the rural-urban divide, running in Miyagi, Tokyo, Osaka, Mie, Kochi, Tochigi, and Chiba. Tanaka's election occurred in the middle of a wave that continued with the success of independent gubernatorial candidates in subsequent elections in Tokushima and Kanagawa. These victories were commonly attributed to voters' desire for a new style of politics characterized by greater citizen involvement in decision-making and a reversal in the flow of power in government, from the top down to the bottom up (Lam 2005b). Kyoko Yanagisawa, a Nagano artist who helped to mobilize citizens' groups to support Tanaka, commented, "We saw what was happening in Kochi, Mie and Miyagi Prefectures and we, too, wanted to demonstrate that the power of one vote could overcome the power of political organizations" (Strom 2001). The "political organizations" that Yanagisawa spoke of are traditional organizations (*koenkai,* PTAs, neighborhood associations, labor unions, chambers of commerce, and so on) aligned with national political parties that are central to voter mobilization, producing an "organized vote" that independent, "floating" voters are seldom able to defeat due to the costs of collective action (Tanaka 2003).

Prior to the election of Governor Tanaka, Nagano had been led by two governors, both former bureaucrats who handpicked their successors, for forty-one years. Tanaka ran on a platform characteristic of successful independent challengers for governor in other prefectures—he rejected support from established parties and mobilized unaffiliated voters; he emphasized transparency in local governance and promoted information disclosure; and he rejected national public works projects that spent taxpayers' money in ways that reflected the narrow interests of an individual politician's narrow base of supporters rather than the common interest (Lam 2005b, 73). Nagano residents, angered by the mismanagement of the 1998 Olympics, which drove the prefecture deeper into debt rather than stimulating the economy, as originally projected, threw their support behind Tanaka. As host city for the Olympic Games, the capital city Nagano spent one billion dollars to build sports facilities, a high-speed train line, a highway, and an airport (Strom 2001). The prefecture shouldered costs in excess of the original investment to maintain these infrastructure projects over the long term.[6] Residents' efforts to hold officials accountable were frustrated because official records were burned.

Shortly after the election, the Nagano Association for Public Opinion Research (2000) conducted an "emergency survey" (*kinkyuu chousa*) to explore

---

6. Prefectural maintenance of skating rinks and a bobsled course alone are in excess of 12 million dollars. Andrew Zimbalist (2010), reporting for the International Monetary Fund, wrote that the Olympics left "various units of Japanese government" with a 11 billion dollar debt (10).

voters' expectations for the new Tanaka administration. Voters' policy preferences remained unclear because the campaign was fought around broad themes that defined a style of governing rather than concrete policies. "Continuity or change," "bureaucracy or the people," "hierarchical organization or grassroots mobilization" were slogans that framed the election as a choice between clientelism and a reform movement to bring politics back to the people. After the election, Tanaka had to express his support for "change," "the people," and "grassroots mobilization" through pragmatic decisions about resolving the enormous government debt, meeting the welfare needs of an aging society, and cutting public works projects with high environmental costs. While it was clear that voters wanted reform, the terms of the campaign made it hard for the new administration to determine how voters were thinking about specific issues.

The Nagano Association for Public Opinion Research (2000) survey found that 57.5 percent of voters surveyed were unaffiliated with any party, and these voters—at 80 percent—were the most satisfied with the election outcome. The largest groups of party identifiers supported the DPJ (16.3 percent) followed by the LDP (13.3 percent). The number one reason voters offered for supporting Tanaka was his "character"; 90 percent of satisfied voters turned out because they thought that change was necessary, and Tanaka's character represented change. The issues that voters hoped the new governor would grapple with were welfare (48.3 percent), education (28.2 percent), environment (24.8 percent), and public finance administration (16.9 percent). These are "common good" issues that speak to broad constituencies. In contrast, demand for traditional pork-barrel issues that mobilize particularistic interests—transportation (15.1 percent), communications (15.1 percent), trade and commerce (15.1 percent) and agriculture and forestry (8.35 percent)—finished well behind the top three public goods. As for their hopes for the prefectural assembly, 91.4 percent of survey respondents agreed that working for better financial health was as important as openness in communication (90.4 percent), and waste management (93.3 percent).

Shifting policy preferences signaled an underlying commitment to a change in political practice in local politics and the dismantling of LDP money-power politics at the grassroots level. Throughout the postwar period, research on mass political participation has shown that voters have supported those politicians that are best situated to deliver pork-barrel benefits to their specific local area (Flanagan et al. 1991; Scheiner 2005, 2006). In contrast, approximately 70 percent of voters who supported the Tanaka administration valued fairness across local areas in administration over a special regard for their own area. In order to achieve a change in policy and democratic practice, 50 percent of Nagano Association for Public Opinion Research (2000) survey respondents wanted to see the governor adopt a more oppositional stance toward the assembly. While a majority of LDP and New Kōmeitō supporters wanted a cooperative relationship between the governor and the assembly, majorities of opposition party supporters and unaffiliated voters wanted a more adversarial relationship to reflect greater openness, deliberation, and debate.

One Nagano Association for Public Opinion Research (2000) finding that warrants closer attention is the 60 percent of survey respondents who turned out to vote *without* being contacted by local political elites; only 20 percent indicated that they were contacted by local elites prior to the election. This finding is salient because it speaks to the breakdown of LDP-style mobilization strategies in local politics and their replacement with new forms of voter mobilization that have not been well-articulated. Tanaka's support base was made up of unaffiliated voters who were outside of traditional voter mobilization networks; they were not contacted by local business and political elites urging them to vote for party candidates.

Many scholars have noted that a combination of women's networks, citizens' networks, unaffiliated voters (*mutouha*), and volunteers are changing the electoral dynamics of local politics in Japan. They have also noted that women are the common thread that holds these coalitions together; women constitute the backbone of citizens' networks, are a majority of unaffiliated voters, and are more likely than men to volunteer to produce electoral upsets. However, new "networks" that are producing upsets in local elections across Japan are fluid, making them difficult to define by traditional measures. Sociologists such as Mario Diani, Roger Gould, and Doug McAdam and political scientists such as Alan Zuckerman (2005, 2007) delineate social networks as sets of "nodes" that are linked by relational "ties." Nodes can be individuals (opinion leaders) or organizations that share concerns for a specific cause. The "networks" that are producing local electoral upsets like Tanaka's in Nagano do not have enduring "nodes," which in the Japanese case have traditionally been local business and political elites and organizations such as neighborhood associations,

PTAs, labor unions, chambers of commerce, and so on that are territori-ally bounded with a physical infrastructure, organizational memory, and a chain of command. The nodes are individual activists and informal groups that meet in public spaces and private homes for a range of social and po-litical purposes. Without identifiable "nodes," the "ties" are hard to trace and the network difficult to define and measure.

Researchers who analyzed Nagano election surveys to understand the coalition of interests that supported Governor Tanaka over several elec-tion cycles found that support for Tanaka was highest among voters who were not plugged into traditional networks. Women who voted for can-didate Tanaka were unaffiliated with any party, they were significantly less trusting of politics and they were less integrated into traditional po-litical networks (for instance, women knew fewer people who were *koen-kai* members than men). Further, women and men belonged to different types of social networks. Rates of group membership among women were highest in study circles, the PTA, consumer organizations, and volunteer associations. In contrast, men were more likely to belong to professional as-sociations, agricultural cooperatives, labor unions, urban planning groups, political parties and *koenkai* (Maruyama et al. 2007). Despite women's low membership rates in these latter, "male-dominated" organizations that have traditionally promoted electoral participation (Flanagan et al. 1991), women who turned out to vote were more likely to remain loyal to Tanaka over several election cycles.

In Japan, the new "networks" are more easily identified by their political practices and goals than by their structure. Robin LeBlanc (1999), Mikiko Eto (2007), Peng Er Lam (2005a), and Foljanty-Jost and Schmidt (2006), among others, have used the case of the Seikatsu Club Network (NET), a consumer cooperative that has successfully elected women to local as-semblies, as one concrete example of a highly elastic and increasingly wide-spread phenomenon. The practices of this "citizens' network" operate across the broad range of what Lam terms "women-centric" networks. NET's "activists and supporters are predominantly female volunteers, espe-cially housewives" (Lam 2005a, 90). NET candidates, active in Kanagawa, Chiba, Saitama, Hokkaido, Nagano, and Fukuoka Prefectures and Tokyo, belong to "local parties" and tailor their campaign appeals to address issues specific to residents; the party is not a "national" party with a central party organization and common platform (ibid.). Candidates do, however, share a commitment to promoting peace, environmental conservation, and social justice. Assembly members who run under the NET banner are replaced after two or three terms to prevent professionalization and the creation of ties to entrenched interests (Foljanty-Jost and Schmidt 2006). Political scientist Yasuo Takao observes that NET and other women's networks "have developed an alternative form of equitable political participation for stakeholders that contrasts with traditional vertical patron-client relationships. Women's organizations, such as the Citizens' Network, are spreading a socially-centered form of governance that draws upon, and coordinates, government and voluntary sector participation, effectively providing an alternative to the traditional system of local government" (Takao 2008). This style of governance was promoted by the Tanaka administration and garnered support from women voters.

Engaging Women

By the time I arrived in Matsumoto City, the "Nagano model" of local government had been fully articulated and the institutionalization process had begun. Fukui-san, my journalist informant, supplied me with an information packet filled with pamphlets and newspaper articles detailing how Nagano was establishing itself as a national model for grassroots democracy. Under Governor Tanaka, citizen activism was spreading across the prefecture, and interest in politics was higher than at any other point in recent history. Governor Tanaka worked in a glass office to symbolize his public commitment to transparency in decision-making and accessibility to residents; he received and, with the help of aides, responded to between 250 and 300 emails from constituents daily; town hall meetings were held twice a month to reach older voters in rural areas; an anti-dam declaration represented Governor Tanaka's official position on wasteful public works spending; and he abolished the press club system and conducted weekly question and answer sessions (Strom 2001; Lam 2005b, 83).

The women I spoke with in Matsumoto City were actively struggling with how to integrate their civic and political practices under a prefectural administration that advocated deepening democracy by bringing more citizens into the local political process. Comparing and contrasting local citizenship practices and elite political behavior enabled participants to imagine how their practices could infiltrate and transform the political arena—locally, regionally, and nationally. This struggle is not specific to Nagano citizens or women voters.

I arrived at Matsumoto City station in Nagano Prefecture on the morning of March 3, 2001, and proceeded to the M-Wing Building, a public space and conference center located in the heart of the city, where a panel discussion on nonprofit and nongovernmental organizations was scheduled for later that day. Fukui-san had recruited a group of eight women in their forties and fifties to share their views of politics in Japan. All were interested in politics, though not directly involved in activities they would classify as overtly political. Instead, they were self-professed students of environmental, health, and welfare issues who were interested in learning how to improve the quality of life for local residents through work on these issues.

Participants expressed that it was their obligation as voters to pay attention to what elected officials are doing because voters are responsible for putting them into power. The ballot gave them the right to demand that elected officials do those things that voters want and to account publicly for actions that oppose the dominant opinion. To enforce public accountability, one participant stressed the importance of everyday people learning what kinds of questions to ask about politics, how to ask them, and how to raise awareness that everyone is entitled to ask for more information. The stress on education recognizes the multiple resource- and status-based limitations that ordinary voters face in performing their citizenship responsibilities and claiming full rights. Ordinary voters lack the knowledge-based resources that support participation in public debates. They do not know the basic facts and, for difficult policy problems, lack the analytical expertise required for critical engagement. While information builds confidence in the ability to participate, talking to others in small groups builds ordinary voters' confidence in their right to defy social conventions against challenging the "higher-ups" while arming them with the tools to do so. Political change is impossible without this minimum level of citizen engagement—seeking information that helps individuals to understand how politics works is fundamental to deciding future political action, individual or collective. This broad overview of the Matsumoto focus group, gleaned from the themes that participants discussed and their patterns of interaction, reflects larger changes in the local political climate.

Nagano women echoed the same sentiments about national politics that I heard time and again among women in Tokyo. Both sets of women were frustrated by the seemingly insurmountable distance between themselves and national politics and the discrepancy between the political practices of corrupt, self-interested politicians and those of ordinary voters at the grassroots level (see chapter 4).[7] The successful election of an antiestablishment outsider in Nagano did set my focus groups apart. Tanaka's success required considerable mobilization of independent, antiestablishment voters. Consequently, there was less distance between Tanaka's political vision and practice and the vision of popular democracy that Nagano residents articulated. The observable efforts of the Tanaka administration to narrow the gap between democratic ideals and practices in government and on the ground had altered citizens' calculations about how citizen activity can influence the pace of political change.

Meanwhile, my Matsumoto City focus group participants were figuring out how to build citizens' confidence in their own opinions about politics. Ordinary voters needed to establish norms for gathering information, comparing notes, and deliberating the findings. Accumulating their own information would increase the chances that officials would take citizens seriously and would enable citizens to challenge decisions that had previously been handed down to them by public officials and accepted without question. Under these circumstances, electoral outcomes would represent the true voice of the people rather than the views of higher-ups in the traditional organizations that faithfully mobilize their memberships to vote for the leadership's preferred party or candidate. From this perspective, the LDP was on thin ice, because if democracy is government by the people, the party would not be able to demonstrate legitimately that it had mass support despite having the largest proportion of Diet seats. Focus group participant Shiino-san, a farmer in her early sixties, reasoned that since

---

7. When I conducted my Nagano focus groups, I had already spoken with three groups in Tokyo. I met with my remaining two Tokyo-based groups in the months following my Nagano experience. Each group was a learning experience. The events in one group were not entirely independent of the events in the ones that followed. I often adjusted questions for clarity. For comparison, I asked about subjects that one group raised that were not independently broached in following groups. If my line of questioning and interpretation of the discussion was biased by preceding groups, my experiences in Nagano were as important in directing my reentry to the Tokyo field site as my earlier Tokyo experiences were in informing the field decisions that I made in Nagano.

voter turnout is 50 percent or less, depending on locale, winners gained their seats with the support of at most 40 percent of eligible voters. When you consider the numbers of citizens who are voting out of obligation to the organizations that they belong to, then it becomes difficult to accept electoral outcomes and the subsequent policies as truly representative. The outcome is, according to Shiino-san "like the relationship between an older male of household and a new bride who is always told what to do and must always defer to his wishes. She is afraid to disagree and he feels that she needs instruction and protection as if she were a child." Matsumoto women were trying to subvert this dynamic by building up their own base of knowledge about politics to enrich their own citizen practices. They were trying to subvert the conventional wisdom that ordinary voters, women in particular, do not know very much about politics and thus cannot be trusted to know their own best interests.

When citizens talk with one another and work through common problems, it unleashes processes that yield a range of political outcomes. At a minimum, exchange of knowledge empowers citizens to go to the polls and vote independently of the recommendations of local political bosses. But forcing information disclosure for public scrutiny has the potential to broaden voters' choices at the polls. The exposure of undemocratic practices mobilizes a broad public to demand fresh candidates who, in turn, introduce new practices that approximate citizens' visions of what democracy should be. Whereas Nagano residents were once satisfied to leave everything up to elected officials, focus group participant Matsuda-san, a housewife in her fifties, observed, "Governor Tanaka is involving ordinary people in public debates... the effect has been that individually people have developed a consciousness of how their opinions and involvement can make a difference. These personal changes influence surrounding people, and that builds momentum that can produce a citizens' movement."

Matsumoto focus group participants were clearly trying to muddle through the process of institutionalizing new norms for engaging with local politics in their own communities of practice. While this group had adopted much of the language of the new Tanaka administration, they—more so than the Tokyo groups discussed in the next chapter—were struggling to integrate these new norms into their everyday lives and practices. The Matsumoto group was as engaged with study, hobby, and volunteer activities as the Tokyo-based groups Neighborhood Friends and Women

Now. However, they had less practice with bridging their different substantive interests to develop a common language for talking about politics. The struggle of Matsumoto women to construct the same narratives that Tokyo women delivered with ease is most likely attributable to the socioeconomic differences between the two groups; the Matsumoto group was less educated overall and had spent less time in professional jobs. They had to work harder to reach common ground, but they did it. The tensions between local and national politics and the distance between ordinary citizens and elected elites were present in the Matsumoto discussion, but these themes had to be extracted from a wide range of stories about personal experiences with politics. Each participant took turns and queried one another in an effort to locate and pin down the experiences and language that best articulated a common ground on a shifting political terrain.

One of my Tokyo participants spoke about women's activism around garbage disposal and recycling in a derisive tone and linked this concern to the amateur politics of conservative housewives. But these "parochial" Matsumoto women used their familiarity with garbage and recycling to talk with greater ease about citizenship practices that are valued equally by more "sophisticated" citizens. Garbage disposal and recycling represent a set of issues with a history of contention and collaboration between local governments and residents. Public debate expanded beyond public health, the siting of landfills and waste disposal facilities, government contracts, and the pragmatic use of tax monies. Deliberation over waste reduction goals forced people to think about the lifestyles they currently live compared to those that they want to live and the tradeoffs that they would have to make individually and as a society to achieve a better quality of life. Matsumoto women claimed that discussions about public works projects helped them to understand that the public was not the primary beneficiary. Better democracy, women discovered, entails the same type of deliberation among ordinary citizens, and between ordinary citizens and political elites, that they practice among themselves.

Nagano after Tanaka

In the summer of 2002, Nagano's prefectural assembly passed a no-confidence motion against Governor Tanaka, marking the first time in twenty-six years that a governor was removed from office. The governor encountered resistance from the conservative prefectural assembly over his public works policy. Across Japan, it is not uncommon for independent executives to be thwarted because legislatures are unwilling to adopt new political goals and styles. Tanaka's cancellation of two previously authorized dam construction projects angered local politicians and construction bureaucrats. Tanaka's position on public works endangered the assembly members' own chances of reelection because they would be unable to deliver pork to their constituent bases in the form of public works contracts. Tanaka's reelection bid offered voters the opportunity to weigh in on his public works policy; they issued him a mandate to stay the course.

When Tanaka lost his seat in 2006 to LDP candidate Jin Murai, approximately 60 percent of voters supported the direction of the Tanaka's administrative reform effort. Despite supporting his opponent, citizens had not lost their interest in furthering the Tanaka reform agenda (*Japan Times* 2006). Voters were, however, tired of the gridlock produced by constant policy disagreements between their independent governor and the entrenched interests that were represented in the prefectural assembly and local bureaucracy (Lam 2005b). Tanaka's style of politics had left an indelible imprint on citizen practices that were expected to continue evolving after Tanaka's departure from office. Tanaka is reported as "boasting" that Nagano residents had learned to express their political opinions freely as a consequence of practices—such as open discussions with residents—that he introduced under his administration (*Japan Times* 2006).[8] Tanaka's successor, a former Ministry of International Trade and Industry bureaucrat and twenty-year Diet veteran backed by business organizations and *koenkai,* is more in the mold of the traditional style of politics that Tanaka had aimed to subvert. Popular democratic practices have heightened mass political consciousness and empowered Nagano citizens to mobilize, should Governor Murai's practices revert to political styles of the pre-Tanaka period.

---

8. Arguably, there is a problem of causality; voter's expectations about citizen participation in democracy had already shifted prior to Tanaka's election, and this shift helps explain why an independent was electable. But the reforms introduced under his administration expanded public venues for deepening these democratic practices.

Changing the Terms of Engagement

I have placed my Matsumoto focus group within the broader context of Nagano prefectural politics and linked the sentiments that emerged from that group discussion to a broader national discourse, represented by JEDS respondents, to argue that these attitudes are expressed in electorally centered patterns of political action across Japan. Understanding the content of these political attitudes yields a more nuanced interpretation of voting behavior that links local and national electoral outcomes. The changing character if the connection between local and national elections is masked by researchers' focus on national elections to the Diet, where there has been more continuity than change. The privileging of national elections has been furthered by the traditional weakness of local party organizations in a highly centralized state. The emphasis on national elections has inhibited researchers from redirecting attention to other parts of the Japanese system where there have been marked changes in political engagement over time.

Scholars have long noted increasing cynicism about national politics in Japan. A decline in political confidence is correlated with a corresponding decline in voter turnout and an increase in unaffiliated voters in the Japanese electorate, but central voting tendencies—the rural/urban cleavage and LDP dominance—have been slow to change. Consequently, Japanese voters appear apathetic when the view is limited to national level change. While national outcomes are the same, the attitudes that underlie patterns of national political participation are changing in ways that promise to upset current practices in the future. In the meantime, the hints of change are evident in local politics.

Patterns of civic and political engagement at the grassroots level tell a very different story about national politics. Everyday citizens are trying to shorten the distance between the center and the periphery by bringing national democratic practices into closer alignment with popular democracy at the grassroots level, thereby changing the political center from the periphery; they are acting locally while thinking nationally and globally. Voting remains the primary mechanism for increasing voice in Japanese democracy. Common efforts to promote direct participation in democracy—referendum and recall movements, citizens' and antiestablishment parties, and the election of independent executives—are increasing in frequency across Japan, and all work through the ballot box. The changing character of local government promises to alter the relationship between local and national politics. Ironically, because voting remains the primary tool by which citizens exercise collective control over elites and is used rarely for referendum or recall, the pattern of change is of quiet changes that go unnoticed until they reach a tipping point. I have tried to map the progression of this quiet transformation in this book.

Falling turnout, the weakening of partisanship, and the decrease in public confidence in national politics does not mean that Japanese voters have abandoned politics or party organizations altogether. Japanese voters reinvest their political resources into local politics where their efforts are most immediately felt. Some voters are engaging in local action that is crafted to send a direct message to national politicians and to effect change from the bottom up. Voters use (or threaten to use) the tools available to them—information disclosure, referendum and recall, and citizen's movements—to alter the local electoral context. Local governments can be more immediately remade according to citizens' visions, even if national political change remains an elusive possibility.

Turnout has decreased at all administrative levels, but participation in local politics has not experienced a drop as pronounced as that in national elections.[9] Higher percentages of voters continue to participate in contests for local office; turnout for the 2007 unified local elections ranged from 50 to 75 percent,[10] and national turnout reached 67.5 percent for the high-profile 2005 House of Representatives election. Higher turnout in local elections, especially town and village elections, is the opposite of what one finds in other democracies, where turnout is higher for high-salience national elections and declines for elections held at lower administrative units. Yusaku Horiuchi (2005) has called this a "turnout twist," which can be explained by voters' calculations about how much their votes will matter. Everyday

---

9. Voter turnout has fallen cross-nationally in established democracies. Japan, however, is not an outlier; its trends are no more or less pronounced than elsewhere. In fact, voter turnout in Japan for parliamentary elections is, depending on the election, much higher on average than during House and Senate elections (40.4 percent of the population eligible to vote in 2006 and 39.5 percent in 2002) and on par with presidential elections in the United States (61.7 percent in 2009, 60.1 percent in 2004 and 54.2 percent of the population eligible to vote in 2000). See the United States Election Project at elections.gmu.edu/ voter_turnout.htm

10. There was tremendous variation across administrative units. Turnout tended to be low in dense urban areas but higher in rural towns and villages.

Japanese correctly conclude that their vote has a higher chance of matter-
ing in local elections. Voters are using citizens' parties; independent and
antiestablishment candidates; and information disclosure, referendum,
and recall to increase the likelihood that their voices will be heard.

Citizens' Parties

Again, I turn to the experience of Ms. Mako Takagi, the local assembly member I introduced in chapter 2. Ms. Takagi was a member of the
220,000-member Kanagawa Network Movement (NET), a grassroots
citizens' party established in 1984 to increase the numbers of women in local
elected office under a banner of participatory reform (LeBlanc 1999; Lassen 2002).[11] NET is an example of a party organization that primarily challenges local assembly seats but also uses local office as a platform to give
citizens more influence in national politics through local initiatives and
transnational collaboration. Ms. Takagi asserted that local parties are fundamental to the democratic process because national parties are limited
by their inability to adjust policies to accommodate the demographic, economic, and geographical differences across Japan.[12] Local parties, in bringing citizens closer to local politics, successfully bring everyday voters that
much closer to national politics because the local level is the foundation for
the operation of politics at higher administrative levels.

Ms. Takagi acknowledged that the influence of local parties in national
politics, like that of everyday people in national politics, is moderate but
growing. Traditional parties in Japan are national organizations without
a strong grassroots presence in the form of local chapters (the exception is
the JCP); this presents a challenge to the DPJ, as its leadership increasingly
acknowledges the importance of establishing itself as a local presence in

---

11. NET is a political group that emerged under the umbrella of the Seikatsu Club Network,
the consumer cooperative that launched a political arm and is the focus of LeBlanc's 1999 book on
the political lives of housewives. In addition to the Kanagawa Net, there are groups in Hokkaido,
Tokyo, Yokohama, and Chiba. Though these local parties spring from the same source, they operate independently of one another. In 2003, Network Yokohama formed and broke away from
the Kanagawa Network.

12. I met with Ms. Takagi on the afternoon of January 18, 2001, at the Kanagawa Network office in Kannai, Yokohama. This account is drawn from my field notes and is informed by a tran-
script of an earlier published interview conducted by a staff writer at a major national Japanese
newspaper.

its efforts to gain more national seats.[13] As the DPJ makes inroads into the local political scene, it must compete with the local citizens' parties that have already begun incorporating into their base the growing numbers of voters who feel disconnected from national politics and parties. The DPJ's 2009 electoral victory was due in large part to its efforts to build local bases of support (Reed, Scheiner, and Thies 2009).

The political influence of local citizens' parties is growing due to the efforts of NET and its support base to build human networks and deepen ties between themselves and citizens' groups in other countries around issues of gender equality, peace, and the environment. I challenged Ms. Takagi to explain how a local party could legitimately aspire to having a global impact. She replied that the bonds that Japanese citizens are capable of building among themselves and with people of other nations are more powerful than the shallow bonds forged at the national level between elites and elites and between elites and citizens. Even when relationships at the elite level, the unit of the nation-state, fracture, the ties between members of the respective civil societies will persist because they have already built a longstanding relationship and mutual trust through working together to solve common problems in their everyday lives.

Independent Executives

My fieldwork corresponded with another important trend in local politics—an increase in independent or antiestablishment candidates for executive offices across Japan. In the 1960s and 1970s, voters installed progressive mayors to provide leadership on pressing social welfare needs. This earlier wave was short-lived because the LDP coopted the policies enacted by

---

13. Since its founding in 1998, the DPJ's victories in national elections have been limited in part because it has not run candidates in every district. The decision not to run candidates in every district was dictated by strategy and resources. The party did not have enough resources to launch candidates in all election districts, so it concentrated on those where the LDP was weakest and its likelihood of winning was high. The party has slowly been able to build its profile and electoral support base; its success the 2007 House of Councillors elections was due to the party's ability to expand beyond urban Japan and win in the LDP's traditional rural stronghold. Running more candidates increases DPJ victories, suggesting that when and where the party does not run a candidate, voters' choices are constrained, which leads to voter frustration. See Weiner (2008) for an empirical discussion of what is at stake at all levels of Japanese politics when the DPJ fails to run more candidates for local offices.

local progressive mayors and implemented the new environmental and social welfare policies nationally (Steiner 1965; Steiner et al. 1980). Electing independents to executive office is not a new strategy for pressuring national elites to increase their responsiveness to voters. That this strategy is being deployed again with renewed vigor in recent years is evidence that the gap between voters and national elites has once again grown too large. This time, this strategy is not being used to protest elites' failure to produce specific policy outputs, as was the case in the late 1960s and 1970s. Rather, support for independent candidates is being used to signal voter dissatisfaction with elite political styles, the disparity between elite political practices and citizens' own visions of democracy on the ground.

Candidates who run for office as independents or with the backing of a citizens' party signal to voters their independence from both interest groups and traditional party constraints. Such candidates are viewed as committed, once elected, to continuing their work on behalf of the ordinary citizens who extended their electoral support. A former assembly member from Gifu Prefecture, Midori Teramachi, writes that once elected, independents are further freed from the usual constraints imposed by traditional interest groups. The expectations of independent candidates' support base are fundamentally different from supporters of traditional party candidates. A vote for an independent candidate is a tacit indication of citizens' approval of and consent to a style of representation that prioritizes discussion, persuasion, and new attitudes within the assembly as a means of improving the common good (Teramachi 2003). Independent and antiestablishment politicians change the political climate and practices within local assemblies. The introduction of deliberative norms that embrace citizens' perspectives will facilitate the passage of policies in the public interest.

Referendum, Recall, and Disclosure Movements

The timing of the JEDS survey coincided with the tail end of a rapid increase in the number of demands for referenda in local politics. The first popular referendum was held in 1995; between December 1995 and March 1999, thirty-seven communities completed signature campaigns to compel their local assemblies to initiate a referendum that would allow voters to express their opposition to public works projects (for instance, nuclear power facilities, dams, stadiums, and waste facilities) (Jain 2000). Of this number, local governments granted approval to initiate a referendum seven times, and six referenda were eventually conducted (Numata 2006). The barriers to referenda are high. Referenda require petitioners to collect and submit signatures from at least 2 percent of the local electorate to the local executive and assembly for a vote; a majority of assembly members can then reject the demand.[14] If the demand is accepted and an ordinance is passed to prepare a yes/no ballot, the decision voiced by a majority of voters is nonbinding; the assembly can still move forward with an unpopular course of action. Consequently, the referendum is a weak tool not worth the high costs that citizens must spend to invoke it. Since 2000, some communities have passed a permanent referendum ordinance that would allow citizens to conduct a referendum—the outcome of which remains nonbinding—without interference from the local assembly if it is able to collect signatures from one-third of the eligible local electorate (Numata 2006). The difference between these two types of referendum lies in the steps that must be taken to start to the procedure. Prior to reform, citizens had to get the permission of the assembly. After reform, citizens can initiate a referendum even in the face of reluctance or outright opposition on the part of the local assembly. Though local assemblies are not bound by the outcomes of either referendum process, the ability of citizens to force a referendum has power that is not merely symbolic. The ability of citizens to overcome the high costs of collectively organizing sufficiently threatens assembly members in advance of subsequent local election cycles.

The increasing incidence of referenda "is one of several indications that voters reject the spectator model of democracy (*kankyaku minshushugi*) and are embracing both the idea of participatory democracy (*sanka-gata minshushugi*) and the political will to institutionalize it" (Jain 2000, 556). That local voters surmount the costs involved in successfully invoking the referendum process speaks to the sense of urgency that many everyday Japanese voters feel. Even though the chances of success for referendum movements are low, the campaign itself is an opportunity for local citizens to voice their opinions and deliberate with one another. Campaigns inspire study groups to organize and energize grassroots movements (Numata 2006, 24).

---

14. Local assemblies can also initiate a referendum.

The increase in disclosure movements and the corresponding increase in taxpayers bringing suit against the government for misappropriation of tax money are inextricable from the increase in referendum and recall movements. When voters initiate disclosure movements and file taxpayer suits, they are often so angered by the information they uncover that they mobilize to demand a referendum or recall. But information disclosure is an easier tool than referenda for tipping the balance of power between voters and public officials, because public exposure damages political careers, creates opportunities for new entrants to politics, and produces new incentives for voters to support political outsiders. Alternatively, the threat of public exposure encourages political incumbents to bring their practices more closely into alignment with citizens' normative ideals if they are to retain their offices.

The national Information Disclosure Act of 1999, passed after nearly two decades during which nearly nine hundred local governments responded to citizen pressures and adopted local ordinances that would enable citizens to demand the release of information that would help them to hold local officials accountable (Marshall 2002). Citizens' groups and opposition parties had been lobbying for over twenty years, since the notorious 1976 Lockheed bribery scandal,[15] the so-called Four Big industrial pollution cases, and mounting evidence of government waste: "Advocates saw a national information disclosure law as a practical tool to combat official secrecy and to root out the causes of government regulatory failures" (Repeta and Shultz 2002). Four thousand information requests were filed during the first week of operation in 2001. Citizens had already had nearly two decades of practice in holding local authorities accountable via local ordinances.

Over the course of the 1990s, information disclosure suits increased tenfold, from ten per year at the beginning of the decade to over one hundred per year by 2000 (Marshall 2002, 11). Local residents filed information disclosure requests to shed light on any number of decisions that affected their quality of life, including the criteria for selecting architects for local projects, for admitting children to public day care, for hiring disabled citizens, and for approving pharmaceutical products (Information Clearing

---

15. During the Watergate hearings, the Japanese (and American) public learned that Prime Minister Kakuei Tanaka had accepted a bribe from the American company.

House Japan n.d.). Local residents across Japan have demanded receipts for expenses that local assembly members incurred while on overseas business and research trips. Information disclosure requests unleashed a flurry of related citizen action resulting in the increase in taxpayer suits by residents who took local officials to court to force them to repay illegally spent public funds to the treasury (Marshall 2002).

Local Participation and National Change: Reining in National Government through Local Action

According to political scientist Purnendra Jain, "Reform, decentralization, transparency, information disclosure, responsibility, efficiency, and public participation have become part of the new political lexicon in Japan's local administrations, most clearly articulated and implemented by the new breed of governors" (Jain 2004, 82). Contemporary political leaders present voters with diametrically opposed options—political change or stagnation. There is more of the former in local politics and more of the latter in national politics. That "new style" leaders have gained more attention than "new style" voters is understandable, given that, by voters' own assessments, leaders have gotten so far beyond voters' control that many voters opt to disassociate from politics altogether. When political leaders attend to voters' interests, their actions are attributed to their own visions for better democracy rather than the agency of voters. Less attention has been given to shifts below the surface of the electorate, specifically changes in how voters interact with one another changes mass attitudes that coalesce in demands for better democratic practices that are embodied in contemporary leaders. Researchers have been slow to entertain the idea that changes in leadership styles may reflect underlying strategic changes in electoral behavior. In other words, leaders are not simply modeling a different type of political engagement; it is a two-way exchange.

Referenda, disclosure movements, and taxpayer suits, while local actions, are a check on national government. Numata (2006) argues that referenda strengthen the bargaining power of local authorities related to the prefectural and central government. The referenda most likely to be approved by local assemblies are on issues that do not supplant the assemblies' own decisions. Indeed, referenda are most likely to be successful when local executives, assemblies, and voters are united in their position against higher-level authorities and intend to reject initiatives from on high. Through referenda, local politicians can demonstrate that their communities are in accord in questioning prefectural and national authority to impose unpopular decisions that were not made with the participation of citizens who will be directly affected.

Sometimes a well-orchestrated signature campaign is enough to deter a local assembly from proceeding with an unpopular plan. Referenda that are carried out send a powerful message to national elites that local citizens are poised for protest and might penalize the party in power in the next election. LeBlanc has termed such referenda movements "an assertive, individualist rhetoric of self-determination" articulated by local citizens' groups, which are "radically altering their participants' experience of Japanese democracy" (LeBlanc 2008, 177). Yet local residents are expressing their radical experiences with Japanese democracy in time-honored fashion. Through the ballot box, citizens voted in new representatives who were sympathetic to their cause and successfully resisted national efforts to complete projects seen as a waste of taxpayer money or a threat to the environment (Jain 2000; Numata 2006; LeBlanc 2008).[16]

In this chapter and the next, my focus on public demands for better elite political practices rewrites a story about an apathetic public that is being spurred to action by strategic elites into one about how everyday people use existing tools and create new tools to assert their voices in politics and their control over elites. In the process, they move elite political practices into closer alignment with popular visions for democracy. The narratives about better democracy that emerge from focus groups and voter surveys indicate that mass attitudes about the capacity to improve democratic practices through public participation began to change in advance of signs of a realigning electorate—independent executives, recalls and referenda, and the proliferation of citizens' parties—that have been seen as harbingers of change to come. Administrative decentralization has provided both incentives and opportunities for voters to redirect their anger and frustration with national politics toward local outlets, where the results of participation are evident in citizens' immediate environment. At

---

16. Both Jain (2000) and LeBlanc (2008) offer case studies of residents who successfully initiated a local referendum to oppose unpopular public works projects.

the same time, changing political dynamics at the grassroots level sends a clear message to national officials that the "electoral connection" between local and national government is shifting (LeBlanc 2008). When citizens use the multiple strategies outlined in this chapter to shake up local assemblies and encourage local elites to strengthen their loyalties to ordinary voters, assembly members no longer function as "reliable grassroots activists" and "significant vote-gathering machines" for the LDP in national, prefectural, and municipal elections (Kohara 2007, 10).

4

Politically Excluded "Commoners"

A Gendered Pathway to Participation

National politics is far removed from everyday voters. This chapter sharpens the focus on Japanese women voters, a segment of the electorate that raises a theoretical and empirical puzzle. As a group, Japanese women face institutional, structural, and cultural constraints that conventionally depress political participation. These conditions have arguably contributed to higher rates of nonpartisanship among women, another factor that correlates with political disengagement. Yet more Japanese women than men have turned out to vote in every election across Japan for over three decades. In this chapter I focus on women because their patterns of electoral participation run counter to what theory would predict. If national politics is far removed from everyday voters, it should be harder for women to close the gap between themselves and political elites. How Japan women both close the gap and exceed expectations can deepen understanding of how to promote participation among disaffected, marginalized, and underrepresented voters in established democracies.

In earlier chapters, I used national survey data to outline the broad parameters of a national discourse about voter dissatisfaction with national politics to establish the generalizability of these views and associated political action repertoires. Men and women are dissatisfied for the same reasons, but the way they come to articulate and act on these views differs. In this chapter, I analyze focus group discussions with women voters to gain a deeper understanding of the experiences and resources that keep women politically engaged. Talking to women provides insight into the factors that help them to overcome multiple demobilizing influences to remain actively engaged in electoral politics for long-term change. Are the factors that bolster women's participation gendered? If so, can the factors that sustain women's participation in an environment characterized by a deep distrust of elite politics be cultivated in less active segments of the electorate?

When Japanese women talk about voting, they invoke larger narratives about self-improvement and community development that are achieved through education and lifelong learning, independently and in the company of others. Election results and policy changes between election cycles tell voters something about how well the linkages between parties and candidates and the public are working. The responsiveness of parties and candidates—or lack thereof—informs voters about how to adjust participatory strategies, often in ways that do not fit neatly into normative and measurable categories of democratic participation. The women in my focus groups vote because they learn something about politics in doing so. The ballot box is a site of knowledge production, the outputs of which become resources that are reinvested in electoral politics and participation in other political spaces. Japanese women revive discussions about education and democracy and provide interesting insights into how marginalized groups generate and use knowledge for their own empowerment. What they learn, how they learn it, and what they do with this knowledge is the focus of this chapter.

A Gendered Pathway to Participation: Women Now and Neighborhood Friends

Participants in my first group, Women Now,[1] were professional women ranging in age from their late twenties to their mid-fifties. All had struggled

---

1. Names of all groups and participants have been changed to preserve confidentiality.

with how to balance work and family responsibilities at some point in their lives. Women in my second group, Neighborhood Friends, were housewives who joined a local group to help foreign students such as myself to negotiate the challenges of living abroad. As discussed below, Women Now participants belong to a community of shared interests that was pulled together for our conversations, though individual members had no prior contact. Neighborhood Friends was a preexisting group whose members had regular face-to-face contact outside of the focus group setting. I select these two groups because the contrasting cast of characters echoes themes about Japanese politics and citizen engagement that are common to all of my groups. Even though the groups' goals and the participants' initial reasons for membership differ, the benefits of participation are similar. These two groups of women see themselves as involved in very different pedagogical enterprises that nonetheless draw attention to how social constructions of gender in Japan are connected to the common challenges women face in their public and private lives. Further, the two groups represent two different types of organizational structure that suggest how women involved in a broad array of civic groups evolve strategies that are functionally similar, but operationally dissimilar, to engage in politics.

Women Now is significant because it belongs to a universe of organizations that uses the internet as its primary hub for recruitment and contact.[2] Internet-based organizations tend to be ephemeral, and the potential for collective organizing via the internet is highly variable (Gottlieb and McLelland 2003).[3] Internet organizations cannot be tied to a place,

---

2. For an overview of women's internet activity in Japan and a closer look at a broad range of groups similar to Women Now, see Onosaka (2003). Popular press reports also track Japanese women's use of the internet for social and economic empowerment (Guth 2000, Kunii 2000).

3. There is a longstanding debate about whether the internet facilitates the building of social capital or contributes to its erosion by displacing face-to-face interaction with computer-mediated interaction between solitary and disassociated individuals. Evidence suggests that the internet does not erode social capital, a resource needed for collective action; it becomes a tool that people integrate into their preexisting social repertoire. People already predisposed toward broadening their scope of social interaction are likely to use the internet in addition to face-to-face interaction with family, friends, and neighbors (Curtice and Norris 2007). Gottlieb and McLelland (2003), in the introduction to *Japanese Cybercultures,* acknowledge that perspectives on the internet as an empowerment tool for marginalized groups are mixed. The internet is inarguably invaluable in connecting individuals and groups with similar concerns who do not share the same physical spaces and, as such, can lower the costs of collective organizing. However, internet users continue to face limitations. As much as it creates potential for organizing, it can also inhibit it. Older generations

members may never meet face-to-face, and resources to cover operating costs are scarce. This internet-based organization frames itself as a reliable source of information about workforce challenges that are specific to women working in Japan. Its "users" self-identify as "working women," a functional label that facilitates connections among single, married, and divorced working women, with or without children. While highly educated professional women are overrepresented, blue-collar women are welcome too.[4] According to Women Now users, the website was a tool to facilitate grassroots activism by helping like-minded individuals to find one another in an ever-changing social milieu. Today the website remains, but the site has not been updated since late 2001. Though the online site has lapsed, my experience with these women suggests that Women Now left its legacy in new groups and relations that cannot be easily traced.

Neighborhood Friends resembles a study circle or hobby group; some members describe participation as an extension of interests and experiences from their school days. Neighborhood Friends is linked to a specific international student dorm and its environs in Tokyo; members live in close proximity to the dorm, which allows them to maintain close contact with one another and the students that they assist. There are countless such "friendship associations" across Japan. Activities vary and include language learning and exchange and cultural events involving different countries. While most of the Neighborhood Friends members had limited or no experience traveling abroad, all were interested in learning more about life outside of Japan through the experience of helping foreign students adjust to the demands of life in Japan.[5]

---

of activists who are not technologically savvy but know a lot about making a "virtual" movement "real" are beyond the reach of younger activists who use the internet as their primary tool for communication and have little on-the-ground experience with organizing. Connecting these two different skill sets and experiences would increase movement potential.

4. It is not inconceivable that white-collar women will find themselves employed in blue-collar jobs later in their life course. Pressure for women to quit their job upon marriage and/or the birth of the first child remains strong in Japan. The structure of the labor market makes it difficult for women who had occupied high-status jobs to reenter the labor force in similar positions. Most women reenter the labor force in part-time and temporary positions (Brinton 1993).

5. I define Neighborhood Friends as more "legible" than Women Now due to the legitimacy that the Ministry of Education has long bestowed on cultural exchange activities. International exchange activities were promoted by local governments and civil and grassroots organizations in the 1970s and 1980s; "promoting mutual understanding through people-to-people exchanges became the task at hand" (Commissioner's Advisory Group 2003, 5). Analogous to the discussion about

Women entered into both these groups because they were facing a problem common to similarly situated women. Broadly defined, the problem was how to establish a space for achieving one's personal goals that exists independent of care-giving roles and other constraints that women face in Japan. Women Now users became involved in the network because they were seeking child care solutions that would allow them to continue careers that they found extremely gratifying before marrying and having children. Hoshino-san was working in the computer industry when she quit to have a baby:

> In my case, I honestly didn't think that there was anything fun about being a full-time housewife. That got me to thinking about why this pattern was still so widespread....I stayed at home for about two and a half years and I began thinking that there was something wrong with that type of lifestyle. So I finally joined a group of mothers who were feeling as stressed as I as a result of staying home and doing housework. It was then that I became aware of gender problems.

Hoshino-san then became involved in citizens' movements focusing on women's lifestyle issues and child development. She joined various circle activities and the ward's cooperative to deepen her interest in quality-of-life issues. Sato-san followed a very similar trajectory. After working for six years as a computer software developer, she quit her job to have a child and become a fulltime housewife. Isolation set in within the first four months, and Sato-san searched for social outlets in her community; as she said, "I found many women who share the same thoughts as I did, and I found peace of mind." She began to volunteer with groups at the ward level that were interested in improving social services and the environment for children. "From there," she said, "I began to look at gender issues." After a while, she decided that she wanted to work again, raising her child while having a part-time job, and took a job with an environmental association that is building an international network. In the meantime, she

---

lifelong learning policies in chapter 5, the state encourages international exchange to promote goals that McVeigh describes as "economic nationalist." For a discussion of the role that "internationalization" plays in defining Japanese national identity among women attending junior colleges, see McVeigh (1996).

participates in and organizes citizens' movements in her neighborhood "as a hobby."

Neighborhood Friends members were mainly housewives who saw the organization as a means to further their own interests while fulfilling family responsibilities. Yamada-san, a five-year veteran of the association, "became involved because it's close to my home and I had an interest in learning about life abroad. And it was something that I could do while my children were young." Miyazaki-san was a member of mothers' clubs at three different YWCAs and joined Neighborhood Friends after meeting a foreign student who had joined one of these groups for mothers. While the guidance that Neighborhood Friends extended to foreign students could be framed as an extension of their care-giving responsibilities, the women in this group took time out from their own families during evenings and weekends. Women often left their families behind when they attended events at the international student resident hall. Even though husbands and children played important supporting roles during the labor-intensive festivals, there was little doubt that the women were the main participants. Whenever students needed assistance, their primary contact was a woman.

Participation in the groups and networks that led my focus group participants to Women Now and Neighborhood Friends helped them to develop a shared narrative about how gender and politics affected their life opportunities and choices. In the case of Women Now, gender troubles motivated women to seek out the network in the first place. These working women were having trouble balancing work and family responsibilities and discussed the cultural, structural, and institutional impediments that they faced. After exhausting available public and private resources in their efforts to strike a balance between work and family, Women Now members realized that they were limited as individual women seeking to live outside dominant, gendered social norms. Owada-san, a medical researcher in her fifties, complained that "since it's still a male-oriented society, I end up being somewhat of an outsider." At the very least, joining a community of online users reassured them that there were other women with similar experiences and concerns.

Neighborhood Friends did not have careers as a site for self-actualization; they joined an existing group that promoted internationalization. While scholars such as Brian McVeigh (1996, 2004) raise the specter of the state's interest in promoting internationalization as a means of defining Japanese-ness through constant comparison with the "other," comparison also exposes fissures in the social construction of gender that then become a focus of group inquiry (Kelsky 2001).[6] While cultural exchange fostered critical comparisons between the status of women in Japan and women in the international contexts encountered by Neighborhood Friends, in all of the focus groups I conducted women asked questions and offered their impressions about the status of Japanese women compared to their American counterparts.

Admittedly, the women in my focus groups, especially those living in Tokyo, are more progressive than the average Japanese voter. Shimabukuro-san, one of the women in the World Café group (see table i.3) who lived near a U.S. army base, used the political views of the Americans she met to contextualize her own views through comparison and contrast. She found that U.S. military personnel were "totally against liberals. They do not like the idea of supporting teenage mothers on welfare or giving money to people who are not working." In contrast, in 2001 the consensus among women in this group and in every other group I interviewed was that Japan's top policy concern should be creating a strong system of social welfare. This is consistent with existing research showing that the LDP is less popular with urban voters and that floating voters are overrepresented in urban electorates. Traditionally, calls for social welfare reforms and attention to quality-of-life issues such as environmental pollution control have originated in urban Japan.

Women Now

In early 2001, I read a news article about a website called Women Now that was devoted to addressing issues in the daily lives of working women in Japan. I contacted Reiko Nakajima, a working mother who was volunteering her time to manage the site, about my project; she agreed to assist me in assembling the website's users for a focus group. On a Saturday afternoon in June 2001, six Women Now users joined me in a conference room at the

---

6. Kelsky (2001) argues that "the West" in the Japanese imagination becomes, in the hands of women, a tool for critiquing and resisting societal expectations about appropriate roles for women over the life course.

Tokyo Women's Plaza, a public space for women located within walking distance of the fashionable Omotesandō, Japan's Rodeo Drive.

There are two stories that I want to tell about Women Now. The first is a story about the practices in which like-minded individuals who are meeting for the first time engage to become a politically concerned group with a shared narrative about politics, gender, and politics and gender. The second story is about the content of the narrative that develops.

"Virtual" Ties to a "Real" Network   At the beginning of our two hours together at the Tokyo Women's Center, Women Now participants gathered quietly, taking seats arranged in a semicircle, and patiently waited for my informant and me to initiate and guide the discussion. Within thirty minutes, everyone was excitedly talking at once and raising their voices to respond to women sitting on the other side of the group. In the second hour, the participants were so engaged in discussion that I feared that we would overstay the two hours for which I had reserved the room; my informant and I had decided that two hours was the most that we could reasonably expect these busy women to commit to in advance. As the second hour drew to a close, it was clear that participants would unofficially continue the discussion over food and drink in a nearby *izakaya* (a Japanese-style tapas bar). Women exchanged contact information before proceeding to the *izakaya* to make sure that opportunities to do so were not lost when individual participants' schedules finally began to impinge upon the day, causing them to drift off one by one. I accompanied them to the *izakaya* for a quick bite to eat but did not keep the tape running. The space was no longer mine; Women Now users had turned the focus group into their own resource.

The focus group was an opportunity to do the business of creating and solidifying new relationships so that the members could continue to meet in smaller groups independently; they transformed a temporary structure into something permanent. The transformation began in the focus group and continued in the *izakaya,* where discussions became more personal over a shared meal. I left early out of respect for the practice of building personal ties in which these women were engaging; I did not want my presence as a researcher-student to undermine the authenticity of this practice, nor did I want to become a permanent member of the group and shed my identity as a researcher-student. Months later, my informant told me that some of my focus group participants had remained in contact and continued to meet.

I was wholly unprepared for—but pleased by—the prospect that the focus group brought together members of a "virtual" group and turned them into a "real" group. This unexpected outcome encouraged me to reflect on my own role as a researcher and the group dynamics that unfolded in producing it. As much as I am a researcher of women and politics, I also positioned myself as a student of women and politics. I make this distinction to underscore the asymmetries in power associated with each position; a researcher is an authority relative to her informants, while the student is a novice. Though Japan researchers warned that I might encounter difficulties in bringing together a set of unacquainted individuals to talk about politics, I found that the biggest challenge was getting women to acknowledge and feel confident that their individual perspectives on politics represented a wealth of information. Women were quick to disavow political "expertise" and could not understand that what they were telling me was of value. I assured them that what people do not know about politics is as interesting as what they do know, because the reasons offered for not knowing are informative. The way that people talk about their knowledge gaps exposes the deficiencies of democracy in linking elites and their constituents. I tried to set aside my expectations about the stories that I should be hearing in my focus groups and entered the room prepared to learn something about women and politics that I did not already know. As "facilitator" of the discussion, I made it clear that I was not there to teach, but to be taught. I asked questions to get the conversation started but encouraged participants to redirect the conversation; I did not assume that I had asked the "right" questions and was looking forward to uncovering unanticipated answers. As facilitator, my role was to make it easy for everyone to talk. Participants quickly shifted from "educating" me to sharing their personal experiences and using that information to find a common ground. Much later, reflecting on my focus group experiences, I realized that I had activated familiar narratives about learning that helped participants to settle into familiar practices of knowledge production.

McVeigh (1996) attends to the "how-to" rituals that accompany learning in Japan. The work of finding a common ground was done in the self-introductions in which Women Now participants verified that they were all members of the same online community who were meeting for the first time. Introductions established a sense of security and trust among participants, as they confirmed that they all occupied a shared ideological space. Women introduced themselves as working mothers, divorcees, professionals in male-dominated fields, and reluctant returnees from work and study experiences abroad. Women used their hobbies, interests, and activities at home, work, and in the community to drop cues and to hint at the social malcontents and political agitators lurking underneath their professional exteriors. Oyama-san, a former Japanese language instructor in her fifties, shared: "I went to the U.S. to study in the 1970s and was stupid enough to return to Japan afterwards. Gender roles were more sharply defined then. You were frowned upon if you wanted a divorce. Happily the bubble economy collapsed, and people's thinking began to change." Self-revelation allowed these women to move quickly to talk about more delicate topics and issues that they were passionate about (quality-of-life issues for women and children), how their passions emerged from the context of their everyday lives, and why they decided to participate in citizens' movements and other political actions to make small practical changes in their own lives while pushing for large-scale policy changes that would change women's status in Japanese society.

User-Generated Knowledge   The story of Nakajima-san, aged twenty-eight, and her entry into the online network and other groups of working women was echoed by other members. After having her first and only child, Nakajima-san began researching child care options so that she could return to her job with a foreign firm based in Tokyo. She was living in Tokyo's Edogawa ward at the time. According to Nakajima-san, the former ward mayor had very traditional beliefs about women's roles. He believed that it was a woman's responsibility to remain in the home to care for children. Nakajima-san believed that the ward mayor's position was important in explaining why Edogawa ward had not changed its public daycare policies to reflect changes that had been instituted in other Tokyo wards and, at the behest of the central government, across Japan.

The national government had promulgated the Angel Plan just two years earlier in an effort to reverse Japan's low birthrate by making it easier for women to remain in the workforce after having children.[7] While the

---

7. For an overview of the plan, see Chitose (2003). "The Basic Direction for Future Child Rearing Support Measures," commonly known as the "Angel Plan," was formulated in 1994 and represented the collaborative efforts of the Ministry of Health and Welfare (MHW), the Ministry

Angel Plan served as a catalyst for change in the local provision of nurseries, other features of public child care that undermined women's ability to balance work and family responsibilities remained intact in Edogawa ward. Edogawa ward had a low ranking among Tokyo's twenty-three wards in its availability of quality child care facilities. Nakajima-san could not enroll her son in a public daycare facility until he had reached one year of age, because there were no facilities for infants. Nakajima-san began to plan her family's move to Bunkyō ward, one of the top Tokyo wards in the provision of child care facilities, to coincide with her son's fourth birthday, because Edogawa ward did not have facilities for children over four years of age either. At the time of the focus group, Nakajima-san and her family had just moved to Bunkyō ward a few months earlier.

Nakajima-san persevered at her job, when similar child care dilemmas cause most Japanese women to quit their jobs as a matter of course. Conditions at home and work were optimal and provided insulation from social censure from neighbors and acquaintances who might be critical of Nakajima-san's decision to continue working while her son was still young. Nakajima-san was very vocal in her belief that she could be a good mother while having a fruitful career. In fact, the two goals were interrelated; she wanted to provide an alternative model of womanhood for her young son. The foreign firm she worked for allowed her to pursue a professional career without the expectations that marriage and motherhood would or should lead to early retirement or fewer responsibilities

---

of Education, the Ministry of Labour, and the Ministry of Construction. The Angel Plan encouraged local governments to adopt measures that would (a) help parents reconcile work and family responsibilities; (b) improve the quality of child-rearing within the family; (c) provide affordable housing to families with children; (d) target child development; and (e) over a five-year period between 1995 and 1999, lower the economic burden imposed by having children. The MHW collaborated with the Ministry of Finance and the Ministry of Home Affairs to prioritize the expansion of daycare, devising the "Five-Year Emergency Measures for Childcare Services" to facilitate the expansion process (Roberts 2002). The 1999 "Basic Principles to Cope with a Fewer Number of Children," formulated by six ministries and referred to as "the New Angel Plan," specified broader objectives within the areas of employment, health, education, housing, and child care. The cabinet's "Basic Direction for Policies Supporting Work and Childcare Compatibility," articulated in 2001, broadened the role of firms and reaffirmed the need to expand child care through longer hours, more flexible services, and the help of local communities (Chitose 2003). The 2002 "Measures to Cope with a Fewer Number of Children Plus One" built upon the prior "Angel" plans and went a step further in its recognition of the need to change working patterns among men as well as women (Chitose 2003).

that would hamper her chances of future promotion. She took a year-long maternity leave that did not impinge upon her opportunities for advancement when she returned to the company. Nakajima-san attributes her ability to pursue her career to a supportive family, both on her side and her husband's side. Her mother-in-law is a foreign-language instructor who firmly believes that a woman should have her own financial resources.[8]

In the three years between her son's first and fourth birthdays, the period during which he could be enrolled in public daycare in Edogawa ward, Nakajima-san found other mothers who were equally frustrated by the inadequate services provided by the ward. Nakajima-san "was thinking we could form our own interest group of working mothers, people who wanted to continue working after becoming mothers, and mothers who wanted to return to work." Together they could raise the consciousness of other women to mobilize enough support to present a petition to the ward offices. Nakajima-san described their early initiative:

> Our first challenge [was] to show why women cannot be completely satisfied as mothers. Society has to change its way of thinking. Of course if you look at today's youth, young men and women, their way of thinking is slowly changing. Young women who enter companies these days still end up quitting. But according to many surveys that ask about consciousness, many more people are saying that they would like to return to work soon after raising their children.

During this period, the ward directly elected mayor was replaced by an equally conservative successor. Though the new mayor did not issue an outright challenge to women to mobilize against him, his conservatism inspired Nakajima-san's group of working mothers to redouble their efforts to convince the full-time housewives in the ward to support their quest for better public child care. According to Nakajima-san, the distance between full-time housewives and working women helped to explain the replacement of the ward mayor with another socially conservative politician and the ability of ward politicians to resist changes in the provision of

---

8. For a discussion of role constraint, its sources and the forms of social censure that non-normative behavior provokes, see Pharr (1981). The experiences of the women activists who are the focus of Pharr's book underscore the importance of role models, often women relatives, in helping young women to live outside of socially prescribed roles.

local child care services that had been mandated by national bureaucrats and politicians. The views of full-time housewives and working women were, in some cases, diametrically opposed; demand for child care among housewives was lower, especially among those who believed that the presence of the mother was vital to a child's development. Nakajima-san, as a working mother, identified herself as a minority in Edogawa ward: "Since there are so many full-time housewives in Edogawa-ku, I realized that I was in the minority as a working mother." Consequently, she changed her strategy to "use tactics suited for working from a minority standpoint." The internet was her key instrument. Nakajima-san complained that many of the housewives in the ward lacked "a consciousness that extended beyond the ward level"; current housewives were unable to see themselves and working women as subject to the same social, economic, and political constraints. Before becoming mothers, they, too, had had to confront the inevitable tradeoff between work and family, a decision constrained by national policies that support a male breadwinner/female caregiver social welfare system.[9]

Nakajima-san saw the internet as offering several benefits to her mission to mobilize working women and mothers to lobby political elites for better provision of child care: "I thought I would have better luck on the internet because I would find fewer housewives and more people like myself." She used the internet "to find information and contacts, and share what I learned" to work toward a society in which women could be both workers and mothers. Her own research led her to conclude that more young women wanted to continue working after having children because they did not accept that motherhood would or should be the role by which they define themselves as individuals. She voiced her belief that her viewpoint would have greater traction with younger women and men, whose perspectives on work and family were changing. The internet enabled her to take her message beyond the boundaries of Edogawa

---

9. For a discussion of how Japan's social welfare policy mix has forced women to make tradeoffs between work and family, see Schoppa (2001, 2006). Over time, increasing numbers of women have chosen to work and delay marriage and family, with some opting out altogether. This has resulted in sub-replacement birth rates that, when combined with the rapidly aging society, are altering the population pyramid to pose a threat to the viability of the pension system and making a labor shortage an inevitability.

ward to build alliances with younger voters while continuing her efforts to forge alliances with housewives locally.

I followed up with Nakajima-san in July 2010. I learned that a member of her working mother's group, who I will refer to as Ono-san, had won a seat on one of Tokyo's ward assemblies where, among her policy priorities, she advocated for better child care. Nakajima-san credits the efforts of her working mother's group for helping a well-qualified, but under-funded candidate win as one of the top vote-getters fielded in the 2007 election. Elections for the ward assemblies in Japan are at-large, meaning that in an election for a council that has forty seats (about the size of Ono-san's assembly), voters cast one vote for their preferred candidate and the top forty vote-getters secure a seat. Ono-san emerged among the top ten. This is an impressive finish for a political newcomer who ran as an independent candidate (unaffiliated with any party). But, members of the working mother's group—even those located in other wards—campaigned vigorously on her behalf, mobilizing their networks and riding in the sound truck to blast her name and slogans throughout ward neighborhoods. A former businesswoman and married mother, Ono-san has been bitten by the political bug and aspires to higher office.

Women's confrontations with the structural conditions that sustain traditional gender roles in their everyday lives and impede attainment of personal goals shape their attitudes about gender, politics, and the relationship between the two. Other Women Now users became active in a variety of groups concerned with the status of women, because soon after quitting their jobs they confronted what they considered the isolation and drudgery of being a full-time housewife and began to think concretely about the broader structural conditions that made the male breadwinner/female caregiver family so desirable, if not widespread. These women's experiences underscored the importance of women creating knowledge for other women that is specifically designed to raise consciousness about gender in society and empower women politically to change their own situations.

Women Now users are "studying" gender problems and politics to share knowledge with other women while preparing themselves for an engagement in politics beyond voting. Some talk about this as a linear process. Oyama-san had "just begun studying" because she plans to become a more active participant in increasing women's participation in Japanese politics and society. Her ultimate goal is to promote women's participation in international causes such as environmental conservation. Maeda-san engaged in the comparative study of cultures and religions because her dream is to found a women's community and learning center devoted to helping women to overcome cultural differences. Study and participation are complementary processes; one informs the other. Nakajima-san learned from her experiences lobbying local political elites for more child care and adjusted her participatory strategies to increase her future chances of success.

Women Now users stress the importance of women assuming responsibility for their own political education and of using their own lives as primary sources, due to the deficiencies of schools, the media, and political parties. Women Now users' critique of political learning in Japan is comprehensive. "The problem with education is that there needs to be more of a focus on how to think about solving political problems rather than just memorizing how old you need to be to vote. Because there is no focus on actual problem solving," argues Owada-san. "I think that consciousness among Japanese is low." Preparation for college entrance exams perpetuates an overemphasis on rote memorization that has direct consequences for political leadership in Japan: "The Japanese elite are people who don't have any questions. They've spent so much time preparing for exams that they did not have time to develop other skills." Political elites struggle to stand outside of the system to critique it when it is in greatest need of change. One group participant suggested that the educational environment should include more content "about the histories of other nations rather than just focusing on Japan. Comparison with other nations would enable us to look at ourselves differently."

In the meantime, mass media coverage of politics was not sufficient to help voters make informed choices. Television and newspapers focus more on gossip than political debate, and the tone of reporting has turned negative. Oyama-san worried that first-time voters lack information: "People who are new to voting don't have any basis for making decisions. If they only hear all of the negative things, they cannot find the positive points in the policy positions of any particular party." Another woman chimed in: "If you depend on the media for information, you end up not being able to make any judgments based on the information that they give." However, even the media faces challenges in producing detailed political coverage rich in policy content when the parties do not speak clearly. In recognition that media content cannot be disentangled from the quality of elite political practices—that is, the failure of politicians to raise and debate important questions—a third voice sneered, "If you took a poll on this, you'd find out that it's a vicious cycle." These are all themes that are echoed by a national random sample of voters, the focus of chapters 1 and 2.

Women Now's website is a portal to a wealth of information and user-generated knowledge that helps women to fill in these critical gaps in political information. The website packages that knowledge in ways that enable women, individually and in groups, to learn about the social conditions that structure relationships between Japanese women and men. Gender-specific constraints also make it difficult to achieve what Owada-san envisions as an "ideal gender balance. Men and women are able live alone and reach their fullest potential as individuals. Shouldn't a partnership between the two lead to a better outcome for both partners?" To accomplish this, society's "way of thinking" must change. The website offers multiple resources that reflect its users' efforts to balance learning with creating and sharing new knowledge that informs their participatory strategies.

The structure of the homepage positions Women Now as a networking organization that links similarly minded people in cyberspace while providing details that give users the option for face-to-face contact with individuals and groups. The first thing that site entrants read is a link to single- or multi-issue interest groups and individuals concerned with improving the status of women and children in Japan across the public and private sphere. The following items appear on the menu of available choices: domestic violence; sexual harassment in the workplace and schools; child abuse; separate surnames after marriage; equal employment; nursery care; single motherhood; and women's medical care and reproductive health. Clicking on one of these issues puts visitors in touch with "informal," inchoate networks of concerned groups and individuals. Scrolling down uncovers another link to "formal," registered organizations. Links to government social services and the texts of laws that specifically address women and children inform women of their rights and welfare entitlements. Considered within the broader context and tone of the site, it is clear that links to governmental sources underscore the state's complicity in generating the constraints that have led women to this site. Women are instructed on how to work within the system to change it. Lists of family-friendly organizations are provided for job-seekers and as models of alternative ways of adapting the workplace to enable women to balance work and family responsibilities. There is a schedule of upcoming events. Finally, there is a link to an English-language page in recognition of the fact that foreign women living in Japan face similar constraints in their own countries and by virtue of living and working as a woman in Japan.

Women Now challenges the still-dominant impression that women know less about politics and therefore are less politically engaged. Women Now users, in generating their own knowledge from the context of their everyday lives and using it to inform political action, are leading by example. They are encouraging other women to empower themselves by studying and sharing their personal experience as a means of collectively generating knowledge about broad social patterns and common structural constraints faced by similarly situated women. This information is used to critique government and to develop strategies to petition elites for political change. Women position themselves as the "knowers" in society; elites should be listening to everyday people. This stance is re-articulated by Neighborhood Friends.

Neighborhood Friends

In June 2001, I met with members of Neighborhood Friends in the cafeteria of the foreign students' dorm where they spend most of their volunteer hours. Our conversation took place at a critical juncture in Japanese politics. Junichiro Koizumi had replaced the unpopular Yoshirō Mori as prime minister only six weeks prior to our meeting, and the House of Councillors election was less than three weeks away. Voters rapidly replaced the cynical tones they had used to talk about the Mori administration with an excitement and optimism about the future of Japanese politics. As noted earlier, the Mori administration's approval ratings had plunged to single-digit lows by the time of his departure. In contrast, Koizumi was elected to the prime minister's office with a record-high approval rating. The new prime minister was called a "maverick" politician, and expectations that he would change the course of Japanese politics ran high. Koizumi's election to the LDP's highest post occurred in an open process in a party known for backroom decision-making, and Koizumi pledged to reform Japanese politics even if it meant destroying the LDP. If Koizumi were to realize any of his campaign promises, voters' chances of influencing political elites would improve.

There are two interlocking stories that Neighborhood Friends tell about politics. One is about the wealth of knowledge held by "everyday Japanese" voters like themselves, and another is about learning about politics through the experience of political exclusion. This group talked about why they did not know what they thought they should know about politics. The fault lies with elites rather than with supposedly "uninformed" voters. Despite all of their efforts to collect information to engage with politics, they were excluded. Instead of disengaging from politics altogether, these women analyze the conditions of their own political exclusion as political output. They transform the reasons for the participatory constraints they face into information about how and why the political system is performing poorly. Like Women Now, Neighborhood Friends turn their everyday experiences into political knowledge. Participation in Neighborhood Friends is one example of how "everyday Japanese" create new learning experiences over the course of life. Lifelong learning, even if not explicitly political, builds confidence in "knowing what I know." Confidence in one's own knowledge and judgment is transferable to politics and is evident in group participants' assured diagnoses of contemporary political dynamics in Japan. What women know is valuable because it is available only from their particular vantage point as "everyday Japanese" voters. Women use their experiences to challenge the legitimacy of elite political knowledge—how elites know what they know and how they come to know it. What political elites know is inherently illegitimate if they have not learned it from everyday voters.

The Value of "Everyday" Knowledge   The members of Neighborhood Friends talked about themselves as "average," "regular," or "everyday" voters. Though gender and class condition their experiences with the political world, they make no claims to a unique perspective that is theirs alone. Rather, these women are members of a politically excluded class of diverse groups and individuals who relate to one another as marginalized democrats. Political elites do not have life experiences in common with everyday voters, and they have little incentive to connect with "average" Japanese because they can be reelected by appealing to a narrow constituency of citizens with interests and experiences that place them outside of what is considered mainstream Japan as well. Though women may be overrepresented among the underrepresented, the experience of political exclusion can also be claimed by men. Women acknowledge that the growing distance between everyday voters and political elites means that more men who occupy similar class positions also stand outside of elite politics. What Neighborhood Friends mean when they say that they are "average" or "non-elite" is that class makes a difference, as becomes clear when this group is compared to an all-male international friendship association and Women Now users.

This all-female group contrasted sharply with another international friendship association with an elite, all-male membership. Upon arriving at the University of Tokyo (Todai), where I was a visiting graduate research student, an older man from an "OB group" (old boys', or alumni group) was assigned to be my mentor. Mori-san, was a spry retired businessman in his seventies whose job had taken him and his family to the Global South where he lived and worked for several years. Many other foreign students had similar mentors who checked on our well-being, invited us into their homes, and took us to interesting sites and events around town. Their job was to help us to navigate the intricate inner workings of the vaunted paths that they traveled and that we would presumably travel in our own work.

The gender and class composition of the group makes a difference in the experiences and resources of members and reflects the different structural conditions that members face in the world. The OB Friendship Association and Neighborhood Friends occupied two very different worlds that were separated by multiple status distinctions, with education and class being most apparent, in addition to gender. Mori-san and his colleagues had first-hand international experiences that many Neighborhood Friends could access only indirectly, through cultural exchange. Further, the Neighborhood Friends did not have the types of associational ties that could gain its foreign friends more "status" points in Japanese society. These cumulative differences are apparent in how members think about and exercise political influence and power. Todai alums are overrepresented among top political, bureaucratic, and business elites. When it comes to political claims-making, they are already on the inside track. These are not people that Neighborhood Friends would consider "average" Japanese.

The Todai OBs have more in common with a political class that Neighborhood Friends characterize as male-dominated, moneyed, and hereditary. Neighborhood Friends echoed an adage common in Japanese politics: only those with *kaban* (financial resources), *jiban* (a local support base), and *kanban* (recognition) can successfully run for office. These resources remain important to candidate success even after electoral reforms intended to eliminate the institutional incentives that made these resources necessary were adopted in the mid-1990s.[10] Women and other political outsiders typically lack the resources needed to navigate a direct route to elite politics. Successful women candidates often have the same "quality" characteristics of their male counterparts and, like men, frequently inherit a *koenkai* (candidate support organization) upon the death or retirement of a male relative. One Neighborhood Friend noted that "Obuchi-san's daughter, even without doing much, has a political base,"[11] and others immediately made the connection between these structural conditions and the overrepresentation of hereditary politicians in the Japanese system. The cultivation of the resources for entry into the national political elite is tightly linked to class background. And women extended this truth to include the bureaucratic and business elite that make up the building blocks of Japan, Inc., a negative term that conjures up collusive relationships between government and business and popularized by the Western press during the miracle years of the 1980s. In the minds of voters, the everyday people on the outside of elite politics, this term is truer today than it was nearly three decades ago.

Neighborhood Friends would consider the Women Now participants' life experiences as distant from their own as those of the OB Friendship Association's members. Women Now users look more "elite" than most of the men that Neighborhood Friends encounter in their everyday lives. Women Now focus group participants were more educated, enjoyed higher-status jobs, and had more international experiences. Despite these

---

10. During the pre-reform era, the single nontransferable vote cast within a multimember district system pitted candidates from the same party against one another, resulting in an emphasis on name recognition and the delivery of pork as candidates were unable to make distinctions on the basis of ideology. Additionally, short and highly regulated campaign periods made it necessary for candidates to evolve some means of maintaining close ties with their support bases between elections. Under the multimember district system, *koenkai* coordinated and maximized votes within districts by ensuring that no one candidate received excess votes that would cost the party district seats that might compromise the electoral chances of another candidate from the same party. *Koenkai* are maintained year-round so that voters can be easily mobilized in the event of snap elections and during the short campaign period. The single-member district system has not undermined the basic need for a loyal base of electoral support (see Flanagan et al. 1991).

11. Keizō Obuchi was prime minister from July 1998 until April 2000. His tenure was cut short by a fatal stroke, and his daughter Yūko Obuchi was elected to his seat the same year. For a discussion of the institutional incentives that benefit politicians' relatives who seek office, see Taniguchi (2008).

differences, Neighborhood Friends valued their experiences as important sources of information precisely because they are mainstream, more common than uncommon. Like Women Now participants, Neighborhood Friends pieced together what they know about politics from the contexts of their everyday lives and saw local knowledge as a resource that elites have dismissed out of hand. They would be happy to talk more about politics if more people, especially elites, asked them.

Neighborhood Friends participants, acutely aware of the national policies at work in their everyday lives, position themselves as the best judges of national government performance on the ground. Participants find government performance lacking across a number of dimensions: transparency, accountability, responsiveness, efficiency, and effectiveness. From their vantage point, democratic processes in Japan are not working well due to the distance between political elites and everyday citizens. There are multiple measures of distance.[12] First, the life experiences of political elites separate them from everyday voters. Consequently, political elites are ill-informed because their life and career paths give them little experience with the world that "average" or "everyday" Japanese inhabit; there is no common ground between elites and voters, making it difficult for elites to intuit what voters need. In the absence of common experiences, the importance of listening to the public to determine the common good increases. Unfortunately, the political process is top-down and not bottom-up. Voters' voices must travel a long path up the political chain. They have to contact politicians indirectly, through national organizations or peak associations. Alternatively, they can participate in citizens' movements, petition campaigns, and demonstrations. In contrast, policies generated by elite decision makers are rapidly evident on the ground in the form of public works projects—roads, runways, cemeteries—that Neighborhood Friends did not ask for and do not need. Indirect channels of interest articulation and direct "pipelines of pork" are a second feature of the political

---

12. The discussion in this paragraph echoes political critiques articulated by Robin LeBlanc's housewife citizens (LeBlanc 1999, ch. 2). They too arrive at the conclusion that elite politics is "far" and use a similar rationale. The political world was distant because housewives had no personal connections to it; they were not intimately familiar with anyone who was a member of the political elite. Housewives said that their values were incompatible with the exclusive and corrupt practices that were characteristic of elite politics and took pains to distinguish their grassroots efforts to promote community change from "politics." Physical barriers also distanced women from elite politics. The halls of national decision-making were far from home and offered none of the supports (for example, child care) that would allow women to enter as valued participants.

distance between voters and elites. Finally, distance is the increasing length of the path between voters and elites; the impression that this path used to be much shorter, but has lengthened with time, is strong. Elite attention to the wealth of information that everyday voters possess is one fundamental step toward erasing literal and figurative distances between voters and elites and setting Japanese politics back on the right path.

The political issues that Neighborhood Friends members did *not* talk about are a striking indication of the gulf that has opened between voters and elites. In the middle of a prolonged economic recession, Neighborhood Friends did not talk about economic reforms or reflect on the era of high economic growth in nostalgic tones, even though these women came from middle-income families that were feeling the pinch of the recession. They expressed few disappointments over continued LDP dominance in politics. Instead, they critiqued the Japanese way of politics and proposed that better outcomes could be attained through better communication between voters and political elites.

People-Power Politics   Taking the citizens' right to question and receive answers from the political system for granted, participants developed explanations for why the social and institutional mechanisms that facilitate communications between citizens and elites do not work as well as they should. Neighborhood Friends saw politics as limited by its own institutional structures and internally generated norms that have become increasingly restrictive over time. Seniority norms in the dominant LDP, for example, constrained the circulation of knowledge among political elites and between voters and political elites. Politicians were routinely promoted to top positions in government and the party on the number of times reelected, with little regard for expertise and policy vision. Leaders without specific policy goals and a long-range vision led to a hollowing out of national electoral politics. Voters were uninformed due to these deficiencies in the political process, despite their best efforts to do their own information gathering. The reasons that focus group participants gave for not knowing what they should know about politics became the very substance of their critique of what ails contemporary Japanese politics.

The primary problem is that politics is top-down and insulated from voters' pressures. Respondents use their primary points of contact with the state, public works projects and street-level bureaucrats in ward offices and local police stations, to talk about politics more generally. Asakura-san calls the ward office every time she notices a new construction project on the same street. Each time she gets a partial explanation for why work crews are there. Sometimes there is a problem with a gas leak; other times it is a sewage problem. Changing, incomplete, and often conflicting information fuels multiple and interlocking diagnoses about what plagues Japanese politics. First, there is no transparency. Officials tell the public about problems only when they can no longer be hidden. "Sometimes we don't even know how long something has been a problem. We only know when it's really bad.... Take the earlier problems with blood donation as an example."[13] Second, bureaucratic administration is fragmented or "piece-meal" (*katawari*); information about overlapping tasks is not shared across jurisdictional boundaries. Third, lack of transparency makes it difficult for taxpayers to track and influence how their money is spent, but unnecessary and redundant public works projects are the visible proof of waste, inefficiency, and corruption. As one Neighborhood Friends member said, "Our taxes are used to build roads that we don't need." Given the opportunity, Neighborhood Friends would tell political elites that they have little need for the seemingly ubiquitous public works projects that they do not see as vital to their quality of life.

According to participants, the "average" or "ordinary" Japanese person does not have the expectation that she can directly contact an elected official. Nor does the "average" Japanese think that her voice, alone or in concert with others, will make much impression on politicians. That participants identified themselves as "average" Japanese was evident in, and substantiated by, the initial confusion that greeted my initial question about the types of people who influenced politics. A long discussion ensued about what "influence" meant; an "ah!" of relief and understanding followed my explanation. It was "natural" that an American would ask this question, since Americans are accustomed to initiating contact with politicians. This was not the case in Japanese politics—although it should be. Rather, as one Neighborhood Friends member said, "There are ways for us to do so indirectly through national organizations." The limitations of this tactic

---

13. This informant is referring to the HIV-tainted blood scandal that broke in 1996 and implicated high-ranking Ministry of Health and Welfare officials who had knowingly released untreated blood products in the 1980s, exposing hemophiliacs to the AIDS virus.

are implicit in the desire "to be a nation where women's thoughts, ideas, perspectives actually do represent fifty percent." Not being heard is a common experience for average women voters.

The discursive thread that links Neighborhood Friends members to Women Now participants is the adamancy that political elites should listen to everyday voters because citizens offer a broader perspective on the "common good." After all, democracy demands that citizens be the principals and political elites be their agents. Though money-power politics has eroded institutional structures and moral norms that enable citizens to hold political elites accountable, everyday people seek strategies for regaining power. Engaging in their own practices of knowledge creation is one means by which voters empower themselves to use existing institutional mechanisms for exercising control over political elites. Voting is just one institutional tool at the disposal of voters interested in accomplishing this task. In recent years, political observers have increasingly laid the blame for ongoing LDP dominance and the government's failure to implement economic and administrative reforms at the feet of voters who are too apathetic, uninformed, and risk-averse to kick the scoundrels out. Neighborhood Friends stress that they are holding up their end of the contract between voters and representatives, thereby absolving themselves of any guilt in perpetuating the status quo, even though other citizens might be implicated. As they shift the remaining bulk of responsibility for creating and correcting these political imbalances to elites, they continue to pressure for change from below.

Voting as Protest

Despite the media buzz surrounding Koizumi's election as prime minister, Neighborhood Friends members had not succumbed to "Koizumi fever." At this particular political moment, Koizumi had yet to prove his staying power, the first obstacle to accomplishing his campaign promises. Japan had had six prime ministers over the preceding seven years. Respondents said that there was little reason to become too invested in the prime minister as a source of political change, because the position is indirectly elected and, in their recent experience, turnover is too rapid. Because the premier is indirectly elected, respondents complained that they did not have the opportunity to approve or disapprove of his past performance, rewarding or penalizing him accordingly. In fact, they were unsure whether the results of the upcoming election would disrupt the partisan balance in the National Diet and threaten Koizumi's newly won position. At this juncture in Japanese politics, it was not clear that Koizumi would become a politician to vote *for,* when voters had grown accustomed to voting *against* political parties and candidates.

Neighborhood Friends problematize the dominant tendency to view national politics narrowly, as a horserace that is all about winning. Rather, voters stay engaged in electoral politics because voting is an iterative game and every election offers parties and voters alike a chance to win. If Neighborhood Friends and "average" Japanese voters have nothing to win, it is not immediately clear how or why voting promises enough utility to warrant showing up at the polls at all. But sometimes winning is about losing. Focus group respondents see turning out as an opportunity to protest by voting against candidates and parties they do not want to win. As one Neighborhood Friends member put it, "To say I have a lot of interest [in elections] means that I absolutely want some person to lose." Rejecting the alternatives is sometimes the best choice a voter can make under contemporary Japanese political conditions. Thus, it would be a mistake to view protest voting as a show of unconditional support for the winner. The winning candidate should not interpret victory as a mandate but rather as a message about what is not working.

If the responses of Neighborhood Friends members are any indication, any conclusions about the depths of women's political interest and engagement made on the basis of who wins elections is necessarily incomplete. How can the depths of individual political interest and engagement be assessed when there is so little for voters to be interested in? The Neighborhood Friends members watch television news and read newspapers but find the candidates' and parties' electoral messages devoid of content. The lack of clarity from parties and candidates, they rightfully complain, makes it difficult for voters to distinguish the differences between the options they have been presented with. They are painfully aware that they are making the best electoral decisions possible with limited information.

Protest voting has precedent in Japanese politics (Reed 1999), especially among women (Iwai 1993; Iwamoto 2001). An oft-noted example is the 1989 House of Councillors elections, when women voters were credited with delivering the LDP its first major postwar loss. Women voters supported the Socialists to protest the LDP's passage of an unpopular consumption tax and Prime Minister Sōsuke Uno's sex scandal. The JSP ran a record number of women candidates, who ran on a "clean politics" platform. Women voters' support resulted in a then-record number of women (twenty-two newly elected women brought the total number of women councilors to thirty-three)[14] candidates elected to the Diet in the "Madonna Boom," and Takako Doi became the first female party leader and speaker of the House of Representatives. This was interpreted as a protest, a warning to the LDP to clean up its act, because this deviation from traditional patterns of support occurred only in the "less powerful" Upper House, and traditional patterns of LDP support seemingly reasserted themselves over subsequent elections.

That "protest" has remained salient in the voting repertoire during otherwise "normal" elections is significant because it provides an impetus for ongoing electoral engagement among voters who might otherwise abstain. But it also indicates a narrowing of choices; voting for the opposition is not an effective protest if the opposition looks just like the party in power. While voting against specific candidates and parties is not the most direct strategy for pressuring national elected officials to adopt a new direction, it is an effective means for choosing the least objectionable option. One Neighborhood Friend member echoed this sentiment. Every election, she looks at all the candidates and concludes that she does not want to be represented by any of them: "I feel as though all of our choices are losing ones."

Voting remains an effective means of bringing about political change. First, as discussed in previous chapters, the voting calculus for individuals and communities changes in subnational elections. Participation in local elections is a means of changing national politics from the ground up. Second, voting works in tandem with other forms of political participation. As Nakajima-san related, when her ward president was replaced by an equally conservative successor, she adjusted her strategies to reach out to the women

---

14. In 1989, there were 252 seats in the House of Councillors and one-half (126) were up for reelection every three years. Twenty-two new women were elected and women held 11 seats that were not up for reelection that year. As a result, the total number of women elected was 33. Nonetheless, 22 successful women candidates elected at one time to the House of Councillors was a record high. In combination with the sitting councillors, the representation of women in the Upper House hit a then-record high (Iwai 1993).

who had helped him to win to produce a different outcome in the next election. Elections and electoral outcomes are a measure of political change, however incremental, and inform voters about other places in the system to reinvest their energies, either to bring about change through alternative avenues or to increase their chances of "winning" in elections the next time around. Third, voting against particular parties and candidates may reproduce the status quo, but it effectively guards against some other possible set of political outcomes. Finally, when we take a long-range view of Japanese politics, we see radical and rapid changes over the course of the postwar period that were enabled by actual or threatened electoral outcomes (Calder 1988). Just as voting is an opportunity to punish, it is also an opportunity to reward.

Increasingly, voters are afforded the opportunity to reward, and they await future possibilities to do so more often. Focus group participants rewarded younger candidates, mavericks, candidates who spoke and listened. They rewarded not policy proposals but political behaviors that they thought should extend to politics as a whole. Candidates who break the mold symbolize a yearning for a more inclusive politics. Change will extend from inclusion, because inclusion means that "average" Japanese will see herself reflected in the political process. Focus groups tell us about the nature of contemporary Japanese politics as seen through the eyes of Japanese women (exclusive), the role they envision for themselves (influential), and their efforts to be more effective principals by assuming responsibility for their own political education. Women prepare themselves to take advantage of opportunities to change politics by engaging in the same types of practices on the ground that they would like to see reproduced in interactions between political elites and citizens.

The strategies that motivate vote choice in Japan are much more complex than originally assumed. We already know that voters protest against the national political establishment by voting against the governing party or casting a "sincere" vote for a fringe party that they support even though it has no chance of winning. According to Kawai and Watanabe (2010), unlike strategic voters whose electoral choices are driven by calculations about how their votes will make the most impact, sincere voters always vote for their preferred candidates and parties even if they have no chance of winning. Strategic voters do not want to "waste" votes. Voters abstain, split their tickets between single-member district and proportional representation seats in the House of Representatives, eschew partisan identification, and move from one category of partisanship from one election period to the next. Voters "divide" government by voting for the opposition parties in House of Councillors elections and the familiar LDP in the traditionally more powerful House of Representatives.[15] Typically, the more local the election, the more nonpartisan it has been. However, nonpartisan conservatives sympathetic to the LDP have held the majority of subnational assembly seats because traditionally it has been beneficial for local politicians to cultivate ties with national LDP politicians to facilitate the flow of public works to their districts (Scheiner 2005, 2006). The increase in local citizens' parties and the DPJ efforts to strengthen its local base to win more national seats offer an additional outlet for voters to send a message to national politicians through their local vote choices. Local elections function as a kind of referendum on national elections, a warning signal to national elites that they will be penalized if they do not adjust their policies and practices in the period preceding the next election.

---

15. Now that the opposition controls the House of Councillors, political observers are revisiting the conventional wisdom that the House of Representatives is stronger than the House of Councillors. The House of Councillors has operated as a rubber stamp throughout the postwar period because the LDP has been the largest party in both houses of the Diet and never faced a unified opposition prior to the current decade.

5

Gender and "Communities of Practice"

Escaping the Regulatory Boundaries of Formal Education

> For my entire education, from elementary school through college, I was
> never interested in things that I was forced to study....I began to enjoy
> studying only *after* I had made it through the educational system and became
> a so-called "member of society." If something interested me, and I could
> study it at my own pace, I was reasonably efficient at acquiring knowledge.
>
> Author Haruki Murakami (2008, 74)[1]

The women in my focus groups provide a glimpse of the wide range of activities available to women that are fundamental to building the types of social capital that "make democracy work." Some of the women who participated in my focus groups belonged to explicitly political groups. Others belonged to groups that fulfilled a range of social functions, from consumer protection to eldercare. But many were involved in study and hobby groups that had the potential to become politicized. At the very least, these groups constitute a dense social network that can be used to mobilize voters during elections. The state recognizes the potential of these groups and

---

1. Murakami, the highly celebrated author of *Norwegian Wood,* among others, is not a woman. But, lifelong learning is not an exclusively female domain, even though I maintain that women are overrepresented among those who are self-consciously augmenting their study over the life course.

has expanded its definition of lifelong learning in an effort to bring these groups under its umbrella.

The Japanese state has tried, at various points along its developmental trajectory and with varying degrees of success, to harness women's knowledge and skills to achieve its own developmental goals. But many women have used their educational resources to render their own interpretation of the state's goals and to pave their own paths to empowerment. This work has been done in their own separate sphere, at their own pace, and on their own terms (Thomas 1985). Understanding study groups as a pedagogical space produced through exchanges between women and the state is crucial to understanding why and how my focus group participants developed a common narrative about education and improvement of self and community. Study groups are sites where female citizens disrupt established norms about what is knowledge, how it is created and transmitted, and who can legitimately claim expertise.

The women in my focus groups expressed a clear discontent with the conventional life course that starts with formal education to a short stint in the workforce and ends with the advent of marriage and childbirth. They wanted to expand their range of activities in political and social life and return to the workforce. Lifelong learning, discussed in this chapter, is one venue that enables women to return to society, intellectual life, and political discussion. Arguably, there is a groundswell of demand for opportunities to extend the learning process over the life course because formal education in Japan concludes in one's mid-twenties in the case of an advanced degree, earlier otherwise. There are no opportunities for Japanese to return to a formal school setting later in life, whether for enrichment purposes or to attain more skills for upward mobility. Accreditation matters. Whereas Americans can return to night school to complete their high school educations or attend accredited institutions—as full- or part-time students—to earn higher degrees later in life, the Japanese adult education system traditionally has not provided learning opportunities at degree-granting institutions. As the Japanese government revamps its lifelong learning infrastructure, it is creating space for new constituencies to emerge. Equipping citizens with knowledge-production resources over the life course may produce successive waves of unforeseen activism.

This chapter examines Japanese women's political participation at the site where women's educational trajectories and state goals meet. I use the new directions that lifelong learning policy took in the late 1980s as a point of entry to a longer history of state interest in women's education. Lifelong learning is one of many wide-ranging reforms adopted by the Ministry of Education, Culture, Sports, Science, and Technology over the past two decades.[2] It is the only education reform policy that directly affects an older learning population. Contemporary lifelong learning builds on formal learning experiences earlier in life that can lead to new feelings of purpose in the minds of citizen participants. I use white papers and statistical data published by the Ministry of Education and an existing literature on education to answer the following questions: What is the state's interest in women's lifelong learning? How does lifelong learning build on formal education? How does lifelong learning dovetail with the general situation of women in Japanese society to change how women think about politics and create, for some, the potential for political activism?

In this chapter, I trace the origins of contemporary lifelong learning in Japan to the gendered social management projects of the developmental Meiji state and the period of military expansion. I then present trends in educational attainment, with a focus on women's education, over the postwar period. In the prewar period, social education was used to develop human capital in a context featuring wide disparities in educational attainment based on age, class, gender, and region. Rapid economic growth in the postwar period produced a highly educated population that shifted the goals of adult learning, for learners as well as the state. Formal education not only provides students with cognitive skills, it also exposes them to multiple models of learning. The extracurricular activities that students participate in during their school days lay a foundation for participation in "communities of practice" over the life course.[3] Years after exiting formal educational institutions, citizens have the knowledge base, material

---

2. The Ministry of Education was renamed the Ministry of Education, Culture, Sports, Science, and Technology (MEXT) in January 2001, when it merged with the Science and Technology Agency as part of Japan's administrative reforms to streamline the bureaucracy. I use "Ministry of Education" when explicitly referencing the ministry prior to 2001 and policies that were initiated prior to administrative reform. Otherwise, I refer to "MEXT."

3. Cave (2004) calls the club activities covering a wide range of interests, from sports to traditional arts to music, that Japanese students participate in during junior and senior high school and at university *bukatsudō*.

resources, and a choice of different learning modes at their disposal for adaptation to new purposes. Past learning experiences become an invaluable resource for citizens seeking new meaning in their lives through study group participation.

Next I look at the rapid proliferation of study circles after completion of formal education and the overrepresentation of women among participants. "Communities of practice" outside of institutions of formal education enrich a dense and vibrant civil society. The internal dynamics of the group—how participants use the conditions of daily life to create knowledge—affect political participation. I uncover political import in the educative function of the group—how it creates knowledge from its socially embedded vantage point, rather than from the social mobilization potential of groups. Even if a group is completely detached from other groups, the interaction among group members creates potential for self-transformation that in turn leads to individual-level engagement with politics. Study circles are, or have the potential to become, consciousness-raising groups, a standard mode of feminist political activism.[4] Self-identified feminists may be among the minority of study group participants. Yet, if one goal of feminism is to empower non-elites to practice alternate modes of inquiry that produce a different and more expansive view of the world to challenge elite perspectives, many study circles would find themselves in agreement with feminists in this regard.

---

4. Here I want to stress the activism rather than the feminism. Consciousness-raising groups bring together individuals whose experiences, in isolation, seem unique. Gathered together, the commonalities that link individual experiences draw attention to shared conditions that are shaped by societal institutions and norms, and that make otherwise invisible hierarchies of power visible. The Chicago Women's Liberation Union (1971) distributed a leaflet, reprinted as an article, as a resource for women interested in starting their own groups. Consciousness-raising, while a trademark of feminist organizing, can be used by groups of women who might propose very different analyses of and prescriptions to the common conditions that they uncover. Similarly, consciousness-raising can be used to examine the construction of class, race, or any other social category that is used to organized society. That said, consciousness-raising has a precedent in the Japanese feminist experience; it is not a strategy that has been transplanted from the Western movement. Still, I do not use the term *consciousness-raising* in this book. Though my informants in chapters 3 and 4 talk about their own "communities of practice" and "consciousness-raising," this is not a term that they themselves use. "Communities of practice" is a more appropriate term because not every study group consciously engages in consciousness-raising, though every group has the potential to do so.

The State in Development: Gender and Modern Citizenship

From the time Japan opened to the West during the Meiji period (1868–1912), educating women has been central to the state's developmental goals (Sievers 1983; Garon 1993; Allison 1996; McVeigh 1998). Improving women's education was an important tool for managing women's social identities to convey an image of Japan as a "civilized" nation for Western onlookers. More importantly, neglecting women's education would be a waste of human capital that could be channeled toward rapid modernization. Through education the state produced good wives and wise mothers (*ryosai kenbo*), that is, "a politicized and managed identity deeply implicated in and reproduced by patriarchy, nation-ness, stateness, and capitalist economic nationalism" (McVeigh 2004, 219). Good wives were household managers responsible for domestic and care work that allowed husbands to engage more fully in economically productive labor that fueled rapid modernization. Wise mothers' care and support produced future workers and soldiers, and the feminization of social welfare responsibilities freed up state resources for modernization and development.

An expansionary "boom" in women's educational attainment occurred between 1895 and 1920; the percentage of school-aged girls receiving elementary education increased from 43.9 percent to 98.8 percent (Garon 1993, 16). The boom in women's education inspired contentious public debates about the curriculum most appropriate for future wives and mothers, the approved social roles for women. More importantly, this boom was a catalyst for the later expansion of civic roles for women during the interwar period (1918–1939) and the emergence of new women's organizations that pursued political rights during Japan's brief period of democratization between 1912 and 1926 (Garon 1993, 16). Women educated during the late nineteenth and early twentieth centuries were well positioned to assume leadership roles twenty years later. Contrary to the dominant thinking among the all-male political and economic elite, women expected space at the decision-making table.

In Japan, the term "social education" has traditionally referred to adult education and can be traced back to the Meiji period, when, at the same time that formal schooling was made available to increasing numbers of girls and young women, the regime instituted social education programs across Japan for adult men and women. The emerging modern state used social education to reach an adult population that was already too old to take advantage of the new universal education system for young people; both systems steered the populace through a period of rapid change and social upheaval, transforming traditional subjects into modern citizens. The Meiji regime used social education to promote innovation and change while preserving traditional social structures and values—contradictory goals. During this period, as now, state-sponsored adult education programming competed with adult education in other social and, potentially, radical spheres. As the government deepened its formal involvement with adult education, the labor and trade union movements carried out their own adult education classes to improve the quality of the labor force (Thomas 1985; Khan 1997).

During the interwar period, information and knowledge transfers to women were a centerpiece of the Japanese state's campaigns to promote rationality and efficiency in public and private life so that resources could be channeled to rapid modernization, military mobilization, and overseas imperial expansion. Women's associational ties were a resource for the social management programs of bureaucrats from the Ministry of Education, which also hosted public lecture series and exhibitions targeting women attendees, who then shared this information with their families, friends, and neighbors. Many women activists saw collaboration with the state as an opportunity to shape new public roles for good wives and wise mothers. Women assisted civil servants in disseminating information and teaching the public new methods for improving diets, personal hygiene and public health, savings and consumption patterns, home economy, and work habits in an effort to create modern subjects (Garon 1993). These same associations were coopted by the military regime for the complete mobilization of society for war.

During the early postwar period (1945–1971), administrative organs that were used by the military regime for social engineering were retooled to implement social education programs for creating democratic citizens and fostering economic recovery. This same infrastructure has been retooled again for lifelong learning to confront contemporary economic and demographic challenges that pose a threat to the viability of the social welfare state, economic recovery, and future growth. Since the late 1980s, the state has relied heavily on physical facilities and social networks built during these previous periods to implement contemporary programs while investing in further expansion. Women made gains in formal educational attainment at each of these junctures: during the Meiji Restoration, the interwar period, the early occupation period, and the contemporary high-growth period of the 1980s. These gains in formal education enabled women to hijack an expanding state infrastructure for social education, later reformed as lifelong learning, to distance their communities of practice from state regulation. The expansion of formal schooling and access to higher education means that adult learners are no longer engaging with social education to "catch-up"; they are launching study groups to deepen their personal interests in a wide range of self-defined topics. Contemporary lifelong learning policies belatedly address fundamental shifts in the material reality and mass attitudes that define the relationship between formal schooling and adult learning.

Democratic Education: Learning to Participate

After Japan's defeat in World War II, the United States-led Allied occupation used formal schooling and social education to indoctrinate the public with attitudes and beliefs consistent with democracy. Many saw the new government as foreign, imported from the West, and imposed upon Japanese society. Public debate about the meaning of democracy and peace facilitated the internalization of "democratic" norms and a true social transformation. Innumerable groups cropped up, led by intellectuals or formed spontaneously by everyday women and men. The loose configuration of small citizens' groups questioned the occupying powers' authority to impose a new order upon Japan and the propriety of the new constitution, envisioning alternative paths that the nation could take to escape its authoritarian past. These initial questions led to a broad questioning of other readily accepted norms, such as "tradition-bound rural communities that showed almost no regard for women's human rights or their personal dignity and left them little freedom to form opinions of their own" (Yamamoto 2004, 164). A tradition of questioning the right of authorities, foreign or indigenous, was already in place.

Techniques that were specifically designed to engage everyday people in critical debate were also widely practiced. The new constitution denounced war, and many Japanese intellectuals led the movement to reconstruct a national identity based on peace. Leftist intellectuals of this period embraced the Chinese Communist Party's "mass line" policy, "which called for learning from the masses instead of teaching them how to act and think." Consequently, "ordinary people acquired an aura of authority in the eyes of intellectual and political activists" who began to record the perspectives and personal histories of ordinary people (Yamamoto 2004, 7). Personal experiences were used as a means of translating new ideas into something consistent with everyday life. Activists encouraged housewives to form informal essay-writing societies to deliver their own interpretation of new democratic ideas. Writers discussed compositions in groups "in order to distinguish between problems they had in common and problems unique to individuals, and try to find solutions to these problems together. It was hoped they would gradually learn how to resolve their problems and begin to ponder what kind of scientific or historical knowledge they should seek if their personal experience alone did not suffice" (Yamamoto 2004, 163). These techniques are still used in Japan today.

Participation in essay-writing groups and other grassroots activities after the war shifted women's perspectives with consequences for their civic participation overall. Women became impatient "with the formal and stifling atmosphere of PTAs, which were under the thumb of a handful of leading officials," and began establishing their own informal groups (Yamamoto 2004, 163). Women left the tutelage of local authorities. Often women who banded together to solve everyday economic problems in the desperate times immediately after the war ended up thinking more broadly about the structural conditions and hierarchies of gender and class. By 1959, the Ministry of Labor's Women and Minors Bureau "noted a sharp increase in the number of such small, independent grassroots groups, and forecast their further growth across the country....Such informal groups no longer required any particular leaders because their members' enthusiasm was so great that they were capable of making independent decisions and acting on them" (Yamamoto 2004, 166). Despite a rich and extensive historical record that shows widespread citizen participation in research and study groups specifically designed to produce a particular type of political subjectivity, work on the relationship of contemporary study groups to the political sphere remains scarce.

Higher Education and Lifelong Learning

Formal educational attainment lays the foundation for extending the process of learning over the life course, independent of and in collaboration with the state. Educational attainment for both men and women increased throughout the postwar period, though the gender gap in post-secondary educational attainment narrowed the most in the 1980s. Figure 5.1 shows that gender differences in higher educational attainment remained relatively constant until the early 1980s, even though 98 percent of all Japanese complete high school. In 1965, 22.4 percent of men and 11.3 percent of women enrolled in institutions of higher education; men were twice as likely to attend college and university. By 1989, the gap had closed altogether, when 36.8 percent of women and 35.8 percent of men of college-age were enrolled in colleges and universities. Over the next decade, the direction of the gender gap reversed, with more women entering colleges and universities between 1989 and 2000. Male enrollment again began to outpace women's enrollments in 2002, likely reflecting renewed efforts to compete in a tighter international labor market; it is too early to tell whether this shift will endure.

Aggregate trends in advancement to higher education disguise important gender differences in the types of institutions that Japanese men and women attend. Figure 5.2 shows that men are more likely to attend

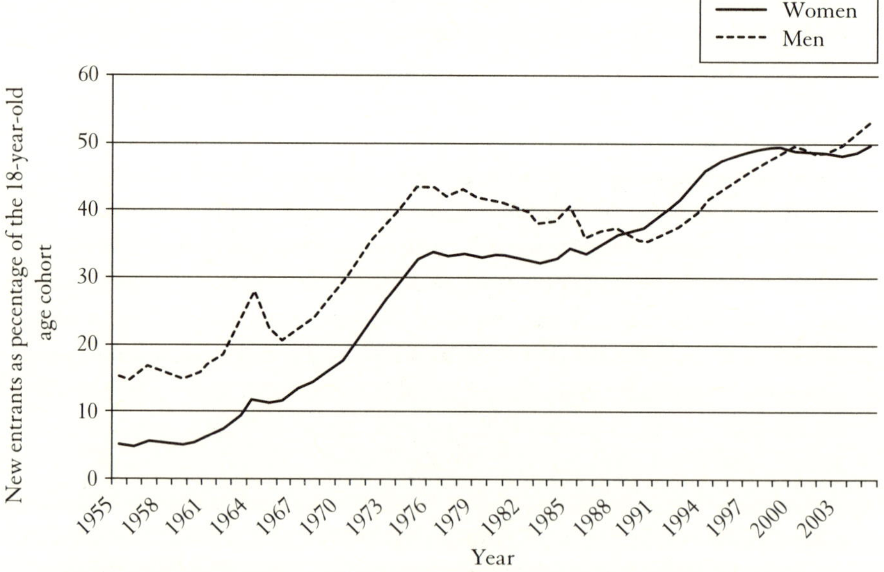

Figure 5.1 Gender gap in higher educational attainment narrows, 1955–2005
Source: Ministry of Education, Culture, Sports, Science and Technology (2006). "Enrollment and Advancement Rate 1948–2005," available at www.mext.go.jp/english/statist/06060808/pdf/013.pdf.

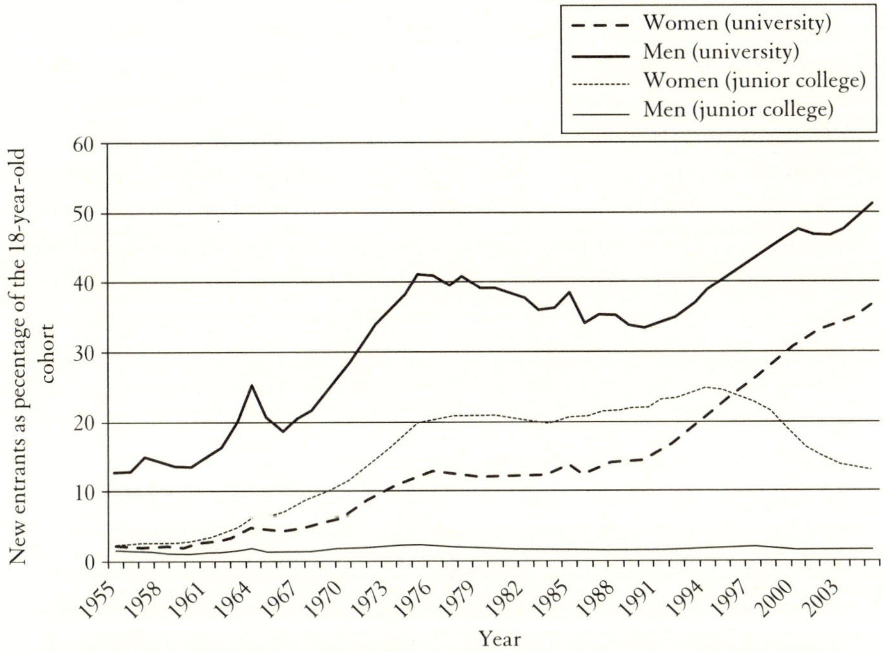

Figure 5.2 Gender differences in enrollment in institutions of higher education, 1955–2005
Source: Ministry of Education, Culture, Sports, Science and Technology (2006). "Enrollment and Advancement Rate 1948–2005," available at http://www.mext.go.jp/english/statist/06060808/pdf/013.pdf.

four-year institutions and that women are more likely to attend junior colleges. Junior colleges are not a stepping stone to four-year colleges, and they provide a qualitatively different type of educational experience. The most popular courses of study in junior colleges—humanities, home economics and domestic arts, and education—prepare women for marriage and homemaking (McVeigh 1996). Though the gender gap in post-secondary education attainment began to shrink in the early 1980s, the gender gap in advancement to four-year universities did not begin to narrow until a decade later, in the early 1990s. The shrinking of the gap was due to the decline, after 1994, in the percentage of women going to junior college and a commensurate increase in the percentage of women attending universities. In 2005, 51.3 percent of men and 36.8 percent of women advanced to universities. The gender gap remains sizable.

Different patterns of education for men and women reflect different judgments about the tools for future success. Throughout the postwar period, it has been common for women to leave the workforce upon marriage or the birth of the first child, and to return to work in the part-time labor force once the last child enters school. To maximize earning potential in a discriminatory labor market that steered women into lower-status office positions (which they were expected to quit upon marriage or childbirth), women opted to pursue degrees at two-year junior colleges rather than four-year institutions (McVeigh 1996). Four-year universities were the reserve of men seeking salaried positions. Recent changes in patterns of educational attainment among women reflect parents' and daughters' changing perspectives on the new paths and life choices becoming available to working women.[5]

Education and Quality Democracy

In each of these earlier periods, education was a motor for social, economic, and political change. Consequently, we should expect contemporary changes in women's education to influence civic engagement. The impact of increased educational attainment for women on how women take action in civil society warrants closer examination, because there have not been commensurable changes in the workforce that support women's participation. Women remain underemployed, an underutilized resource. Women have an excess of human and social capital that seeks alternative outlets.

Formal education provides basic cognitive skills that promote citizens' engagement with politics, and it also closes the gap between dominant and subordinate groups in society, but social scientists recognize that individuals often fail to convert educational achievement into knowledge for empowerment (Burns et al. 2001). Gender-based disparities in political participation narrow significantly but do not completely disappear as women close the education gap. A better understanding of what intervening factors help women to convert formal education into an effective political resource is

---

5. Sociologist Keiko Hirao of Sophia University is researching the impact of economic and demographic changes in Japan on the choices that parents make about investing in their daughters' educations in order to understand the dramatic change in women's patterns of higher educational attainment in recent years.

important, not only because it can help eradicate gender differences in political influence but also because higher education is credited with changing the quality of mass engagement with political elites.

Political scientists Ronald Inglehart (1977, 1990, 1997) and Russell Dalton (2000) see education as a fundamental ingredient in producing the elite-challenging behaviors observable in mass publics from the 1960s onward, when democratic electorates erupted with student protest activity and social justice movements. Inglehart and Dalton attribute the increase in citizen demands for direct participation in established democracies around the world to the rise of affluent and well-educated publics able to use the resources of a high-tech and information rich environment to bypass traditional channels of interest articulation such as political parties. Citizens would rather think for themselves than be told by elites what to think about politics. Publics with large proportions of voters who convert their formal schooling into political power—"cognitively mobilized" publics—are often characterized as more politically engaged, deliberative, and inclusive.

Unfortunately, the process through which formal education slips its regulatory functions to become an instrument for challenging elites is not well specified by cognitive mobilization theory (Cassel and Lo 1997). Formal education is often experienced during one's youth and early adult years in well-delineated institutional spaces in which dominant modes of instruction can reproduce existing inequalities.[6] Models of political participation that limit measures of education to formal schooling are unable to capture how learning through experience and study, individually and in groups, over the life course can lead to personal empowerment with consequences for how people engage in politics. Limiting measures of education to formal schooling limits our understanding of how citizens who face high barriers to participation can augment existing resources to expand their repertoire.

Education is a resource that Japanese women enjoy in relative excess. The process by which women extend their research and study experience

---

6. For example, Japanese students learn about proper gender roles when teachers routinely call all boys before all girls when taking attendance rather than calling on students alphabetically. This experience implicitly teaches students that boys are more important because they come first. Margolis et al. (2001) call these experiences the "hidden curriculum."

beyond formal educational institutions deepens our understanding of how individuals convert education into political power. Women alter their learning environment—what is learned, who can claim expertise, what is taught, how and for what purposes—in significant ways that fundamentally reshape individual engagement with the political sphere. Lifelong learning not only arms women with the cognitive capacity to negotiate the political sphere, it also empowers them to question social norms and challenge the political elites who delegitimize women as political actors by questioning the epistemological origins of what women as a group know about politics and how they know it.

Formal Training and Informal Learning

Peter Cave (2001, 2004) has written extensively about the social regulatory functions of formal schooling in Japan.[7] Along their educational journeys, both men and women experience *bukatsudō* (extracurricular school clubs), alternative spaces of learning that lay a foundation for learning later in the life course. *Bukatsudō* are sports and culture clubs that have a long tradition in Japanese secondary education. Students devote three hours a day and, depending on the activity, up to seven days a week all year long to club activities. Clubs are funded by the school fees that each student pays, and teachers work as coaches and supervisors. Unlike sports teams, orchestras, bands, and the numerous other activities in the life of the average American teenager, membership is open to all participants and is not awarded on a competitive basis to those with the most talent.

Bukatsudō serve multiple purposes and function as alternative sites of learning to the classroom environment. On the one hand, *bukatsudō* are another channel for state regulatory control. Their emphasis on hierarchy, conformity, physical endurance, self-control, and self-improvement acquaint students to the demands they will face as adults. On the other hand, *bukatsudō* offer students the chance to choose from many different activities—freedom from the constraints of the classroom environment. *Bukatsudō* are places where students can develop a sense of self-worth through practicing skills and talents that are not associated with academic

---

7. This section draws heavily on Cave's (2004) work on *bukatsudō*.

success. These sites of learning challenge the rigidities of the competitive educational system that marginalizes so many young adults and often forecloses paths to privileged occupational categories.

Universal experience with *bukatsudō* in the formal schooling environment, in high schools and colleges and universities, provides men and women with a basis for discarding the regulatory functions that these activities served while retaining the transformational potential for realization later in life. In *bukatsudō,* experienced students transfer their knowledge and skills to new members who learn through observation and disciplined practice. This is one means by which *bukatsudō* allow alternative models of learning to thrive within institutions of formal education in Japan. The "classroom model," in which "a teacher transmits masses of propositional knowledge to individual learners," competes with the "club model," which employs apprenticeship-style patterns of learning that prepare participants to "act as informal participant-learners or participant-teachers in other settings, including workplace settings" (Cave 2004, 414).

The "study group" is a point of entry to the multiple and overlapping spaces that Japanese citizens, especially women, use as pedagogical sites after formal education is completed. As discussed below, women passed men in participation in "study groups" by 2006, right on the heels of the increases in formal education for women over the two preceding decades. As more women have gained *bukatsudō* experience and higher education, they have honed their skills for replicating these practices in self-guided groups in their civic lives.

Dangerous Minds: Upending Politics through Study

Through lifelong learning, the Japanese government—as documented online and in published white papers—is seeking to achieve multiple goals that will change the relationship between citizens and government. Lifelong learning was first and foremost adopted to create a more flexible education system by expanding opportunities for citizens to continue gaining new skills over the life course and stimulate more flexibility in an increasingly competitive global labor market. Lifelong learning aims to offset the inflexibility of formal schooling that is the exclusive reserve of children and young adults by creating opportunities to continue personal development and professional advancement later in life. A rigid tracking system and fierce competition for entry to the nation's top universities, which are dominated by the economic and political elite, have been blamed for driving up education costs and causing an increase in social problems among youths that include bullying, truancy, and suicide. Thus, lifelong learning is meant to resolve problems at both ends of the life course, alleviating pressures on young adults by making their projected life course more flexible while keeping elderly citizens engaged in public life.

Lifelong learning was originally one part of a larger package of education reforms initiated in the 1980s that targeted girls and boys, women and men. Since 2000, lifelong learning has been increasingly framed as a means for raising public consciousness about the connections between gender inequality and the current demographic crisis. Contemporary lifelong learning policies make an already existing women's associational universe visible and grant it legitimacy by providing infrastructure and resources and acknowledging a broad range of activity as learning. The state has elevated the value of women's communities of practice by endorsing work that dovetails with its own goals or that can be adapted to them.

The practices, if not the stated mission, of contemporary study groups across Japan are consistent with a style of citizen protest and pressure politics that emerged in the 1960s, when citizen study groups using the term "supra-party politics" devoted themselves to airing voices representing "socio-political blindspots" that had been ignored by national political parties. In the early 1970s, Japanese women activists, annoyed at finding themselves relegated to support roles in student movements with a predominately male leadership, sought to raise consciousness about women and inequality by distributing *mini-komi*[8] and participating in thousands of self-study and problem approach seminars (Jones 1975, 722). From this period onward, women's organizations mobilized around consumer rights, pollution control, defense of Article 9 (the provision in Japan's constitution that forbids acts of war), child care facilities, education policies, and all manner of social protections. This high rate of grassroots activism led to "housewives being called the Ralph Naders of Japan" (Jones 1975, 722). By the mid- to late 1970s, there emerged an observable trend of voters exiting national

---

8. *Mini-komi* are mini-communications, newsletters published by individuals and small groups designed to inform readers about specific problems and provide networking information for collective problem-solving. *Mini-komi* can be found at women's centers throughout Japan.

parties. These trends—a rise in nonpartisanship, a proliferation of women's study groups, and a rise in women's grassroots activism—have continued unabated and are arguably connected to each other and to the increase in women's educational attainment.

Changes in women's education and corresponding changes in political engagement such as abandoning political parties and eschewing national organizations are all consistent with Inglehart's and Dalton's expectations about elite-challenging electorates. Though Japanese women are not co-alescing into the violent protests that we associate with the 1960s, women who participate in small study groups over the life course are the backbone of "an empirical, individual, and amateur political movement in confron-tation with statism and nationalism, independent of party but bound to-gether by commitment to democracy" (Jones 1976, 228). Political actions, themselves diverse, span a large range of topics; the common thread is better democracy.

Over the course of the last two decades, the Japanese state has instituted a series of political and administrative reforms to respond to widespread cynicism and citizen demands for more citizen involvement in politics and decision-making. Information disclosure laws were followed by a rise in taxpayer suits (Marshall 2002); the proliferation of nonprofit associations (Kawato and Pekkanen 2008); administrative decentralization, which re-vitalized local parties and autonomy movements (LeBlanc 2008); and the Basic Law for Gender Equality, which provided a legal framework for grassroots women's groups to renew their efforts to increase the numbers of women on all decision-making bodies across Japan and combat discrim-inatory practices in public and private life. The range of citizen actions to promote better democracy, like the range of study activities that constitute learning, is so broad and seemingly disconnected that it has been hard to locate the common thread. By examining the inner workings of communi-ties of practice, we gain a sense of what better democracy means and how it shapes deliberative political engagement.

"Communities of Practice" over the Life Course

The Ministry of Education, Science, and Culture began retrofitting the so-cial education infrastructure for lifelong learning when it reorganized the Social Education Bureau to create the Lifelong Learning Bureau in July

1988. To signal a substantive policy shift, the ministry initiated policy kick-off fairs to raise public consciousness and motivation in 1989. For the next ten years, the ministry devoted a section of its annual white paper to developments in this policy arena. The ministry provided broad guidelines and subsidies to local governments to facilitate the expansion of lifelong learning programs across Japan. Within the first five years, 26 of 47 prefectures had established lifelong learning councils; 37 had promulgated basic policies for promoting lifelong learning; and 54 municipalities had declared themselves "lifelong learning communities" (Ministry of Education, Science and Culture 1994). Within seven years, 33 prefectures had lifelong learning councils, 42 had a basic policy framework, and 1,877 local municipalities (50 percent) were "lifelong learning communities" (Ministry of Education, Science, Sports and Culture 1995). Even before this rapid expansion of infrastructure and opportunities, 64.5 percent of Japanese polled by the Prime Minister's Office (Ministry of Education, Science, Sports and Culture 1996) were familiar with the term "lifelong learning."

The initial push for lifelong learning came after the United Nations Educational, Scientific, and Cultural Organization's advocacy in the late 1960s; UNESCO pushed the philosophy that education was essential to the worldwide promotion of democracy and social justice. The Japanese national government began cooperating with local governments to establish women's centers in the 1980s to carry out policy initiatives to address concerns and goals that emerged from the United Nation's International Women's Year in 1975 and the International Decade for Women (1976–1985). This dovetailed with UNESCO's lifelong learning agenda, which included a specific platform for improving the status of women through education.

Throughout the 1990s, the Ministry of Education and its Lifelong Learning Bureau sought to alleviate the social pressures associated with employers' preoccupation with academic credentials, on the one hand, and the increasingly competitive and rigid academic environment, on the other. Promoting lifelong learning would be especially important if Japan sought to maximize the social and human capital of a rapidly aging population when the pace of economic and social change was quickly rendering their skills obsolete. The bureau sought to re-value achievements that Japanese citizens had accrued later in life while also transferring new skills. Consequently, the bureau expanded its definitions of "education" and "learning" to include sports and health activities, hobby groups, volunteerism, "refresher" courses, and efforts by local governments to inform the public about welfare for the elderly, the importance of gender equality, *machi tzukuri* (rural revitalization), environmental protection, and traffic safety. Bureaucrats expanded the range of acceptable "learning methods" to include texts (magazines, books, pamphlets), telecommunications media (radio, TV, and internet), and face-to-face groups (classes, seminars, and lectures). Learning could happen in community centers, citizens' halls, and private learning centers. The bureau encouraged "intelligent facilities," physical facilities offering a range of activities, featuring information and communications technologies, and providing comfortable meeting spaces, all linked to form a cohesive network.

The mission of lifelong learning evolved and expanded for a decade until 1999, when, according to white papers, the Ministry intensified its efforts to reform formal education. Activity on the lifelong learning front regained some of its lost momentum in 2005, when the Lifelong Learning Bureau began to link its mission to two potentially oppositional goals: building stronger linkages between schools, communities, and families to enhance children's social education and promoting learning opportunities for achieving gender equality. Under the Abe administration, lifelong learning programs were targeted as venues by the conservative prime minister with the goals of fostering a controversial moral education agenda and a sense of patriotism. But once the state provided the initial infrastructure, citizens had the resources to initiate their own learning programs and to move lifelong learning outside of the government's framework.

Who Participates? When? Where?   The Ministry of Education, Culture, Sports, Science, and Technology has restructured the Japanese school system.[9] The system that had been in place prioritized formal accreditation (advanced degrees, correspondence courses); the new system includes much more emphasis on grassroots and nontraditional modes of education (see figure 5.3). In the three cells in the top left-hand corner of the diagram is

---

9. While MEXT provides the most comprehensive data on trends in lifelong learning nationally, I also consulted a growing literature that focuses more closely on specific sites, specific types of participants, and specific activities. Among these sources are: Kawanobe (1994); Maehira (1994); Yamada et al. (2003); Kinoshta (2005) Oda (2006).

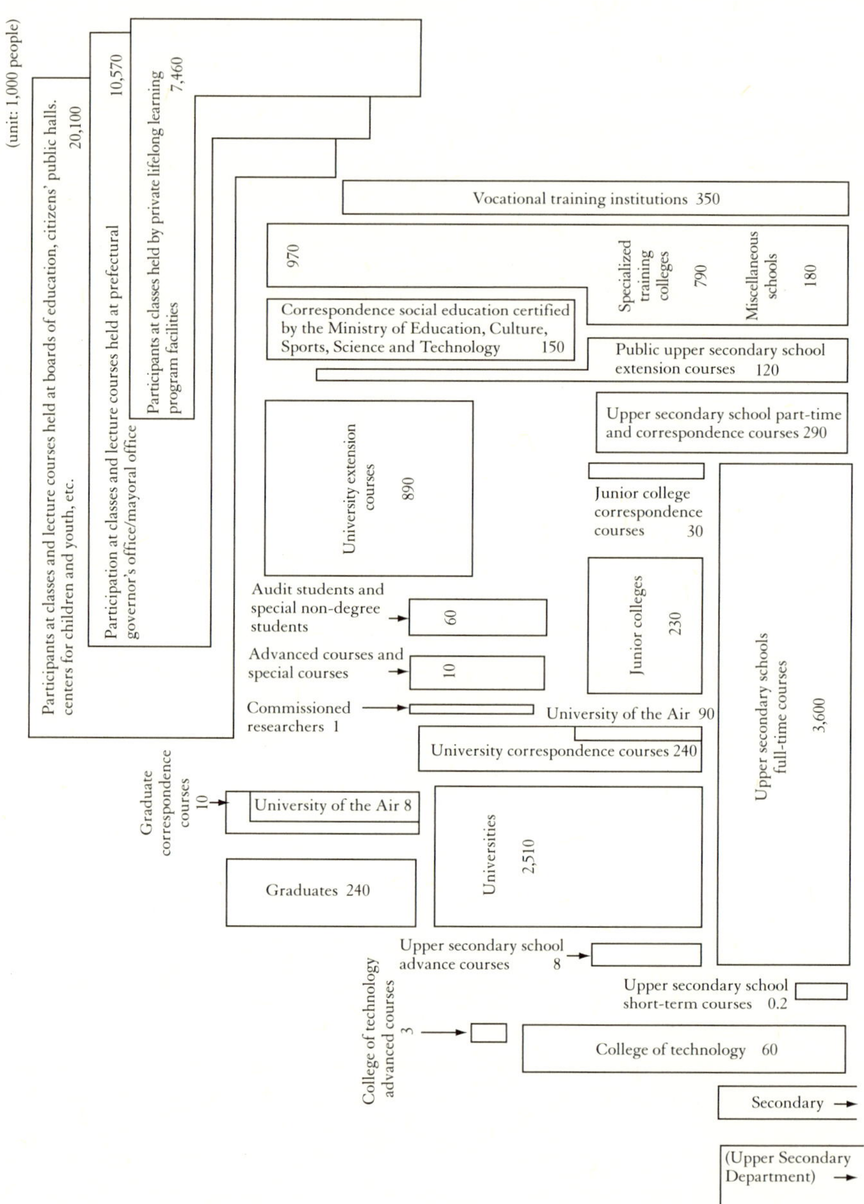

Figure 5.3 Learning population

Note: Time of survey varies.

Sources: MEXT, *School Basic Survey* (2004), MEXT, *Social Education Survey* (2002), MEXT, *Survey on Juku and Related Matters* (1993), etc. This image of Japan's learning population appears in MEXT's

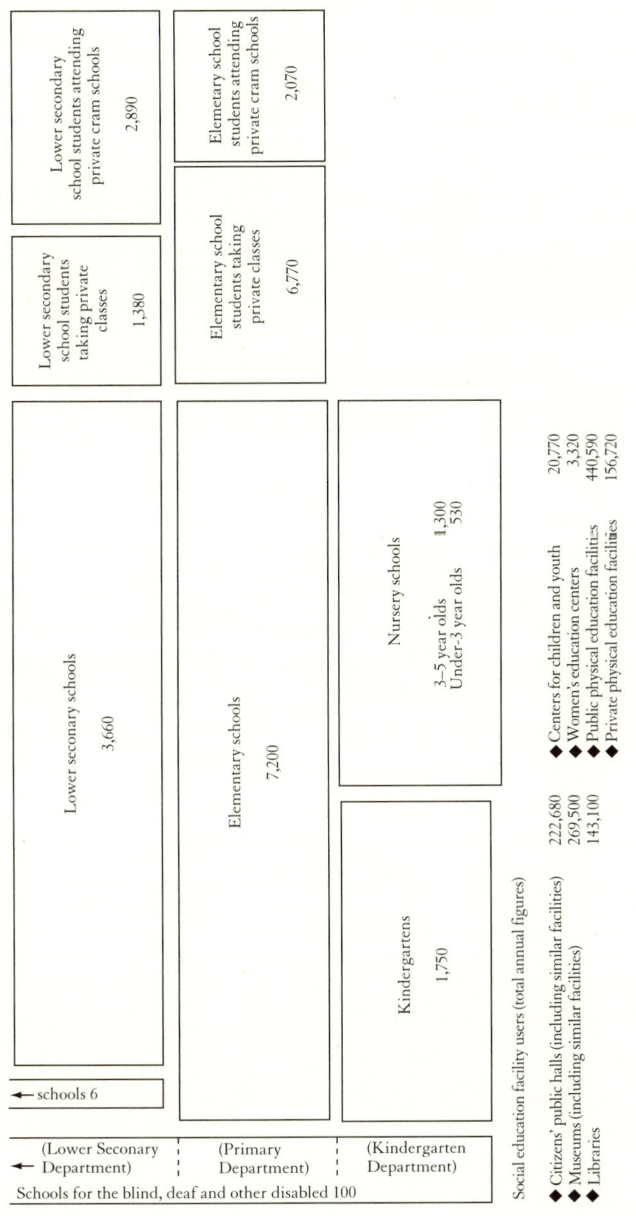

online publication, *Japan's Education at a Glance 2006,* posted at http://www.mext.go.jp/english/ statist/04120801/004.pdf.

a new category that captures lifelong learning—engagement in an informal pedagogical setting during a point in the life course where, previously, education had usually been considered complete. Included in the learning population are the nearly 7.5 million participants in classes offered in the private sector, 8.1 million participants in classes sponsored by prefectural and municipal governments, and 22 million participants in courses held in publicly funded citizens' centers. This diagram does not capture the 40 percent of Japanese who claimed to meet independently with other people with similar skills and interests.

The profile of lifelong learners presented at the beginning of this chapter is largely correct; women and the elderly are overrepresented. Even though participation rates decline over the life course (discussed below), the elderly make up a large absolute number of participants because the Japanese enjoy the world's longest life expectancies (86 years for women and 78 years for men). Government statistics do not permit empirical claims about the class and educational composition of lifelong learners. One can infer, however, from the high levels of overall educational attainment and citizen self-identification as "middle class" that these variables do not predict participation very robustly. Tellingly, the Japanese government does not use education and income in discussing patterns of participation in lifelong learning. That is not to say that these factors do not matter. They do not matter in predicting who will participate as much as they matter in predicting what types of learning a participant selects and where she will engage in it. The significant distinctions lie in who is more likely to be a hobbyist, resident, careerist, or activist and whether a participant will engage in learning in a public or private facility (Rausch 2004). Younger participants and men are more likely to engage in learning activities that will advance their careers. Socioeconomic differences, which correlate with urban/rural residence, are significant predictors of who is most likely to extend their learning in the public or private sector. A 1999 survey on lifelong learning found that Japanese citizens prefer, by a 3:2 ratio, programs in public facilities to those in private facilities, although both are popular with women (Naikakufu Daijin 1999). The population density, higher incomes, and looser social networks in urban areas create a vibrant market for private companies offering a variety of learning opportunities. In contrast, rural residents are more likely to rely on offerings at publicly funded community centers.

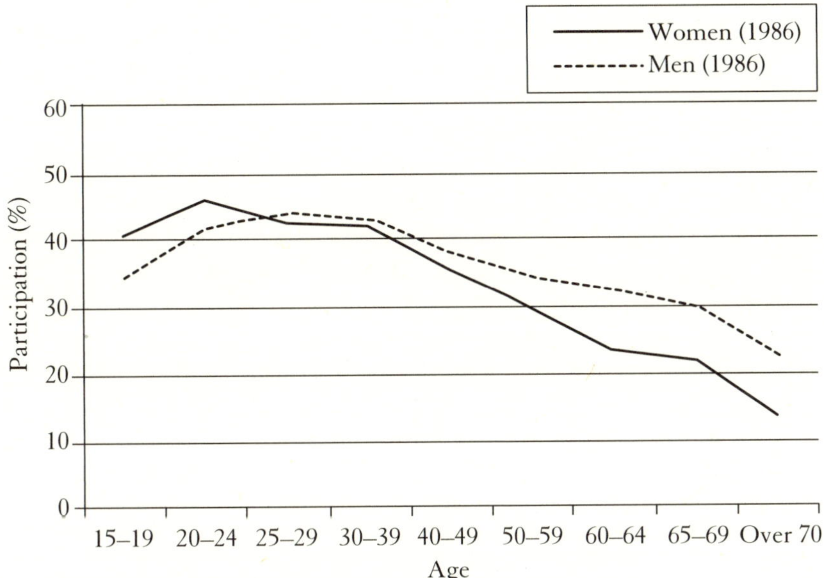

Figure 5.4 Participation in study and research groups, 1986
Source: Statistics Bureau, Management and Coordination Agency (1987), 699.

Figures 5.4 and 5.5 represent patterns in the rates of participation in learning opportunities over the life course for men and women in 1986 and 2006, respectively. I generated these graphs with the *Survey on Time Use and Leisure Activities* data reported in the *Japan Statistical Yearbook,* compiled annually by the Ministry of Internal Affairs and Communications.[10] The participation rates are for study and research activities outside of formal educational institutions. Respondents were asked about their participation in study and research activities in the following categories: foreign language study, vocational studies, nursing and care-related activities, home economics and housework, humanities and the social and natural sciences, art and culture, and current events. These data provide an estimate of a universe of practice that extends beyond the official spaces. Despite many limitations, it is our best estimate of citizen participation in

---

10. The survey is a sample of the population; the rates and patterns of participation are taken as representative of the entire population. These rates do not allow me to say anything definitive about the actual numbers of Japanese who participate in lifelong learning.

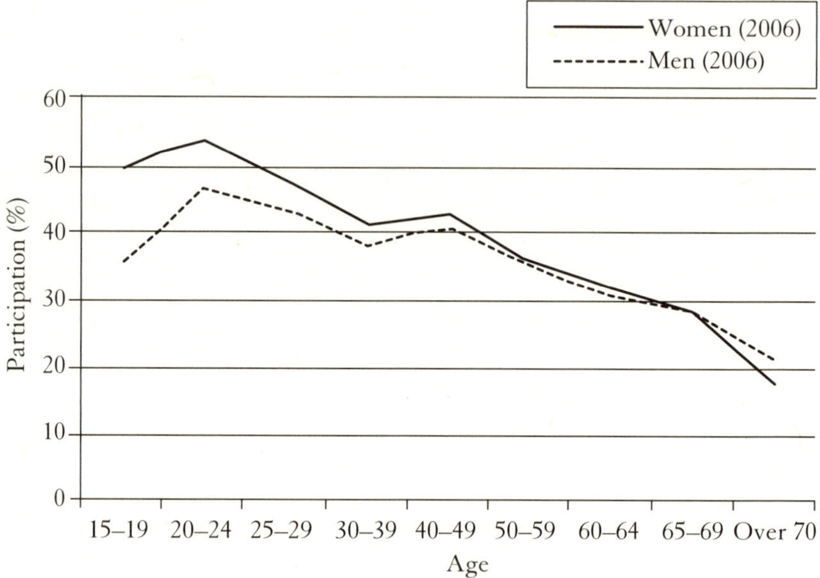

Figure 5.5 Participation in study and research groups, 2006
Source: Statistics Bureau, Management and Coordination Agency (2007), 754.

study and research groups outside of formal education institutions.[11] These rates alert us to the potential existence of a multitude of other groups that are independently organized.

The figures reflect similar participatory patterns for women and men over the space of twenty years. First, participation rates for women and men have increased at every age along the life course; more Japanese were involved in lifelong learning in 2006 than in 1986. It is safe to say that the Ministry of Education's campaigns to increase the overall participation in lifelong learning from the late 1980s onward contributed to the observed increase that is evident across women and men of every age group. Second, the participation rate is high among young women and men in their late

---

11. It very likely underestimates participation, since respondents are likely to underreport participation in independent study and informal pedagogical settings. For example, participants may be likely to report attending activities at their local citizen's halls but less likely to report groups that meet in coffee shops or private homes. Further, underreporting might be higher among older respondents because many of the response options are limited to vocational skills (computing and business related skills) for which demand is probably higher among younger respondents.

teens but peaks when both groups are in their early twenties. As women approach their marriage and childbearing years, participation begins to taper off and gradually decreases over the remainder of the life course. Young men exhibit a similar pattern with an initial drop in participation that coincides with their career-building years, followed by a gradual decline over the life course.

Despite similarities in the participatory patterns, women and men exhibit distinct differences in their rates of participation over the life course. The 1986 figure features a pronounced gender gap, which by 2006 had closed—indeed, the numbers for women are slightly higher in the later data. In 1986, females had the higher participation rate below the age of 25 (40 percent and 46 percent for females aged 15–19 and 20–24, respectively, as compared to 34 percent and 42 percent for males) but dropped below the male rate from age 25 onward, with the gap getting wider with age. Twenty years later, in 2006, women decisively out-participate men in research and study groups early in the life course. The gap narrows as both groups age, but women maintain a slim advantage until the very late stages of life. Declining rates of participation over the life course are offset by the long life expectancies and the rate of population aging; the population pyramid in Japan is barrel shaped. Consequently, the absolute number of older lifelong learning participants approximates the number of younger participants.

The data in figures 5.4 and 5.5 measure the rate of participation in lifelong learning activities without shedding light on the actual numbers of participants involved. Table 5.1 provides the requisite data. The number of individuals using their local citizens' centers for their own purposes is twice the number of individuals who enrolled in center-sponsored classes and lectures, and the number of individual users is only a small portion (14 percent) of the number of groups that convened for any number of purposes in these same spaces. The same dynamic is at work in women's centers, where the number of groups far exceeds of the number of individual users. The discrepancy between the number of individual users and groups is a product of the way the data were tabulated—single groups that met multiple times were counted as separate groups; however, it is probably also true that many people had overlapping memberships. The discrepancy between the number of classes and lectures available to citizens in 2005 and the number of groups that convened outside of these state-sponsored learning opportunities suggests the immense scope of the

TABLE 5.1. Tapping into the "official" lifelong learning universe, 2005

	No. lecture courses	No. courses for women	No. course participants	No. individual facility users	No. group facility users
Boards of Education	164,632	8,988	7,973,000	—	—
Citizens' centers	472,697	55,866	12,449,000	25,751,000	185,451,000
Women's education centers	7,555	—	—	318,000	2,533,000

Source: Statistics Bureau, Management and Coordination Agency (1987).

lifelong learning universe that exists outside the regulatory boundaries of the state, albeit with the help of state-provided resources.

What accounts for the elimination of the gender gap in study and research activities over the life course over a mere twenty years, as figures 5.4 and 5.5 indicate? The most likely answer is the overall increase in educational attainment among women and the state's promotion of lifelong learning programs. As noted earlier, more women began to pursue higher education and enter four-year colleges and universities in the 1980s and into the 1990s. This is consistent with an increase in women's participation in study and research activities, especially among women aged forty-five and younger in 2006. And the corresponding increase in state involvement during this period has already been established.

The elimination of the gender gap in participation results from substantial gains across the board; the only group of women that did not increase was the 30–39 cohort. Men not only failed to make comparable gains, they even lost ground (see table 5.2). Over this same period, women continued to face the same constraints in balancing work and care responsibilities over the life course, with the consequence that a large segment of the expanding pool of women in the workforce still experience an interruption in work and are overrepresented among part-time and temporary workers. In short, women have the opportunities and the incentives to search for other outlets for self-improvement, a fact demonstrated by the increased participation in study and research activities. In 2000, the Economic Planning Agency reported in *National Lifestyle: Volunteering Enriches Societies with Taste-Linked Human Relations* that one in four Japanese citizens were participating in voluntary activities, and housewives comprised the bulk (42 percent) of participants, followed by retirees (16 percent). Here, I consider voluntarism one type of community

TABLE 5.2. Change in gender and rates of study group participation between 1986 and 2006

Age	Men	Women
15–19	0.8	9
20–24	4	7
25–29	–1.6	4.7
30–39	–5	–1
40–49	2.6	6.6
50–59	0.4	5.5
60–64	–2.4	7.8
65–69	–1.8	6
over 70	–1.7	3.5

Note: Calculations are based on the same data used to generate figures 5.4 and 5.5 and represent the difference in average participation rate reported in years 1986 and 2006. Positive numbers indicate higher participation in 2006 than 1986; negative numbers indicate lower participation in 2006 than 1986.

of practice. The top rate of volunteer participation for women occurred in their thirties and forties, while participation for men was highest among those sixty and over. Women's advances in higher education was offered as a reason for high participation among housewives (Economic Planning Agency 2001, 14).

Japanese Adult Learners in Comparative Perspective   Lifelong learning is a worldwide movement. The Fifth International Conference on Adult Education held in Hamburg, Germany, in July 1997 revealed a clear global trend in nations promoting lifelong learning to facilitate democracy, social justice, gender equality, conflict resolution, social and economic development, and environmental sustainability and scientific innovation. Intergovernmental agencies such as the World Bank, UNESCO, and the Organization for Economic Cooperation and Development have been crucial in providing an international forum for discussion and debate and facilitating the emergence of a common discourse around lifelong learning: "Although the adult education enterprise varies in scope, philosophy, and structure in different nations, it is not unusual for approaches to adult education developed in one region or country to spread" (Imel 2000). The movement has seen cross-national diffusion of policies alongside wide variations in grassroots practices.

Variation in scope, philosophy, and structure is a tremendous challenge to developing cross-national measures of lifelong learning.[12] The United States continues to privilege measures of the role of adult education, or lifelong learning, in building human capital in purely economic terms, that is, the attainment of work-related skills. Adult education surveys track participation in formal and informal work-related training and learning for personal interest. When lifelong learning is defined strictly as adult education, measures exclude less formal learning (organized activities in churches, senior centers, and voluntary associations) and informal learning (what is learned from everyday life experiences), precisely the types of organizations that I am interested in (Young and Rosenberg 2006). Japanese government statistics are more successful at capturing less formal learning, while informal learning is beyond the scope of current measurement practices. Nonetheless, I use participation in personal interest courses to draw some comparison between the United States and Japan; personal interest courses in the United States are the category of adult education that most closely corresponds to social education courses offered in Japan (discussed above in tables 5.1 and 5.2). By these measures, the rate of participation in personal interest courses is higher in Japan than in the United States. In 2000–2001, one in five (21 percent) American adults over the age of 16 participated in personal interest courses. This estimate is much lower than Japan, where the participation rate is 35.2 percent; indeed, participation rates for adults over the age of 70 years approximates 20 percent, the total participation rate for the United States.

As in Japan, American participants tended to be women, and participation declined over the life course. Similarly, participants were more likely than nonparticipants to have completed at least some college education, to have work experiences in professional or managerial occupations, to have continuing education requirements for their occupation, and to have never

---

12. For example, there is a distinction between "second-chance" and "expanded-chance" education in lifelong learning that corresponds to a given nation's level of economic development. "Second-chance" education tends to be the predominant goal in middle-income countries, while "expanded-chance" education is more prevalent in upper income countries; there is a shift from one to the other as nations move along the developmental trajectory (World Bank 2003).

been married. The same general tendencies are evident in Japan, but they are not as pronounced as in the American case. In Japan, lifelong learning looks like a buffet of choices that draws frequent visitors from across the socioeconomic spectrum and life course.

The role of employer incentives in the promotion of adult learning activities in the United States makes participation more compulsory in the American than in the Japanese case (Kim et al. 2004). Americans tend to participate in learning activities that are specifically geared toward their participation in the labor market. Even individual participation in personal interest courses in the United States increases when there are are employer incentives to participate. In contrast, Japanese adult learners are more likely to be self-motivated.

The Japanese resemble the Europeans in how they think about the goals of lifelong learning and where they locate and envision pedagogical spaces. The 2003 Eurobarometer shows that Europeans define lifelong learning in broad terms, as learning work-related skills and knowledge that contributes to self- and community improvement. Like Japanese, most Europeans agreed that they learn best in informal settings within the context of their everyday lives: at home (69 percent), in meetings with other people (63 percent), and through their leisure/recreational activities (51 percent). Other informal learning settings included libraries and local resource centers (32 percent), traveling abroad (30 percent), and social and political work (21 percent) (CEDEFOP 2003).

Deregulated Knowledge Production

John Dewar Wilson (2001) views lifelong learning in Japan as a "lifeline" for (a) political elites trying to learn how the social problems of late capitalism are experienced on the ground; (b) senior citizens, who can present themselves as community resources rather than a collectively shared burden; (c) a nation concerned about the effects of globalization; and (d) a society with a modern workforce that seeks to take full advantage of the potential of currently marginalized members such as women, older workers, and workers without privileged educational backgrounds. The proliferation of study groups within a highly educated and heavily female population makes state regulation difficult, if not impossible. Policy feedback has not come merely in the form of data on participation rates, program content, and facility usage. Feedback has also rebounded in the form of grassroots pressure on elites to practice a more inclusive democracy if their aim is to produce communitarian responses to contemporary social challenges; program participants identify elite practices as one of the problems of late capitalism.

Conclusion

Engendering Knowledge and Political Action

On the afternoon of February 29, 2008, approximately two hundred people marched by Osaka's prefectural assembly building to protest the planned closing of the Dawn Center, one of Japan's leading public institutions devoted to promoting gender equality. The demonstration was organized by the We Love the Dawn Center Association, founded earlier in the month following Governor Tōru Hashimoto's announcement of the planned closure and sale or privatization of the center and twenty-four other public facilities to rein in the prefecture's mounting debt.[1] A group of predominantly female protesters presented a list of invaluable services that make the center a model for women's centers across Japan.[2] The Dawn

---

1. Ironically, as a candidate, Hashimoto campaigned on a platform promising improved child care and won the support of a majority of women voters. Child care, one of the many services offered at the Dawn Center, is a cornerstone of national policies to help women to balance work and family responsibilities to bolster Japan's low birthrate.

2. The group reported that both men and women marched to protest the center's closing, but the photos that appeared in the newspaper (Terano 2008) and on the We Love the Dawn Center website (www.sukiyanen-dc.com) show that the marchers were predominantly women.

Center has been an exemplary case that fulfills an evolving national policy agenda, encouraging adult-centered educational programming in local communities and local initiatives to further gender equality through life-long learning.

The Dawn Center, a seven-story structure centrally located in Osaka, contains meeting and conference rooms, a library, an auditorium, a recording studio, a kitchen, and child care facilities. Its library holdings offer a wide range of information related to women and gender, and the center offers training workshops to help visitors to use its resources. Professional counselors are available to help individuals with a range of problems encountered by women in their daily lives, from domestic abuse to assistance in managing work and family responsibilities. A variety of support groups meet regularly to aid women living in Osaka, foreign-born and native, to develop collective solutions to individual problems. The center's programming is diverse: public screenings of gender-themed movies, training workshops that cover topics ranging from career development for working women to gender sensitivity training for public employees; there is also a lecture series. In addition to the programming, members of the general public can also rent rooms for a fee to conduct independent activities. When these activities are devoted to furthering gender equality, the center reduces its rental fees. There is an annual newsletter and numerous center publications. The center creates and shares information with other women's centers across Japan as well as with nonprofit organizations and foreign agencies.[3]

Every year hundreds of thousands of women visit the Dawn Center as participants in seminars, workshops, lectures, hobby groups, and study circles, to empower themselves and transform their lives. Nearly four hundred thousand people visit the Dawn Center each year, giving it an average of fifteen hundred visitors every day. Over eight thousand people made use of the center's counseling services in 2007. Bracket its gender equality mission, and the Dawn Center is a hub that provides access to a vibrant layer of Japanese civil society that is made up of an expansive range of activities carried out in "communities of practice," defined as "groups of people who share a concern or passion for something they do and learn how to

---

3. See the Dawn Center's website at www.dawncenter.or.jp.

do it better as they interact regularly" (Wenger n.d.). Study circles are a prevalent feature of the Japanese political landscape, and women make up the majority of participants. Millions of Japanese women study in groups, regularly convening in any available space, from citizen's public halls and women's centers to private homes and coffee shops. The shared concerns or passions that bring them together include but are not limited to hobbies, sports, arts and culture, political and current events, voluntarism and community service, travel and foreign language study, and classes one might find listed in the course of study at any liberal arts institution.

The Dawn Center's services provide a sense of the scope of the official lifelong learning programs and the accompanying facilities that, in turn, provide a baseline for imagining the overall size of a universe of study opportunities that use official brick-and-mortar centers as a springboard for launching independent learning activities. The Dawn Center is a part of a loosely configured nationwide network of citizens' public halls, libraries, museums, sports and culture facilities, schools and universities, and programming facilities in companies and offices that serve as adult education sites. There, citizens can engage in a broad range of sports, hobbies, volunteer activities, vocational programs, liberal arts classes, and study circles that, whether sponsored by the state, a firm, or private citizens, fall under a nearly two-decades old Ministry of Education initiative to revamp and expand its social education program into a comprehensive lifelong learning program.

It was remarkable that Osaka's governor and prefectural assembly members had targeted such a heavily trafficked public venue for closure. The decision to close the Dawn Center seems especially ill-conceived because it goes against an evolving national policy agenda. More surprising, however, is how much elite political actors underestimated the extent to which center supporters would protest the proposed closure. The day after the Osaka protest, the We Love the Dawn Center Association posted its version of events on its website. The association deemed the march a success; it had attracted the attention of the mass media, with broadcast as well as print journalists reporting on the event. That same day, the public gallery overlooking the prefectural assembly was filled to capacity. The association and the website continued to expand over the spring and into the summer months as the assembly deliberated its final decision about the future of the Dawn Center. The website posted announcements, maintained an archive, and provided ready-made petitions for sympathizers to down-load. We Love the Dawn Center may be powered by political amateurs, but they are using high-tech, politically savvy strategies to mobilize public opinion and pressure the political pros to change their budgetary priorities. The Dawn Center remains open, though its budget has been reduced.

The Dawn Center movement is the rare physical manifestation of broad changes in women's political orientations that, at the level of attitudes and the norms and practices governing everyday life, have passed unobserved. The We Love the Dawn Center Association is testimony to the potential for adult education to deepen democratic practices, directly and indirectly, among everyday citizens. The women-centered focus of the Dawn Center and its commitment to building resources specifically designed to subvert a patriarchal order, while not inconsequential, should not divert attention from basic pedagogical practices that are common across different spaces of adult learning. Women's centers constitute a minority of the spaces of learning where majorities of Japanese women predominate. By asking how using the Dawn Center's services—the information network, international exchange programs, counseling services, cultural programs, and enlightenment programs—alone or in tandem, change the terms by which its heavily female clientele engages with the political world, I tether questions that I ask of a broader universe of practice to a specific location in order to make my object of study tangible for another moment.

In this concluding chapter, I offer concrete examples of political action by women and for women that is inextricable from the cognitive processes that are mobilized in political conversation, study and lifelong learning, and local political action. I examine how the state's interest in bringing citizens into collaborative relationships to solve problems coalesces with citizens' demands for direct participation. I have placed Japanese women at the center of a struggle to harness human capital to achieve state developmental goals. Through Japanese women's experience we gain insight into whether lifelong learning operates as a vehicle for the state to coopt women or empowers women to influence the practices that make up the state. The process by which everyday citizens convert basic education into knowledge for empowerment raises important questions for further research on the potential for lifelong learning to empower underrepresented and socially disadvantaged groups in the political process. This work is especially salient when nations worldwide are reexamining the importance of lifelong learning as a means of strengthening democracy and economies. I conclude with reflections on how my work generates questions for future research agendas in comparative education and democracy, gender and inequality, and Japanese politics.

Training Women for Politics

Public spaces like the Dawn Center make visible the important connections linking lifelong learning, gender-specific patterns of political engagement, and changes observable in contemporary Japanese politics. In this section, I focus on two grassroots efforts specifically geared toward increasing women's knowledge-based resources and expanding their networks to overcome the chronic structural and institutional barriers that disproportionately bar women from the political world: backup schools and women's simulated assemblies.

Starting in the late 1990s, "the concept of providing training for prospective candidates spread throughout grassroots groups across the nation" (Takao 2008). Backup schools are training academies staffed by incumbent assembly women, academics, government officials, journalists, and management professionals to introduce women to successful electioneering and legislative processes and policy-making. Women participants gain hands-on experience working on assembly members' campaigns and in their offices. "Everyday women" enrolled in political training programs to deepen their knowledge about democratic politics and its practice. Conveners of training programs hoped to equip some subset of women with the tools to run for elected office. A decade later, these programs are credited with contributing to the record number of women elected to local assemblies in every unified local election since 1991 (Ogai 2004; Takao 2008). Even though the percentage of women elected to local assemblies currently stands at 10.9 percent, the rate of increase over the last two decades has been more rapid than in the preceding five when women's representation reached a plateau and held at 2 percent (Martin 2008; Ministry of Internal Affairs and Communications 2009).

Women's simulated assemblies (*josei kaigi*) fill local assembly seats for a day with community women who follow legislative procedures, discuss policy, and make decisions as if it were a typical day when the assembly is in session. Women's assemblies demystify legislative politics for everyday voters. The number of successful women candidates in local politics who trained in backup schools and attended simulated assemblies is an indication that this is a significant and legitimate path for women to break into politics (Ogai 2004). Generally, backup schools and simulated assemblies increase interest and participation in politics among the hundreds of ordinary women who never run for office.

Spaces of lifelong learning for women such as the Dawn Center are launching pads for the increasing numbers of women who are running for seats on local assemblies across Japan. Backup schools and simulated women's assemblies are planned in, recruit women from, and stage their activities in sites of learning for women. Local women across Japan started backup schools and mobilized their own networks to "go about making a network for political amateurs to study, exchange information and determine [their] own election agenda" (Moriya n.d.). Backup schools and simulated women's assemblies were started because most women were not in labor unions or political parties where they would have received exposure to how to make policies, organize supporters, raise money, speak in public, and market themselves (Moriya n.d.). Women had to train themselves to become viable candidates while amassing resources to overcome the traditional barriers to entry that all political outsiders have to overcome, regardless of gender. These innovations for breaking women into politics at the grassroots level are extensions of capacities for creating and sharing knowledge, problem-solving, and networking that lifelong learning seeks to build.

The Dawn Center has hosted a backup school twice a month for six months of every year.[4] It has also posted online reports on these efforts to narrow the gender representation gap on local assemblies across Japan, itself an indicator of the conscious linkages that are being made between lifelong learning in communities of practice and empowering women to participate in the political system. Participation in study and hobby groups is not peripheral to the political attitudes professed by focus group

---

4. The Fusae Ichikawa Memorial Association's Center to Promote Women's Involvement in Politics is another prominent sponsor of "backup" activities that draw participants from around Japan, many of whom successfully run for local office. See www.ichikawa-fusae.or.jp/110/index. htm, accessed August 21, 2010.

participants and voters across Japan and the patterns of local political action that they produce. Gender equality activists are calling contemporary patterns of women's political engagement the "Third Wave" as grassroots women all over the country develop effective movements to increase their visibility in the political sphere without the help of charismatic national figures (Moriya n.d.). Movements are powered by the everyday efforts of ordinary voters. Consequently, this wave of energy to make the political sphere more inclusive of women merits comparison to the prewar movement for women's suffrage and the 1989 Madonna Boom (Iwamoto 2001). The strength of the current wave is that its activities are rooted in local communities, a foundation that makes this wave "steadier and more sustainable than the First or Second Wave" (Moriya n.d.). Practices internal to study and hobby groups are vital to the larger effort to deepen Japanese democracy.

Bringing Citizens Back In

In this book, I have argued that closer examination of puzzling political behavior pronounced among women voters in Japan—people who think that all of their electoral choices are losing ones, yet turn out to vote anyway—can tell us about how the institutional reforms, rapid demographic change, and mass accumulation of resources that facilitate political engagement coalesce to promote higher rates of political participation than the conventional wisdom might lead us to expect. Political science has long maintained that rational voters would stay home because the likelihood that any one vote makes a difference is very low; the costs of voting outweigh the benefits. A well-developed sense of civic duty, not to mention a well-oiled political machine, can mobilize voters to go to the polls on Election Day. But voting is a low-grade political activity. What motivates citizens not only to vote but also to work between elections to increase the likelihood that their votes will matter? In this book, I argue that discursive practices in study groups over the life course have the potential to change citizen's expectations about democracy and calculations about how and where their participation matters for bringing local and national political practices into closer alignment with their new expectations. Study and hobby group activity over the life course helps to produce and sustain a civic culture that is associated with a more active local politics that might, over the long term, become the foundation for a new form of citizenship and engagement with the potential of altering the national political arena.

For women voters, political change is not achieved simply through an alteration in power and an increase in women candidates; it is achieved through changes in the way that democracy is practiced. New expectations about politics are shaped in the context of women's everyday lives and the groups that they belong to, which are themselves embedded within a larger and evolving socio-institutional context. Women such as Reiko Nakajima in chapter 4 are finding that women in their communities express a broad range of gender role norms that influence their understandings of equality and how it is produced; there is no one way to be a woman or a man.

Women are grappling with how to bridge divergent perspectives in their groups and communities, practices not evident in the political world even though deliberation and consensual decision-making should be constitutive of democracy. In the weeks before the unified local elections of 2007, female politicians and grassroots activists came together for the third time since 1999 to raise public consciousness about the underrepresentation of women in elected office and its ramifications for democracy. For the first time, groups made explicit demands for electing more men and women who would pursue gender-equal policies (*Yomiuri Shimbun* 2007). Feminists such as academic and activist Keiko Higuchi and the nonpartisan activist Midori Teramachi acknowledged that increasing the number of women on elected assemblies would not change politics or women's lives if "they're people who prioritize the logic of political parties or other organizations" and do not challenge traditional gender roles (*Yomiuri Shimbun* 2007). As the number of elected women has increased, voters have learned that change is not possible if the numbers are not matched by an increase in the range of perspectives that are represented (*Yomiuri Shimbun* 2007).

The DPJ's 2009 electoral victory did produce change along many of the dimensions indexed by the Japanese Election and Democracy Study respondents in chapter 1. The composition of the House of Representatives changed radically. In kicking out the LDP incumbents, voters installed the highest percentage of politicians elected for the first time in sixty years. Thirty-three percent of seats were filled by politicians who were elected to the Diet for the first time; within the DPJ, 46 percent of winners were first-time politicians (Izumi 2009). Women now hold a record fifty-four Diet seats, with forty held by DPJ women. The average age of DPJ members (49.4 years) is the lowest in the Diet. Descriptive change in the Diet promised to bring about a substantive change in political practices and policy outcomes. A DPJ heavily populated by politicians elected to national office for the first time also meant that the party had fewer *zoku giin,* Diet politicians who are policy specialists, among its ranks; fewer *zoku giin* means fewer ties to entrenched interests and bureaucratic entities. And the party promised to put the people back in charge by exercising greater control over the bureaucracy (Izumi 2009).

In late November 2009, two months after the election, the Female Politicians Network held its meeting at DPJ headquarters to pass an action plan linking the pursuit of gender equality within the national DPJ to the local autonomy movement aimed at giving voters greater access to and control over policy processes in local and national government (Democratic Party of Japan 2009). This initiative aims to increase the number of female politicians at every level of government while also shortening the divide between politicians and voters through better and more open communication. In the aftermath of the 2009 House of Representatives election, women are emerging as a vital resource for the DPJ in its continued efforts to build its local base.

The DPJ's newness undermines its efforts to make inroads with all voters who anticipate change. Aside from the small number of incumbents that constitute the party leadership, the rank and file of the DPJ lacks the policy expertise and the networks amassed by the LDP. This not only made for a rocky transition, it has also compromised the DPJ's ability to keep its campaign promises. For example, Prime Minister Hatoyama had to retreat from his campaign pledge to renegotiate the terms of the relocation of the U.S. Marine Corps Air Station at Futenma incited mass protests and demonstrations on Okinawa, ultimately becoming a major factor that resulted in Prime Minister Hatoyama's June 2010 resignation and the DPJ's loss of its majority in the July House of Councillors election.

Still, the DPJ's commitment to restore "popular sovereignty" through administrative reforms that have further opened the bureaucracy has added momentum to changes already in motion, making their reversal impossible even if the LDP is restored to power. In his October 26, 2009, policy speech, former Prime Minister Hatoyama acknowledged the proliferation of grassroots movements and their utility to state and society in resolving "everyday issues like those relating to child-rearing, nursing care, education, and community-building on their own." Like the women I interviewed, Hatoyama described these civically engaged citizens as "people who support young parents—who tend to become isolated with child-rearing concerns—by hosting community classes so that parents can openly share their experiences and have a place where they belong." And, as I have argued throughout this book, participation in these groups can inspire facilitate political participation: "Among the parents who receive such support are some who go on to participate in activities to support others, thereby finding a new "role to play" in society which takes advantage of their own experiences" (Democratic Party of Japan 2009).

Lifelong Learning and Democracy

Lifelong learning is rooted in a broad, cross-national debate about how to reduce gender, racial/ethnic, and class-based disparities in political participation to increase political voice among underrepresented groups in established democracies. Education is central to discourses about equality because it is the symbol of equal opportunity (Gamson 1992, 97). While formal education is an important prerequisite for critical political participation, social scientists recognize that individuals often fail to convert educational achievement into knowledge for empowerment. An increase in education narrows gaps in political participation between dominant and subordinate groups, but it does not erase it entirely. Established democracies are struggling with the problem of adapting learning institutions to widen access and address social inequality by providing wide-ranging skills to foster lifelong citizen engagement in all sectors of public life.

Globalization has produced renewed interest in lifelong learning as a tool for democratic states searching for innovative ways to weather social, economic, and political changes. Sweden has long been the standard in this regard. Sweden is a "study circle democracy" where citizens "strongly believe that adult education should be voluntary, democratic, and participatory with educational methods chosen to enhance freedom of choice, exchange of ideas, critical thinking, leadership, and application of knowledge to everyday life" (Oliver 1987, xvii–xviii). The Swedish study circle model "transformed the economic, political, and social base of their society in just two generations" (Oliver 1987, 144). Democracies around the world are renewing their commitment to lifelong learning "for the personal development of all citizens and for participation in all aspects of society from active citizenship through to labor market integration. Lifelong learning has emerged as an overarching strategy for enabling citizens to meet new challenges" (Kalis and Pilos 2005). In 2006 the European Parliament established the Lifelong Learning Programme for Community Action in the Field of Lifelong Learning, to run for seven years (2007–2013).

Efforts to promote lifelong learning among EU member states have produced wide variation in outcomes over the course of the past decade. There are enough cases to launch large-scale comparative studies to determine whether lifelong learning can deliver all that it promises. How does lifelong work at the individual level, the community level, nationally, and globally? Does it produce greater social cohesion? A more vibrant civil society? Does lifelong learning assist in democratic consolidation? Does it help economies achieve global competitiveness? Under what conditions can lifelong learning realize each of these very disparate goals?

The Japanese state is actively encouraging increased citizen participation in agenda-setting and problem-solving given its own limited capacity to address the challenges of rapid demographic change. The population is rapidly aging, fertility rates are below the replacement level, rural towns and villages are depopulated, and the nation has entered a period of overall population decline. These trends are shrinking the labor force, stressing the social welfare state, and threatening the sustainability of the world's third-largest economy. Administrative decentralization and deregulation and the movement of social service provision from the public to the private sector demand that citizens assume responsibility for innovating local solutions to the problems of rapid demographic change (Ogawa 2010). State initiatives that charge citizens with many of the responsibilities that it has performed to date coincide with an already evolving groundswell of everyday citizens demanding increased participation in decision-making as a means of strengthening their control over political actors. Lifelong learning is a mediating force, promoted by the state as a means of equipping citizens with the knowledge and skills to assume new social service responsibilities (even as citizens have long since launched their own independent practices to empower individuals and communities relative to the state). Who is controlling whom? Is the state crafting citizenship, or are citizens crafting the state? And how do women's study group practices, enabled by lifelong learning policies, help to sort out this web of causality?

Ogawa argues that "the newly advocated knowledge is disciplinary in nature: lifelong learning is primarily expected to contribute to the quality of the public sphere, which is called the *New Public* [*atarashii kōkyō*] in Japanese society" (2010, 87). In response, "people at the grass-roots level are trying to construct citizenship through dynamic, spontaneous participation in lifelong learning activities in public lifelong learning facilities" (2010, 87). From this perspective, the state controls the very terms of cognitive mobilization and channels the increased capacity for civic engagement in directions that serve its purposes and its own reproduction. Ogawa, drawing upon the work if Aihwa Ong, sees citizenship as a "dual process of self-making and being-made, with webs of power linked to the nation-state and civil society" (2010, 96). In this book, I have argued that lifelong learning creates opportunities for citizens to hijack a state-sponsored infrastructure to bring about political changes that are unanticipated by elite proponents of education reform. I detail the shift in the balance of power from the state to citizens; the emphasis is on "self-making" and how that process empowers citizens to compel agents of the state to change how they practice democracy, rather than on citizens "being made" to carry out the business of the state.

Education arms women with the cognitive capacity to negotiate the political sphere, and group activity over the life course can empower them to question social norms and challenge political elites. Women's roles were at the center of historic debates about what kind of political subject and nation the Japanese education system should produce, and they remain at the center of contemporary debates about education. However, women are not only subjects in this debate, they are active agents lobbying government as mothers of school-aged children, as students seeking equal opportunity in employment, and as adult learners. In each of these roles, women are producing an educated self that they think is appropriate to the context of their own lives. While politics stays the same, women's lives reflect the broad socioeconomic changes that are shaping their plans for the future (Schoppa 1991, 22–23). Education is a resource for changing politics to bring national policy outcomes into alignment with their lived experience. Social transformations are moving inside the institutions of higher education, spilling over to the lifelong learning environment, and rippling out to mobilize a broader community for political change.

Normative debates about the relationship between education and democratic citizenship and empirical evidence position lifelong learning as an important site of struggle between state and society over the processes of individual and group transformation that give rise to demands for political change. At the heart of this debate about lifelong learning policy is the recognition, by citizens and elites, that universal education creates the potential for the mobilization of knowledge to achieve vastly different visions of state-society relations (Sato 2004, 2003). Several factors lend credibility to the claim that women's study and hobby groups are sites of self-transformation in the name of broad socio-political change.

Flexibility, malleability, creativity, and transformative change characterize the ways that women have worked within the structural constraints that women face as a group to mobilize for a more inclusive political sphere. But these terms also capture a change in popular perspectives that voters want political elites to embrace to revitalize society. This change in perspective has large-scale implications for Japanese politics as more women (and men, as well) find themselves at loose ends in a society that demands flexible labor and mobile knowledge but traditionally has offered no opportunities to citizens interested in returning to school and pursuing new career paths later in life. One's life options are determined by the quality of one's early education; upon graduating from high school or university, the average Japanese citizen followed a fixed career path with little room for deviation over the life course. The problem of limited options has been especially acute for women. Women regularly fall off their career tracks because they are unable to balance employment with care-giving responsibilities over the life course. Once career women leave the labor market, they reenter in lower-status jobs with little opportunity for advancement. Study circles, whether state-sponsored or not, offer Japanese citizens who "fall off the escalator" a way back into society where none previously existed. The proliferation of study circles as citizens seek outlets for personal growth outside of the workplace and family suggests that rigid social structures are eroding and being replaced by outlets that foster diversity and individuality. Learning over the life course enables adults to extend their toolkits in ways that promote and sustain a different type of engagement with politics.

Japanese women's experiences with study groups as a vehicle for engagement in public life provide insight into how interpreting one's individual and shared experiences creates knowledge and mobilizes political capabilities in unexpected ways that promise to strengthen the quality of democratic participation: "Some of the capacities that are useful in attaining equal political influence in deliberations include; autonomy, which enables citizens to develop authentic preferences; 'the effective use of cultural resources' such as knowledge and language; cognitive capabilities; and skill at discussion" (Conover et al. 2002, 42). Schooling provides the foundation for these capacities, but lifelong learning furthers their development and helps to even the playing field for less educated members of society as well as those whose school days are long past. At a minimum, it helps people to meet a basic threshold for equal participation when their material resources are unequal in other respects. At most, learning over the life course helps to increase political equality at the individual and group levels by empowering more individual women to participate. Lifelong learning helps subordinated groups that include women, the old, and the poor to enter public discussions by disrupting the institutional, structural, and cultural conditions that depress participation.

The narratives that emerge from women's focus groups discussions are not marginalized. Rather, women articulate a political worldview that has found purchase across Japanese society. Indeed, their attitudes about politics, what is wrong with it and how it can be fixed, are frequently echoed by men. The political worldviews that participants construct resonate on a larger scale and provide insight into the attitudes that underpin the patterns of local political action that have been unfolding across Japan for a over a decade. Women's study practices contribute to a national discourse about how better democracy can be achieved from the grassroots level. More importantly, they shed light on otherwise unobservable changes in attitudes that underpin political actions such as voting that seem relatively mundane until it becomes apparent that voters' motivations and goals have changed even as they continue to engage with the political system through normative venues. The discursive practices within study and hobby groups are an important mechanism for creating and framing new forms of political knowledge that subvert existing ones, and these communities of practice are vital to the process of diffusing attitudes that give rise to new ways of engaging with the electoral apparatus.

New trends in local action have erupted across Japan—recalls and referenda, information disclosure movements and taxpayer suits, the election of independent executives, and the proliferation of citizens' parties. People who find that their local political contexts are corrupt and controlled by old-style political bosses are more likely to carry over these expectations to national politics as well. In contrast, citizens who believe that local politics conform to, or can be bent to, their shared understanding of what democracy is are more likely to have a positive outlook on the potential for national-level politics to follow the same patterns (Hiskey and Bowler 2005). They are more likely to believe that they can make the national government over in their own image. In Japan, citizens are finding that local politics can be made to conform to look and act like democracy as they define it at the ballot box. Local experiences have demonstrated that everyday voters can wrestle politics away from local elites who are not governing in the public interest and replace them with officials who are more likely to respect and promote the practices of popular democracy. Over time, popular democracy can be mobilized from the ground up.

References

Allison, Anne. 1996. "Producing Mothers." In *Re-Imaging Japanese Women,* ed. Anne E. Imamura, 135–55. Berkeley: University of California Press.

Almond, Gabriel, and Sidney Verba. 1963. *The Civic Culture.* Princeton, NJ: Princeton University Press.

Anderson, Christopher J., André Blais, Shaun Bowler, Todd Donovan, and Ola Listhaug. 2005. *Losers' Consent: Elections and Democratic Legitimacy.* New York: Oxford University Press.

Asahi Shimbun. 2001. "LDP in Trivial Maneuvers to Choose Next Prime Minister." March 21.

Benford, Robert D., and David A. Snow. 2000. "Framing Processes and Social Movements: An Overview and Assessment." *Annual Review of Sociology* 26: 611–39.

Bickford, Susan. 1996. *The Dissonance of Democracy: Listening, Conflict, and Citizenship.* Ithaca, NY: Cornell University Press.

Bowler, Shaun, and Todd Donovan. 2002. "Democracy, Institutions, and Attitudes about Citizen Influence on Government." *British Journal of Political Science* 32: 371–90.

Brinton, Mary. 1993. *Women and the Economic Miracle: Gender and Work in Postwar Japan.* Berkeley: University of California Press.

Burns, Nancy, Kay Lehman Brady, and Sidney Verba. 2001. *The Private Roots of Public Action: Gender, Equality, and Political Participation.* Cambridge, MA: Harvard University Press.

Calder, Kent E. 1988. *Crisis and Compensation: Public Policy and Political Stability in Japan.* Princeton, NJ: Princeton University Press.

Cassel, Carol, and Cecilia Lo. 1997. "Theories of Political Literacy." *Political Behavior* 19: 317–35.

Cave, Peter. 2001. "Educational Reform in Japan in the 1990s: 'Individuality' and Other Uncertainties." *Comparative Education* 37 (2): 173–91.

——. 2004. "*Bukatsudō:* The Educational Role of Japanese School Clubs." *Journal of Japanese Studies* 30 (2): 383–415.

Chicago Women's Liberation Union. 1971. "How to Start Your Own Consciousness-Raising Group." *Black Maria.* Available at http://www.cwluherstory.com/how-to-start-your-own-consciousness-raising-group.html, accessed September 20, 2010.

Chitose, Yoshimi. 2003. "Policies Targeted to Families with Children: Policy Responses to Declining Fertility." In *Child Related Policies in Japan.* Tokyo: National Institute of Population and Social Security Research.

Commissioner's Advisory Group on International Cultural Exchange. 2003. *About the Future Promotion of International Cultural Exchange.* Agency for Cultural Affairs, Japan.

Conover, Pamela Johnston, Donald D. Searing, and Ivor M. Crewe. 2002. "The Deliberative Potential of Political Discussion." *British Journal of Political Science* 32 (1): 21–62.

Crozier, Michel. 1977. *The Governability of West European Society.* Colchester: University of Essex.

Curtice, John, and Pippa Norris. 2007. "Isolates or Socialites? The Social Ties of Internet Users." In *British Social Attitudes,* ed. Alison Park, 59–84. London: Sage.

Curtis, Gerald. 2010. "Japan's New Leaders Must Show Leadership." *Financial Times,* April 22.

Dalton, Russell J. 2000. "Citizen Attitudes and Political Behavior." *Comparative Political Studies* 33: 912–40.

——. 2006. *Citizen Politics: Public Opinion and Political Parties in Advanced Industrial Democracies.* Washington, DC: CQ Press.

Dalton, Russell J., Ian McAllister, and Martin P. Wattenberg. 2000. "The Consequences of Partisan Dealignment." In *Parties without Partisans: Political Change in Advanced Industrial Democracies,* ed. Russell J. Dalton and Martin P. Wattenberg, 37–63. Oxford: Oxford University Press.

Democratic Party of Japan. 2009. "Female Politicians Network Meeting Assembly Decides on New Action Plan." November 25. Available at www.dpj.or.jp/english/news/?num=17362, accessed December 20, 2009.

Diamond, Larry. 1997. "Consolidating Democracy in the Americas." *Annals of the American Academy* 550: 12–41.

Diani, Mario. 2007. "Networks and Social Movements." In *Blackwell Encyclopedia of Sociology,* ed. George Ritzer, 4455–58. Malden, MA: Blackwell Publishing.

Easton, D. 1965. *A Systems Analysis of Political Life.* New York, Wiley.

Economic Planning Agency, Government of Japan. 2001. "Volunteering Enriches Societies with Taste-Linked Human Relations." *White Paper on the National Lifestyle Fiscal Year 2000.*

The Economist. 1998. "Japan's Amazing Ability." September 24.

———. 2005. "Survey: New Politics, Old Politicians." October 8.

———. 2008. "Why Japan Keeps Failing." February 23.

Eto, Mikiko. 2007. "Vitalizing Democracy at the Grassroots: A Contribution of Post-War Women's Movements in Japan." *East Asia* 25: 115–43.

European Centre for the Development of Vocational Training (CEDEFOP). 2003. *Lifelong Learning: Citizens' Views.* Luxembourg: Office for Official Publications of the European Communities.

Fackler, Martin. 2008. "Memo from Tokyo: Populist Appeals in Election, and Claims of Political Theater." *New York Times,* September 16.

Field, John. 2005. "Social Capital and Lifelong Learning." *Encyclopedia of Informal Education.* Available at www.infed.org/lifelonglearning/social_capital_and_lifelong_learning.htm, accessed November 3, 2008.

Flanagan, Scott C. 1991. "Mechanisms of Social Network Influence in Japanese Voting Behavior." In *The Japanese Voter,* eds. Flanagan, Scott C., Shinsaku Kohei, Ichiro Miyake, Bradley M. Richardson, and Joji Watanuki, 143–97. New Haven: Yale University Press.

Flanagan, Scott C., Shinsaku Kohei, Ichiro Miyake, Bradley M. Richardson, and Joji Watanuki, eds. 1976. *JABISS: The Japanese Election Study, 1976* [Computer file]. ICPSR04682-v1. Irvine, CA: University of California, Irvine, Center for the Study of Democracy [producers], 2007. Ann Arbor, MI: Inter-university Consortium for Political and Social Research [distributor], 2008-02-27. doi:10.3886/ICPSR04682

———, eds. 1991. *The Japanese Voter.* New Haven: Yale University Press.

Foljanty-Jost, Gesine, and Carmin Schmidt. 2006. "Local Level Political and Institutional Changes in Japan: An End to Political Alienation?" *Asia Europe Journal* 4 (3): 381–97.

Frederick, Jim. 2005. "Standing Tall." *Time,* December 18.

Fretwell, David H., and Joe E. Colombano. 2000. *Adult Continuing Education: An Integral Part of Lifelong Learning: Emerging Policies and Programs for the Twenty-First Century in Upper and Middle Income Countries.* Washington, DC: World Bank.

Gamson, William A. 1992. *Talking Politics.* New York: Cambridge University Press.

Garon, Sheldon. 1993. "Women's Groups and the Japanese State: Contending Approaches to Political Integration, 1890–1945." *Journal of Japanese Studies* 19 (1): 5–41.

———. 1998. *Molding Japanese Minds: The State in Everyday Life.* Princeton: Princeton University Press.

Gelb, Joyce. 2003. *Gender Policies in Japan and the United States: Comparing Women's Movements, Rights, and Politics.* New York: Palgrave Macmillan.

Gottlieb, Nanette, and Mark McLelland, eds. 2003. *Japanese Cybercultures.* New York: Routledge.

Guth, R. A. 2000. "Your Career Matters: Net Lets Japanese Women Join Work Force at Home." *Wall Street Journal,* February 29, B1.

Haddad, Mary Alice. 2007. *Politics and Volunteering in Japan: A Global Perspective.* Cambridge: Cambridge University Press.

———. n.d. *Making Democracy Real: Power to the People in Japan* (unpublished manuscript).

Harris, Tobias. 2010. "Kan Presses the Reset Button." Observing Japan (blog). September 19. Available at www.observingjapan.com.

Hartsock, Nancy C. M. 1987. "The Feminist Standpoint: Developing the Ground for a Specifically Feminist Method." In *Feminism and Methodology: Social Science Issues,* ed. Sandra Harding, 157–80. Bloomington: Indiana University Press.

Hatoyama, Yukio. 2009. Policy Speech at the 173rd Session of the Diet. October 29, 2009. Available at www.kantei.go.jp/foreign/hatoyama/statement/200910/26syosin_e.html, accessed May 19, 2010.

Hayao, Kenji. 1993. *The Japanese Prime Minister and Public Policy.* Pittsburgh: University of Pittsburgh Press.

Hiskey, Jonathan T., and Shaun Bowler. 2005. "Local Context and Democratization in Mexico." *American Journal of Political Science* 49 (1): 57–71.

Horiuchi, Yusaku. 2005. *Institutions, Incentives and Electoral Participation in Japan: Cross-Level and Cross-National Perspectives.* New York: RoutledgeCurzon.

Hosaka, Tomoko A. 2009. "Japanese Voters Empowered by Historic Election." Associated Press, August 31, 2009. Available at http://abcnews.go.com/International/wireStory?id=8454743, accessed December 10, 2009.

Ikeda, Ken'ichi, and Sean Richey. 2005. "Japanese Network Capital: The Impact of Social Networks on Japanese Political Participation." *Political Behavior* 27 (3): 239–60.

Ikeda, Ken'ichi, Yoshiaki Kobayashi, and Hiroshi Hirano. 2007. *Nation-wide Longitudinal Survey Study on Voting Behavior in the Early 21st Century, 2001–2005* (Japanese Election Study III). Available at the University of Tokyo, Institute of Social Science, Social Science Japan Data Archive. http://ssjda.iss.u-tokyo.ac.jp/en/.

Imel, Susan. 2000. "International Perspectives on Adult Education." *International Perspectives on Adult Education,* Trends and Issues Alert No. 14.

Information Clearing House Japan. n.d. Selection from "Information Disclosure: One Hundred Samples." Available at www.foi-asia.org/Japan/Japan_Index.html, accessed August 14, 2008.

Inglehart, Ronald. 1977. *The Silent Revolution: Changing Values and Political Styles among Western Publics.* Princeton, NJ: Princeton University Press.

———. 1990. *Cultural Shift in Advanced Industrialized Society.* Princeton, NJ: Princeton University Press.

———. 1997. *Modernization and Postmodernization: Culture, Economic, and Political Change in Forty-Three Societies.* Princeton, NJ: Princeton University Press.

Inoguchi, Takashi. 2003. "Executive Turnovers in 2003." *Japanese Journal of Political Science* 4(2): 349–51.

Inter-Parliamentary Union. 2010. "Women in National Parliaments." Available at http://www.ipu.org/wmn-e/classif.htm.

Ito, Joichi. 2007. "In Japan, Stagnation Wins Again." *New York Times,* September 18, 27.

Iwai, Tomoaki. 1993. "The Madonna Boom: Women in the Japanese Diet." *Journal of Japanese Studies* 19(1): 103–20.

Iwamoto, Misako. 2001. "The Madonna Boom: The Progress of Japanese Women into Politics in the 1980s." *PS: Political Science and Politics* 34 (2): 225–26.

Izumi, Hiroshi. 2009. "Historic Victory, Ticklish Transition." The Tokyo Foundation. Available at www.tokyofoundation.org/en/articles/2009/historic-victory-ticklish-transition, accessed May 18, 2010.

Jain, Purnendra. 2000. "*Jumin Tohyo* and the Tokushima Anti-Dam Movement in Japan: The People Have Spoken." *Asian Survey* 40 (4): 551–70.

———. 2004. "Local Political Leadership in Japan: A Harbinger of Systematic Change in Japanese Politics?" *Policy and Society* 23 (1): 58–87.

Japan Times. 2001. "870,000 Subscribers Make Koizumi e-zine No. 1?" June 16.

———. 2006. "Nagano Bids Maverick Goodbye." August 10.

Jones, H. J. 1975. "Japanese Women in the Politics of the Seventies." *Asian Survey* 15 (8): 708–23.

———. 1976. "Japanese Women and Party Politics." *Pacific Affairs* 49 (2): 213–34.

Johnson, Chalmers. 1982. *MITI and the Japanese Miracle: The Growth of Industrial Policy, 1925–1975.* Stanford, CA: Stanford University Press.

Kabashima, Ikuo, Jonathan Marshall, Takayoshi Uekami, and Dae-song Hyun. 2000. "Casual Cynics, or Disillusioned Democrats? Political Alienation in Japan." *Political Psychology* 21 (4): 779–804.

Kalis, Emmanuel, and Spyridon Pilos. 2005. "Lifelong Learning in Europe." In *Statistics in Focus: Population and Social Conditions.* Luxembourg: Eurostat. Available at http://libserver.cedefop.europa.eu/vetelib/eu/pub/eurostat/2005_0002_en.pdf.

Kawai, Kei, and Yasutora Watanabe. 2010. "Inferring Strategic Voting." Available at SSRN: http://ssrn.com/abstract=1402891.

Kawanobe, Satoshi. 1994. "Lifelong Learning in Japan." *International Review of Education* 40 (6): 485–93.

Kawato, Yuko, and Robert Pekkanen. 2008. "Civil Society and Democracy: Reforming Nonprofit Organization Law." In *Democratic Reform in Japan: Assessing the Impact,* ed. Sherry L. Martin and Gill Steel, 193–210. Boulder, CO: Lynne Rienner.

Kelsky, Karen. 2001. *Women on the Verge: Japanese Women, Western Dreams.* Durham, NC: Duke University Press.

Khan, Yoshimitsu. 1997. *Japanese Moral Education Past and Present.* London: Associated University Presses.

Kikkawa, Takeo. 2000. "Beyond the 'Lost Decade.'" *Social Science Japan Newsletter* 34: 3–5.

Kim, Kwang, Mary Hagedorn, Jennifer Williamson, and Christopher Chapman. 2004. *Participation in Adult Education and Lifelong Learning: 2000–01 (NCES 2004–050).* U.S. Department of Education, National Center for Education Statistics. Washington, DC: U.S. Government Printing Office.

Kinoshita, Miyuki. 2005. "Library Services for the Women's Empowerment: Activities of the Library, Osaka Prefectural Women's Center Library." *Lifelong Education and Libraries* 5: 69–76.

Kohara, Takaharu. 2007. "The Great Heisei Consolidation: A Critical Review." *Social Science Japan Newsletter* 37: 7–11.

Krauss, Ellis S., and Robert Pekkanen. 2008. "Reforming the Liberal Democratic Party." In *Democratic Reform in Japan: Assessing the Impact,* ed. Sherry L. Martin and Gill Steel, 11–37. Boulder, CO: Lynne Rienner.

Kronsell, Annica. 2005. "Gendered Practices in Institutions of Hegemonic Masculinity: Reflections from Feminist Standpoint Theory." *International Feminist Journal of Politics.* 7 (2): 280–98.

Kunii, I. M. 2000. "Japanese Women Get Equal Billing on the Net: Online Startups Give Them a Chance They Never Had." *Business Week,* March 13.

Lam, Peng Er. 2005a. "Competing Modes of Election Campaigning in Japan." *Asian Perspective* 29 (1): 79–98.

———. 2005b. "Local Governance: The Role of Referenda and the Rise of Independent Governors." In *Contested Governance in Japan,* ed. Glenn G. Hook, 71–89. New York: RoutledgeCurzon.

———. 2007. "Japan's Quest for 'Soft Power': Attraction and Limitation." *East Asia* 24: 349–63.

Lassen, Mary M. 2002. "A Promising Dilemma: Reflections on the Status of Japanese Women in the Year 2002." New York: The Japan Society of New York. Available at http://www.japansociety.org/content.cfm/a_promising_dilemma.

Lave, Jean, and Etienne Wenger. 1991. *Situated Learning: Legitimate Peripheral Participation.* Cambridge: Cambridge University Press.

LeBlanc, Robin M. 1999. *Bicycle Citizens: The Political World of the Japanese Housewife.* Berkeley: University of California Press.

———. 2008. "The Potential and Limits of Antiparty Electoral Movements in Local Politics." In *Democratic Reform in Japan: Assessing the Impact,* ed. Sherry L. Martin and Gill Steel, 175–92. Boulder, CO: Lynne Rienner.

———. 2010. *The Art of the Gut: Manhood, Power, and Ethics in Japanese Politics.* Berkeley: University of California Press.

Luker, Kristin. 1984. *Abortion and the Politics of Motherhood.* Berkeley: University of California Press.

Machidori, Satoshi, and Kengo Soga. 2007. *Nihon no Chihou Seiji.* Nagoya, Japan: University of Nagoya Press.

Mackie, Vera. 2003. "Creating Publics and Counterpublics on the Internet in Japan." In *Japanese Cybercultures,* ed. Nanette Gottlieb and Mark McLelland, 174–90. New York: Routledge.

Madriz, Esther. 2003. "Focus Groups in Feminist Research." In *Collecting and Interpreting Qualitative Methods,* 2nd ed., ed. Norman K. Denzin and Yvonna S. Lincoln, 363–88. Thousand Oaks, CA: Sage Publications.

Maehira, Yasushi. 1994. "Patterns of Lifelong Education in Japan." *International Review of Education* 40 (3–5): 333–38.

Mahmood, Saba. 2005. "The Subject of Freedom." In Saba Mahmood, *Politics of Piety: The Islamic Revival and the Feminist Subject,* 1–39. Princeton: Princeton University Press.

Mainichi Japan. 2010. "Kan Cabinet Public Approval Rating Rises to 64 Percent Following Reshuffle." *Mainichi Shimbun,* September 20. Available at http://mdn.main ichi.jp/mdnnews/news/20100920p2a00m0na008000c.html.

Margolis, Eric, Michael Soldatenko, Sandra Acker, and Mariana Gair. 2001. "Peekaboo: Hiding and Outing the Curriculum." In *The Hidden Curriculum in Higher Education,* ed. Eric Margolis, 1–20. New York: Routledge.

Marshall, Jonathan. 2002. "Here Comes the Judge: Freedom of Information and Litigating for Government Accountability." *Social Science Japan* 23: 8–13.

Martin, Sherry L. 2008. "Keeping Women in Their Place: Penetrating Male-dominated Urban and Rural Assemblies." In *Democratic Reform in Japan: Assessing the Impact,* eds. Sherry L. Martin and Gill Steel, 125–49. Boulder: Lynne Rienner Publishers.

Maruyama, Masao, Ryosuke Takaki, Shigeru Kubota, Naoto Higuchi, Mitsuru Matsu-
tani, and Takaya Yabe. 2007. "The Electoral Defeat of Tanaka Yasuo: Bottleneck in
the Base of Democracy and Populism." English translation. In *The Age of the Governor: Introduction to Comparative Political Sociology,* ed. Naoto Higuchi et al. Tokyo:
Chijikenkyukai.

Massey, Joseph A. 1975. "The Missing Japanese Leader: Japanese Youth's View of Political Authority." *American Political Science Review* 69: 31–48.

Maynard, Michael L., and Senko K. Maynard. 1995. *101 Japanese Idioms: Understanding Japanese Language and Culture Through Popular Phrases.* Lincolnwood, IL: Pass-
port Books.

McVeigh, Brian J. 1996. "Cultivating 'Femininity' and 'Internationalism': Rituals and
Routine at a Japanese Women's Junior College." *Ethos* 24 (2): 314–49.

———. 1998. "Linking State and Self: How the Japanese State Bureaucratizes Subjectivity through Moral Education." *Anthropological Quarterly* 71 (3): 125–37.

———. 2004. *Nationalism of Japan: Managing and Mystifying Identity.* Lanham, MD:
Rowman and Littlefield.

Miller, Arthur. 1974a. "Political Issues and Trust in Government." *American Political
Science Review* 68: 951–72.

———. 1974b. "Rejoinder." *American Political Science Review* 68: 989–1001.

Ministry of Education, Culture, Sports, Science, and Technology (MEXT). 2006. "Enrollment and Advancement Rate 1948–2005." Available at www.mext.go.jp/english/
statist/06060808/pdf/013.pdf.

———. 2008. *White Paper on Education, Culture, Sports, Science and Technology,* ch. 2.
Available at www.mext.go.jp/b_menu/hakusho/html/hpaa200901/1283098_005.pdf,
accessed April 23, 2008.

———. 2003–2006. *White Paper on Education, Culture, Sports, Science and Technology.*
Available at www.mext.go.jp/english/wp/index.htm, accessed April 23, 2008.

———. n.d. *Japan's Modern Education System.* Available at www.mext.go.jp/b_menu/
hakusho/html/hpbz198103/index.html, accessed April 23, 2008.

Ministry of Education, Science and Culture. 1994. *Japanese Government Policies in Education, Science and Culture 1994.* Available at http://www.mext.go.jp/b_menu/
hakusho/html/hpae199401/index.html, accessed on April 23, 2008.

Ministry of Education, Science, Sports, and Culture (MEXT). 1989–2002. *Japanese
Government Policies in Education, Science and Culture.* Available at www.mext.go.jp/
english/wp/index.htm, accessed April 23, 2008.

Ministry of Education, Science, Sports and Culture. 1996. *Japanese Government Policies
in Education, Science and Culture 1996.* Available at http://www.mext.go.jp/b_menu/
hakusho/html/hpae199601/index.html.

———. 1995. *Japanese Government Policies in Education, Science and Culture 1995.* Available at http://www.mext.go.jp/b_menu/hakusho/html/hpae199501/index.html.

Ministry of Internal Affairs and Communications. 2009. Members of Local Assemblies
by Sex (data file). Available at the National Women's Education Center's Gender
Statistics Database winet.nwec.jp/cgi-bin/toukei/load/bin/tk_sql.cgi?bunya=10&hn
o=0&rfrom=1&rto=0&fopt=1, accessed January 20, 2010.

———. 2009. Report of the Results of Elections (data file). Available at the National Wom-
en's Education Center's Gender Statistics Database winet.nwec.jp/cgi-bin/toukei/

load/bin/tk_sql.cgi?hno=155&syocho=49&rfrom=101&rto=120&fopt=3, accessed January 20, 2010.

Morgan, David L. 2004. "Focus Groups." In *Approaches to Qualitative Research: A Reader on Theory and Practice,* ed. Sharlene Hesse-Biber and Patricia Leavy, 263–85. New York: Oxford University Press.

Moriya, Yuko. n.d. "Gender-Free Perspective in the Legislature." "DAWN" Newsletter of the Dawn Center. Available at www.dawncenter.or.jp, accessed November 17, 2008.

Mulgan, Aurelia George. 2000. "Japan's Political Leadership Deficit." *Australian Journal of Political Science* 35: 183–202.

Murakami, Haruki. 2008. "The Running Novelist: Learning How to Go the Distance." *New Yorker.* June 9–16, 72–77.

Muramatsu, Michio, and Ellis S. Krauss. 1987. "The Conservative Policy Line and the Development of Patterned Pluralism." In *The Political Economy of Japan, vol. I,* ed. Kozo Yamamura and Yasuba Yasukichi, 516–54. Stanford: Stanford University Press.

Nagano Association for Public Opinion Research. 2000. *Shin shiji to kensei ni Nozomu.* Available at www.nagano-yoron.or.jp/pdf_report/2000/sinchiji.pdf, accessed January 6, 2010.

Naikakufu Daijin Kanbou Seifu Kouhou Shitsu. 1999. *Shogai Gakushu ni Kansuru Yoron Chousa.* Available at http://www8.cao.go.jp/survey/h11/gakushu/, accessed June 11, 2008.

Nakane, Chie. 1970. *Japanese Society.* Berkeley: University of California Press.

Nishizawa, Yoshitaka, Hiroshi Hirano, Ken'ichi Ikeda, Ichiro Miyake, and Aiji Tanaka. 2001. *Japanese Election and Democracy Study 2000,* 3rd release. December.

Norris, Pippa. 2000. "The Impact of Television on Civic Malaise." In *Disaffected Democracies: What's Troubling the Trilateral Countries?,* eds. Susan J. Pharr and Robert D. Putnam, 231–51. Princeton, NJ: Princeton University Press.

———. 1999. "The Growth of Critical Citizens." In *Critical Citizens: Global Support for Democratic Government,* ed. Pippa Norris, 1–30. New York: Oxford University Press.

Numata, Chieko. 2006. "Checking the Center: Popular Referenda in Japan." *Social Science Japan Journal* 9 (1): 19–31.

Nyblade, Benjamin, and Ellis S. Krauss. 2005. "Presidentialization in Japan? The Prime Minister, Media and Elections in Japan." *British Journal of Political Science.* 35: 357–68.

O'Donnell, Guillermo. 2007. "The Perpetual Crises of Democracy." *Journal of Democracy* 18 (1): 5–11.

Oda, Yukiko. 2006. "The Kitakyushu Forum on Asian Women and Japan's Gender Centers." Paper presented at International Political Science Association Conference. Fukuoka, Japan. July 10.

Ogawa, Akihiro. 2010. "The Construction of Citizenship through Volunteering: The Case of Lifelong Learning in Contemporary Japan." In *Japan's Politics and Economy: Perspectives on Change,* ed. Marie Söderberg and Patricia A. Nelson, 86–98. New York: Routledge.

Ogai, Tokuko. 2004. "From the Personal to the Political: Women Activists in Japan." In *Promises of Empowerment: Women in Asia and Latin America,* ed. Peter H. Smith, Jennifer L. Troutner, and Christine Hunefeldt, 88–102. Boulder: Rowman and Littlefield Publishers, Inc.

Oliver, Leonard P. 1987. *Study Circles: Coming Together for Personal Growth and Social Change.* Washington, DC: Seven Locks Press.

Oliver, Pamela E., and Hank Johnston. 2000. "What a Good Idea! Frames and Ideologies in Social Movement Research." *Mobilization* 5: 37–54.

Onosaka, Junko R. 2003. "Challenging Society through the Information Grid: Japanese Women's Activism on the Net." In *Japanese Cybercultures,* ed. Nanette Gottlieb and Mark McLelland, 95–108. New York: Routledge.

Ōtake, Hideo. 2000. "Political Realignment and Policy Conflict." In *Power Shuffles and Policy Processes,* ed. Hideo Ōtake, 125–51. Japan: Japan Center for International Exchange.

Pateman, Carole. 1970. *Participation and Democratic Theory.* Cambridge: Cambridge University Press.

Pekkanen, Robert. 2006. *Japan's Dual Civil Society: Members without Advocates.* Stanford: Stanford University Press.

Pharr, Susan J. 1981. *Political Women in Japan: The Search for a Place in Political Life.* Berkeley: University of California Press.

———. 1997. "Public Trust and Democracy in Japan." In *Why People Don't Trust Government,* ed. J. S. Nye Jr., P. D. Zelikow, and D. C. King, 237–52. Cambridge, MA: Harvard University Press.

Pharr, Susan J., and Robert D. Putnam. 2000. *Disaffected Democracies: What's Troubling the Trilateral Countries?* Princeton, NJ: Princeton University Press.

Putnam, Robert D. 1993. *Making Democracy Work: Civic Traditions in Modern Italy.* Princeton: Princeton University Press.

Rausch, Anthony. 2004. "Lifelong Learning in Rural Japan: Relevance, Focus, and Sustainability for the Hobbyist, the Resident, the Careerist, and the Activist as Lifelong Learners." *Japan Forum* 16 (3): 473–93.

Reed, Steven R. 1999. "Strategic Voting in the 1996 Japanese General Election." *Comparative Political Studies* 32 (2): 257–70.

Reed, Steven R., Ethan Scheiner, and Michael F. Thies. 2009. "New Ballgame in Politics." *Oriental Economist* 77 (10).

Reed, Steven R., and Michael F. Thies. 2001. "The Causes of Electoral Reform in Japan." In *Mixed-Member Electoral Systems: The Best of Both Worlds?* ed. Matthew Soberg Shugart and Martin P. Wattenberg, 152–72. New York: Oxford University Press.

Repeta, Lawrence, and David M. Shultz. 2002. "The 2001 Information Disclosure Law, and a Comparison with the U.S. FOIA." Available at www.freedominfo.org/features/20020705.htm, accessed August 14, 2008.

Richardson, Bradley M. 1974. *The Political Culture of Japan.* Berkeley: University of California Press.

———. 1997. *Japanese Democracy: Power, Coordination, and Performance.* New Haven: Yale University Press.

Roberts, Glenda S. 2002. "Pinning Hopes on Angels: Reflections from an Aging Japan's Urban Landscape." In *Family and Social Policy in Japan: Anthropological Approaches,* ed. R. Goodman, 54–91. Cambridge: Cambridge University Press.

Rosenstone, Steven J., and John Mark Hansen. 1993. *Mobilization, Participation, and Democracy in America.* New York: Macmillan.

Sakamoto, Eiji. 2008. "Opinion: Parties Dodge Tough Issues to Score Populist Points." *Nikkei Shimbun.* September 25.

Samuels, Richard J. 2003. *Machievelli's Children: Leaders and Their Legacies in Italy and Japan.* Ithaca: Cornell University Press.

Sato, Katsuko. 2003. *Shougai gakushuu ga tsukuru koukyou kuukan.* [The Production of Public Space Through Lifelong learning]. Tokyo: Hakushobou.

———. 2004. *NPO no kyoiki ryoko: shougai gakushu to shiminteki koukyousei* [The Educational Practice of the NPO: Civic Activism and Lifelong Learning]. Tokyo: Tokyo Daigaku Shuppankai.

Scheiner, Ethan. 2005. "Pipelines of Pork: Japanese Politics and a Model of Local Opposition Party Failure." *Comparative Political Studies* 38 (7): 799–823.

———. 2006. *Democracy without Opposition in Japan.* Cambridge: Cambridge University Press.

Schoppa, Leonard. 1991. *Education Reform in Japan: A Case of Immobilist Politics.* London: Routledge.

———. 2001. "Japan, the Reluctant Reformer." *Foreign Affairs* 80 (5): 76–90.

———. 2006. *Race for the Exits: The Unraveling of Japan's System of Social Protection.* Ithaca: Cornell University Press.

Sievers, Sharon L. 1983. *Flowers in Salt: The Beginnings of Feminist Consciousness in Modern Japan.* Stanford, CA: Stanford University Press.

Southwell, Priscilla L. 2008. "The Effect of Political Alienation on Voter Turnout, 1964–2000." *Journal of Political and Military Sociology* 36 (1): 131–45.

Statistics Bureau, Management and Coordination Agency. 1987. *Japan Statistical Yearbook.*

———. 1990. *Japan Statistical Yearbook.*

———. 1996. *The Statistical Handbook of Japan.*

———. 1998. *Japan Statistical Yearbook.*

———. 2007. *Japan Statistical Yearbook.*

———. 2008. *Japan Statistical Yearbook.*

Steiner, Kurt. 1965. *Local Government in Japan.* Stanford, Stanford University Press.

Steiner, Kurt, Ellis S. Krauss, and Scott C. Flanagan. 1980. *Political Opposition and Local Politics in Japan.* Princeton, NJ: Princeton University Press.

Steinhoff, Patricia G. 2008. "Political Ties of Visible (Right) and Invisible (Left) Social Movements in Contemporary Japan." Paper delivered at the Association for Asian Studies Annual Meeting. Atlanta, GA, April 2–6, 2008.

Strom, Stephanie. 2001. "Governors Taking a New Broom to Japan's Politics." *New York Times,* January 10.

Sugeno, Mikio. 2008. "Maverick Style Leaves Mixed Feelings among Public, LDP." *Nikkei Shimbun.* October 13.

Sugita, Atsushi. 2003. "'Karera' to wa chigau 'Watakushi tachi.' Toitsu-chihosen no minii wo kangaeru." *Sekai.* June, pp. 20–25.

Tajima, Yoshisuke. 1996. "Jumin keishi no kokusaku ni hanran." *Asahi Shimbun Weekly AERA.* August 19–26.

———. 2003. "Kaku chi ni miru jimin jichi undo to tochi naibunken no kanou." *Toshi Mondai* 94 (4): 17–28.

Takao, Yasuo. 2008. "Women in Japanese Local Politics: From Voters to Activists to Politicians." *Japan Focus.*

Tanaka, Aiji. 2003. "Decline of Trust in Japanese Party System, 1976–2001: Why Has the LDP Stayed in Power? And What is the Consequence?" *Waseda Political Studies* 35: 35–59.

Taniguchi, Naoko. 2008. "Diet Members and Seat Inheritance: Keeping It in the Family." In *Democratic Reform in Japan: Assessing the Impact,* ed. Sherry L. Martin and Gill Steel, 65–80. Boulder, CO: Lynne Rienner.

Tarrow, Sidney. 1998. *Power in Movement: Social Movements and Contentious Politics.* Cambridge: Cambridge University Press.

Teramachi, Midori. 2003. "Senkyo dake shiminha." *Shukan Kinyoubi.* April 11, pp. 30–31.

Terano, Akemi. 2008. "Pioneering Women's Center in Osaka Slated for Closure." *Japan Times,* March 28.

Thomas, J. E. 1985. *Learning Democracy in Japan: The Social Education of Japanese Adults.* London: Sage Publications.

Tilly, Charles. 1983. "Speaking Your Mind without Elections, Surveys, or Social Movements." *Public Opinion Quarterly* 47: 461–78.

Ueno, Hisako, and Bruce Wallace. 2008. "Japan Adrift as Another Premier Resigns." *Los Angeles Times,* September 2.

Verba, Sidney, Norman H. Nie, and Jae-on Kim. 1978. *Participation and Political Equality: A Seven Nation Comparison.* Cambridge: Cambridge University Press.

Wallace, Bruce. 2006. "The Buzz on Japan's New Premier: Too Old School." *Los Angeles Times,* December 31, p. A5.

Walsh, Katherine Cramer. 2004. *Talking about Politics: Informal Groups and Social Identity in American Life.* Chicago: University of Chicago Press.

Weatherford, M. Stephen. 1991. "Mapping the Ties That Bind: Legitimacy, Representation, and Alienation." *Western Political Quarterly* 44 (2): 251–76.

Weiner, Robert. 2008. "Prefectural Politics: Party and Electoral Stagnation." In *Democratic Reform in Japan: Assessing the Impact,* eds. Sherry L. Martin and Gill Steel, 151–74. Boulder: Lynne Rienner.

Wenger, Etienne. n.d. "Communities of Practice: A Brief Introduction." Available at www.ewenger.com/theory/, accessed May 7, 2008.

White, Aaronette M. 1991. "Talking Feminist, Talking Black: Micromobilization Processes in a Collective Protest against Rape." *Gender and Society* 13 (1): 77–100.

Wilson, John Dewar. 2001. "Lifelong Learning in Japan—A Lifeline for a 'Maturing' Society?" *International Journal of Lifelong Education* 20 (4): 297–313.

World Bank. 2003. *Lifelong Learning in the Global Knowledge Economy: Challenges for Developing Countries.* Washington, DC: World Bank.

Yamada, Kanehisa, Yoshihiro Tatsuta, Hiromi Sasai, and Yukiko Sawano. 2003. "New Trends and Challenges of Lifelong Learning Policies in Japan." Paper presented at the International Policy Seminar coorganized by the International Institute for Educational

Planning/UNESCO and Korea Research Institute for Vocational Education and Training, Seoul, Korea, June 24–26.

Yamamoto, Mari. 2004. *Grassroots Pacifism in Post-War Japan.* New York: Routledge-Curzon.

Yokoyama, Keiji. 1999. "Chihou kara chuo no seiji o kaeru." *Shukan Kinyoubi.* April 2, pp. 21–23.

Yomiuri Shimbun. 2007. "Japan: Political Gender Equality Takes a Turn: Election Campaigners Call for More Pro-Women's Rights Female Candidates." March 28. Available at www.wunrn.com/news/2007/04_07/04_16_07/042207_japan.htm, accessed September 29, 2008.

Yoshida, Shin'ichi. 2002. "Distrust in Politics: Will Voters Transform the Nature of Governance?" In *Governance for a New Century: Japanese Challenges, American Experience,* ed. Thomas E. Mann and Sasaki Takeshi, 14–28. Tokyo: Japan Center for International Exchange.

Young, Iris Marion. 2002. *Inclusion and Democracy.* Oxford: Oxford University Press.

Young, Kelly, and Ed Rosenberg. 2006. "Lifelong Learning in the United States and Japan." *Lifelong Learning Institute Review* 1: 69–85.

Zimbalist, Andrew. 2010. "Is It Worth It?" *Finance and Development,* 8–11. Available at www.imf.org/external/pubs/ft/fandd/2010/03/pdf/zimbalist.pdf.

Zuckerman, Alan S. 2005. "Returning to the Social Logic of Political Behavior." In *The Social Logic of Politics: Personal Networks as Contexts for Political Behavior,* ed. Alan S. Zuckerman, 3–20. Philadelphia: Temple University Press.

———. 2007. "The Social Logic of Political Choice: Picking a Political Party in the Context of Immediate Social Circles." *Politische Vierteljahresschrift* 48 (4): 633–48.

Index

Note: Page numbers in *italics* indicate figures; those with at indicate tables.